TURKEY AND THE TURKS

SULTAN ABDUL-HAMID II. AT THE AGE OF THIRTY-FOUR.

TURKEY AND THE TURKS

AN ACCOUNT OF

THE LANDS, THE PEOPLES, AND THE INSTITUTIONS OF THE OTTOMAN EMPIRE

BY

W. S. MONROE

ILLUSTRATED

LONDON
DARF PUBLISHERS LIMITED
1985

First Published 1908

New Impression 1985

ISBN 1 85077 061 1

Printed and bound in Great Britain by
A. Wheaton & Co. Ltd, Exeter

TO
𝔐r. George Lawrence Stimson
WHO, DURING FOURTEEN MONTHS, WAS THE AUTHOR'S TRAVEL-
LING COMPANION IN EUROPE AND SHARED THE TRAVELS
DESCRIBED IN THIS VOLUME, "TURKEY AND THE
TURKS" IS AFFECTIONATELY DEDICATED.

PREFACE

THE author has endeavoured to give in this book a brief but unified picture, gained through study and travel, of the incoherent Ottoman Empire and its complex civilization. A Scotch philosopher has remarked that if one wishes to give a strong and emphatic description of a country he must not linger long enough to be annoyed with contradictions.

It has not been an easy matter to condense within the limits set for this volume a subject so rich in material and so varied in interest, but the author has been guided (1) by the reactions of the audiences to whom he has presented most of the chapters of this book in lecture-form, and (2) by the topics which appealed most strongly to his own interests during his brief sojourn in Turkey.

Since physiography has been a dominant factor in the growth of the Ottoman Empire in Europe, a geographic study of the structure of the Balkan peninsula seemed a fitting introduction.

Two chapters have been devoted to the history of the empire — one to its rise and one to its decline — wherein it is noted that in less than three centuries the followers of the Prophet acquired Transylvania, Hungary, Moldavia, the Crimea, Albania, Herzegovina, Bosnia, Greece, Wallachia, Ragusa, and Rumelia in Europe, not to mention the immense territories in Asia, Africa, and the Mediterranean. But within an equally brief period most of these countries were lost to Ottoman power.

A chapter is given to the significant events in Turkish history during the past thirty years, including the last war with Russia and the farcical doings of the European concert.

But the lion's share of the book is given to matters of purely human interest — the numerous races with their varied customs and activities. Like the audience that listened to St. Paul on the day of Pentecost, the inhabitants of the Ottoman Empire "are out of every nation under heaven."

Eight chapters have been given to Constantinople, — its monuments, characteristic quarters, street scenes, bazaars, baths, khans, fountains, mosques, and dervishes; and, when not otherwise stated, the illustrations are of the Imperial City and its environs.

The author is under a large measure of obligation to the many friends who have aided him in the collection and verification of the data embodied in his book, but for reasons which will be obvious, after reading Chapter XI, personal recognition to his friends and correspondents in Turkey has been withheld.

Most of the American and English books on the Ottoman Empire have been consulted, and they have been frequently cited in confirmation and disagreement with the author's viewpoints on controverted subjects. Reference is made to these books in the foot-notes and the select annotated bibliography at the end of the volume. For the use of these books he is indebted to the City Library at Springfield, Massachusetts, probably one of the most select and best administered public libraries in the United States.

The spelling of Turkish words is unsettled and contentious; but the simplest forms approved by good American and English usage have been followed.

WILL S. MONROE.

CONTENTS

PAGE

CHAPTER I

Geographic position and natural advantages of European Turkey — Structural divisions — The Balkan range, the Dinaric Alps, and the Macedonian highland — The river basins — Mount Olympus, the abode of the gods — The Morava valley — Mount Athos, the mountain of the monks — Climatic zones in European Turkey — Area and political divisions of the Ottoman Empire — Centre of gravity in Asia — Population and important cities   1

CHAPTER II

Tribal beginnings of the Osmanli Turks — Migration from the Desert of Gobi to Persia and Asia Minor — Osman the first Sultan — Conquests of Nicomedia and Nicæa by Orkhan — Murad I. crosses the Hellespont and captures Adrianople, Philippopolis, and Rumelia — Bulgaria added to the Ottoman Empire — Reign of Bayezid I. — The interregnum — Murad II. and Mohammed I. — Mohammed II. and the conquest of Constantinople — Servia, Bosnia, Trebizond, and Karaman added to the empire — The rebellious Jem and the pious Knights of St. John — Selim the Grim and conquests in Persia, Kurdistan, Syria, and Egypt — Possession of the caliphate — Suleiman the Legislator and the acquisition of Belgrade, Rhodes, Tripoli, and Algiers — Selim the Drunkard and the war with Ivan the Terrible — Georgia taken from Persia — Ottoman Empire at the time of Mohammed III. . .   12

Contents

CHAPTER III

Causes of decline — The reigns of Ahmed and Mustafa — Wars with Poland and Persia — Occupation of Crete — Unsuccessful war with Austria and loss of Transylvania, Hungary, Slavonia, Podolia, Dalmatia, Morea, and Azov — War with Peter the Great — Moldavia and Wallachia taken by Catherine of Russia — First European alliance for the maintenance of the balance of power — Napoleon's invasion of Egypt — Rebellion in Servia — Destruction of the Janissaries — The Crimean war — Abdul-Aziz deposed 26

CHAPTER IV

Brief reign of Murad — Abdul-Hamid II. on the throne — Rebellions in Herzegovina, Bulgaria, Montenegro, Servia, and Rumania — War with Russia — The treaty of Berlin and disintegration of the Ottoman Empire — Armenian troubles — Rebellion in Crete and war with Greece — Macedonian outbreaks — Work of the commission — Growing influence of Germany — The future of Turkey 39

CHAPTER V

Origin of the Osmanli Turks — Ethnic stock — Asiatic home — Race intermixture — The physical type — Mental characteristics of the Turks — Turkish women — Polygamy — Legal rights of Moslem women — Occupations and amusements — The Turkish home — Democratic social ideals — Dress and habits — Alterations in the Turkish character — Effect of contact with the Christians — The blindness of human beings 59

CHAPTER VI

Diversity of races in Turkey — Their relative moral worth — Greeks — Their numerical strength — Physical and mental characteristics — Deficiency in practical ethics — Religion and education — Armenians — Geographic limits of the province — The ethnic stock — Habits and character — Lack of personal courage — The Gregorian church — Intellectual progress of the Armenians — Hebrews — Their degraded condition in Turkey — Relation to Judaism 79

CHAPTER VII

Kurds — Their origin and relation to the Mohammedan religion — Tribal life — Conflicts with the Armenians — Albanians — Strong muscular type — Low intellectual attainments — Occupations — Persians — Commercial enterprises — The Constantinople colony — Circassians — Emigration to Turkey — Beauty of their women — Wallachians — Connection with the Latin races — Physical and mental type — Bulgarians — Their Asiatic origin — Industries — Gypsies — Their degradation — Ethiopians — The eunuch type 98

CHAPTER VIII

Theocratic nature of the Ottoman government and its relation to the Mohammedan religion — Beginnings of the faith of Islam — Life of the founder — Effect of the flight from Mecca — Conflict of spiritual ideals and temporal power — Pathological mental condition of the Prophet — Factors in the spread of Islamism — Nature of the religion — Mohammedan creed — Sunnites and Shi'ites, the two great sects — Their differences 117

CHAPTER IX

Nature of the Ottoman theocracy — The Sultan's ministry — Grand Vizier — Sheik-ul-Islam — Political divisions of the empire — Local administration — Basis of Turkish law — Rights of foreigners — The army — Military reforms — War strength — Navy — Finance — Imperial taxes — Revenues and expenditures — National debt — Turkey an irredeemably corrupt despotism 133

CHAPTER X

Agriculture the mainstay of the people — How the lands are held — Chief agricultural products — Forests — Fisheries — Industries — Their primitive nature — Commerce — Foreign trade — Exports and imports — Customs duties — Commercial importance of Constantinople — Mercantile navy — Turkish railways — Postal service   150

CHAPTER XI

Place of education in the Koran — Education and the state — Mosque schools and their courses of study — A Moslem child's first day at school — The mosque colleges — Nature of the college instruction — Special and technical schools — The paper university at Constantinople — Schools maintained by the Greeks — Schools of the Christian missions — Robert College — Other American institutions — Roman Catholic schools — Newspapers — Press censorship — Publication of books — Index expurgatorius . . .   161

CHAPTER XII

Constantinople the continuous seat of empire for nearly sixteen hundred years — As rebuilt by Constantine — The seven hills — Its unrivalled geographic position — Natural divisions — The land-walls — Prison of the Seven Towers — At Meidan, the ancient Hippodrome — The Serpent Column — The Egyptian obelisk — The Burnt Column — Column of Constantine — Columns of Mercian and Arcadius — The Imperial Museum of Antiquities — The Cisterns   .   128

CHAPTER XIII

Nature of the population — Beauty and wonders of the site — Characteristic quarters — The Phanar, the Greek quarter — Balat, the Hebrew quarter — Eyub, the sacred suburb of the Turks — Sweet Waters of Europe — Pera and Galata — Scutari — Cemeteries — Princes' Islands — Prinkipo and Halki   194

Contents   xiii

PAGE

CHAPTER XIV

Characteristic street scenes — Mark Twain quoted — The bridges of boats — Bridge of Valideh Sultan an open air salon — The dogs — Hamals or porters — Sedan chairs, caïques, and barcas — Fields of the Dead — Fires and fire brigades — Cafés — Turkish coffee .   208

CHAPTER XV

The bazaar an Oriental department store — The Grand Bazaar — Diversity of commodities — Egyptian Bazaar — Drugs and perfumes — Khans — Turkish baths — Their social function — What they are not — Fountains — Ahmed Fountain   223

CHAPTER XVI

Ancestry of the present Sultan — Early death of his parents — How his childhood was passed — Inaptitude for studies — Dorys's life of the Sultan — Varying estimates of Abdul-Hamid's character — Mental illness — Yildiz Kiosk — Why selected — The imperial harem — Its organization and administration — Education of the harem women — Occupations and amusements — The Sultan's sons — Fast of Ramazan — Feast of the Bairam — The Selamlik . . .   233

CHAPTER XVII

The Seraglio a cluster of kiosks — Present uses of these — Chamber of Execution — Hall of the Divan — Library of Mustafa — Imperial palace treasury — The Bagdad Kiosk — Dolma Bagtché Palace — Palace of Beylerbey — Cheragan Palace — The Sublime Porte   254

CHAPTER XVIII

Origin of the mosques of Constantinople — Their dependencies — St. Sophia — Some of its materials — Its dedication by Justinian — Capture by the Turks — The disappointing exterior — Beauty of the interior — Mosque of Sultan Ahmed — Its minarets — Richness of its decorations — Its tombs — Mosque of Mohammed the Conqueror — Its impressive size — Mosque of Suleiman the Magnificent — Interior decorations — Mosque of Eyub, and other mosques. . . 262

CHAPTER XIX

Monastic orders not recognized by the Koran — Opposition of Turkey — The Turlakis, or nude dervishes — Bektashee, or free-thinkers — Whirling dervishes — Their movements — Religious significance — Howling dervishes — Nature and purpose of the religious excitement — Its counterpart in Protestant and Roman Catholic churches 279

CHAPTER XX

The ancient Lesbos — Nature of the island — Its prominence in Greek history — Mitylene to-day — Smyrna — Foundation of the city — Early history — Ancient ruins — Character of the population — Commercial importance of the city — Ephesus — The ancient city — Temple of Diana — Other ruins at Ephesus — Connection of Ephesus with Christianity . . . 281

CHAPTER XXI

Triangular nature of the question — Three sides of the triangle — Nations interested — Russia's foothold on the Black Sea — The policy of Catherine — Appearance of England — Pitt's failure — The Greek war of liberation — The Crimean war — Duke of Argyll's defence of England's attitude — Bulgarian barbarities — Congress of the Powers — Porte rejects suggested reforms — War with Russia — Treaty of San Stefano — Shameful policy of England — Congress and treaty of Berlin — The defenseless Armenians — The subsequent massacres — Austria, Germany, France, and Italy 308

LIST OF ILLUSTRATIONS

	PAGE
SULTAN ABDUL-HAMID II. AT THE AGE OF THIRTY-FOUR . . . . *Frontispiece*	
MOSQUE OF SULEIMAN THE MAGNIFICENT (*See page 273*) .	22
TOMBS OF MAHMUD II. AND ABDUL AZIZ . . .	38
ARMENIAN PEASANTS	48
A TURKISH WOMAN OF QUALITY	65
ARMENIANS WEAVING	88
A KURD PEASANT	100
A KURD WOMAN	102
A CIRCASSIAN	108
A GYPSY GIRL	114
AN ETHIOPIAN EUNUCH	116
AN OFFICER IN THE TURKISH ARMY	141
TURKISH WAR-SHIPS IN THE GOLDEN HORN . . .	143
A TURKISH PEASANT	150
A TURKISH SCHOOL	170
ROBERT COLLEGE, AT RUMILI HISSAR	174
THE SECOND HILL OF CONSTANTINOPLE	184
THE SEVEN TOWERS	187
HIPPODROME: — EGYPTIAN OBELISK, SERPENT COLUMN, AND MOSQUE OF SULTAN AHMED	188
SARCOPHAGUS OF ALEXANDER THE GREAT (End view) .	192
CASCADES AT THE SWEET WATERS OF EUROPE . .	200
PERA AND GALATA	202
ENGLISH CEMETERY AT SCUTARI	204
TURKISH WATER PEDDLER	208
THE NEW BRIDGE	212
THE DOGS OF CONSTANTINOPLE	214
THE FIELDS OF THE DEAD, IN THE HEART OF THE CITY .	217

List of Illustrations

	PAGE
A Turkish Café	221
Spice Bazaar at Constantinople	226
Fountain of Sultan Ahmed III.	232
Yildiz Kiosk and Mamidieh Jam Mosque	242
A Turkish Odalisque	246
Entrance of the Old Seraglio	250
The Selamlik: — The Sultan Entering His Mosque	252
Seraglio Point	254
Dolma Bagtché Palace	258
Palace of Beylerbey	260
Mosque of St. Sophia	264
Mosque of Sultan Ahmed	270
Turkish Beggars in Front of the Mosque of Suleiman the Magnificent	274
Pigeon Court of the Mosque of Sultan Bayezid	278
Whirling Dervishes	282
A Howling Dervish	284
River Meles, near Smyrna, the Reputed Birthplace of Homer	291
General View of Smyrna and the Acropolis	292
The Quays of Smyrna	294
Ephesus and the So-called Prison of St. Paul	295
Ephesus and the Ruins of the Temple of Diana	297

TURKEY AND THE TURKS

CHAPTER I

GEOGRAPHY OF THE BALKAN PENINSULA

Geographic position and natural advantages of European Turkey — Structural divisions — The Balkan range, the Dinaric Alps, and the Macedonian highland — The river basins — Mount Olympus, the abode of the gods — The Morava valley — Mount Athos, the mountain of the monks — Climatic zones in European Turkey — Area and political divisions of the Ottoman Empire — Centre of gravity in Asia — Population and important cities.

THE Balkan peninsula is the most easterly of the three great arms of land that project southward from the continent of Europe. Its northern boundary is a line drawn from the Gulf of Fiume to the source of the Kulpa, and along that river, the Save, and the Danube to the Black Sea. It is united to the mainland by a longer land boundary than either the peninsulas of Italy or Spain. In geographic position and natural advantages, it outranks both. It is less unwieldy in outline than Spain; and it surpasses Italy in variety of physiographic features. Its coasts are washed by four important seas; it is fringed by more than two score islands; and it has numerous drowned valleys and good harbours.

The word Balkan means mountain or mountain pass, and the peninsula is composed of such a variety of irregular mountain ranges and ridges that it is no easy task to organize geographic unity out of so great a variety of structural forms. So far as the peninsula has system, it classifies into three reasonably well defined plateaus — (1) the Balkan proper, in the northeast and east, (2) the Dinaric Alps, in the west, and (3) the Thracian-Macedonian highland between.

The Balkan range is the immediate continuation of the Carpathian mountains, and extends from the plain of Sophia in Bulgaria to Cape Emineh on the Black Sea; and forms the boundary between Bulgaria and eastern Rumelia. It subdivides into three sections. The first extends south from the Carpathians through eastern Servia, and is composed of crystalline schist and limestone ridges, which rise to an elevation of 6,500 feet; the second section extends eastward in a uniformly high central ridge with summits as high as 7,800; the third is composed of broken-down ridges, which gradually merge into the plain. The eastern coast along the shores of the Black Sea is steep, the only sharp indentation being the Gulf of Burgas in the middle.

The second structural section of the Balkan peninsula is formed by the Dinaric Alps in the west, an offshoot of the Alpine system, which connects the Julian Alps with the mountains of Albania and Greece and covers southern Croatia, Dalmatia, Herzegovina, and their diverse ramifications, rising at several points to an elevation of 6,500 feet, and separating the basin of the Save from the regions watered by the Kreka, the Narenta, and other streams flowing to the Adriatic. The stony and barren plateau is separated by longitudinal valleys; and, where the Drin, the Semen, and the Narenta break through the soft schistose chains, wild and picturesque ravines are formed, which shelter the marauding Albanians. In the western barrier of the Dinaric region are numerous rich plains and mineral deposits, and, under a stable and progressive government, they might easily maintain a dense population. The narrow plains extend to the mouth of the Drin, and from there north and northwestward to Fiume. Their coasts are mountainous and fringed by numerous long and narrow islands and peninsulas, separated by straits and bays, the result, doubtless, of the partial submergence of a folded mountain region. Mt. Olympus, the abode of the Celestials, and famed by Homer and other poets as the throne of the gods, is the most historic peak in the Dinaric Alps. It is in the Thessaly mountain range on the border of Macedonia, and rises to a height of 9,745 feet.

Between the Balkans and the Dinaric Alps lies the mountain highland of Thrace, Macedonia, and western Servia, an irregular mass of broad and flat crystalline hills, penetrated by numerous deep ravines and river valleys. One of these furrows forms the broad valley of the Morava, which flows north through the fertile hills of Servia to the Danube. The new railway from Vienna to Constantinople, through Belgrade, Sophia, and Adrianople, follows in the main the Morava valley. Another furrow branches southward from the Morava and is traversed by the Vardar River. These highland basins are the highways of

Geography of Balkan Peninsula 5

commerce and they contain the most populous of the Balkan cities. In this highland are the wild mountain ridges of the Rhodope, attaining an altitude of nearly 10,000 feet in such peaks as Rilodagh and Muss-Alla. Mt. Shardagh, in upper Macedonia, west of the Vardar valley, is more than 10,000 feet above sea-level, the highest peak in the Balkan peninsula.

Three rocky promontories project southward from the Balkan peninsula into the sea. The most easterly, known as the Athos promontory, is forty miles long, with an average width of four miles. The promontory is composed of a series of ridges; and, just below the point where Xerxes is said to have cut a canal, between the Gulf of Istillar and the present Gulf of Monte Santo, rises the historic peak of Mount Athos to an elevation of 6,350 feet. A sort of an ecclesiastical state, composed of thousands of hermits and saints of the Greek Orthodox church, circles the lower slopes of the holy mountain. The monks are held in high veneration in countries where the Orthodox religion is practised; they live in twenty monasteries, and they lead pious and retired lives. A company of soldiers is stationed at the neck of the promontory to prevent the sacred soil from being desecrated by the footsteps of women; and even the resident Turkish official on the peninsula is not permitted to have his harem with him. Not only women, but female animals in general are not allowed to approach the mountain of the hermits, which fact has led an English wit to apply the remark of Pliny to the holy mountain — "not a female of any kind, not a cow, nor a hen, nor a she-cat, nor a mare, nor an ewe." Nevertheless it is currently reported among the ungodly and the infidels in Turkey, that two American women a few years ago donned male attire and visited the sacred peninsula.

The topography and geographic position of the Balkan peninsula necessarily give it a variety of climate. The central portion and the eastern coast, as far as the Bosporus, have warm summers and cold winters, the thermometer not infrequently going below zero Fahrenheit. Constantinople, in spite of the fact that it is ten and a half degrees nearer the equator than London, has colder winters than the English metropolis. The winds from the Black Sea in winter are cold and bleak; the Golden Horn was frozen over in 1880, and in 1428 the ice in the Sea of Marmora was so thick that it injured the sea-wall. The rainfall on the eastern coast is less than in the central sections, but it is more uniformly distributed throughout the year. The southern coast of the peninsula has a sub-tropical climate similar to that of the Mediterranean countries. The Adriatic coast also has a relatively mild climate. It is exposed to the warm sea-breezes, and is protected by mountains from the changeable winds from the north, and it has heavy rainfall at all seasons. The climate is most trying in the north central section of the peninsula where the seasonal variations are greatest. Oranges, lemons, limes, figs, olives, and subtropical evergreen shrubs grow luxuriantly on the west coast; in the south the vegetation is scant, and in the central portions of the peninsula one finds the forest and orchard vegetation of northern Europe. The Adrianople plain is grassy and not unlike the steppes of Asia and is largely devoted to grazing.

The Balkan peninsula, however, is no longer the exclusive territory of Turkey. Greece, Rumania, Servia, and Montenegro are independent kingdoms; Bulgaria and eastern Rumelia are practically autonomous, notwithstanding the fact that an imperial Ottoman commissioner resides in Bulgaria; Bosnia and

Herzegovina have been occupied and administered by Austria and Hungary since 1878; Crete, with the adjacent islands, constitutes an autonomous state under a commissioner appointed by Great Britain, France, Italy, and Russia, subject to the suzerainty of the sultan, but without tribute; Cyprus is administered by Great Britain, the Porte receiving an annual tribute of half a million dollars; Samos, while forming a principality under the suzerainty of Turkey, is under the guarantee of France, Great Britain, and Russia; and Macedonian autonomy in the three vilayets of Monastir, Saloniki, and Adrianople, is almost an accomplished fact.

The area of the Balkan peninsula of European Turkey, including autonomous and tributary provinces, is only 64,600 square miles, or about that of the New England states with New Jersey added. Deducting, however, the provinces not under the immediate control of the Porte, European Turkey is reduced to the shabby pittance of 26,018 square miles, or about three times the area of the small commonwealth of Massachusetts or less than that of the state of South Carolina.

The centre of gravity of the Ottoman Empire is no longer in Europe but in Asia Minor.

The Asiatic provinces of the Porte include Armenia, Kurdistan, Mesopotamia, Syria, and Arabia — in area ten times greater than European Turkey. Egypt, Tripoli, and the Egyptian Sudan in Africa sustain a loose relationship to the Porte; so that all told the area of the Ottoman Empire nets more than a million and a half square miles, making Turkey territorially, after Great Britain and Russia, the third largest European nation.

The eleven vilayets of Asia Minor and Kurdistan contain the Porte's most obedient subjects. Armenia is not loyal; the interior of Arabia is controlled by independent rulers, and the provinces of Syria and Mesopotamia are only nominally under the control of governor-generals sent out by the Porte. Federation is even looser in Africa than in Europe. An Ottoman high councillor resides at Cairo; but Egypt can scarcely be called a tributary state of Turkey. She possesses full power of concluding commercial treaties with foreign nations and of maintaining an independent army. Tripoli, while nominally a Turkish vilayet, is more or less under the direct control of predatory Bedouins, and the Egyptian Sudan, since 1899, has been administered jointly by Great Britain and Egypt. Thus, what purports to be one of the largest empires of Europe, is, after all, a relatively small country.

Measured by population, Turkey is also a very small country. The whole Ottoman Empire — European, Asiatic, African, and Mediterranean, and including states that are only nominally subject to the sultans — barely reaches forty million souls, or less than the population of the British Isles; while the immediate Turkish possessions in Europe. have a population of but six million people, or about that of the New England states of the American Union. Osmanli Turks number only a tenth of the population of European Turkey, the other nine-tenths being Greeks, Albanians, Bulgarians, Wallachians, Hebrews, Servians, Magyars, Gypsies, Armenians, Circassians, and divers other races.

Contantinople, the capital, has a population (probably) of a million and a quarter of inhabitants, or about that of Philadelphia. Among the other important towns in European Turkey are Saloniki, an important shipping centre, with 105,000 inhabitants; Adrianople, which has had a large domestic traffic since the completion of the railway to northern Europe, with 81,000 inhabitants; and Dedeagatch at the mouth of the Maritza, which has a considerable export trade in Bulgarian wheat.

CHAPTER II

RISE OF THE OTTOMAN EMPIRE: 1300 - 1603

Tribal beginnings of the Osmanli Turks — Migration from the Desert of Gobi to Persia and Asia Minor — Osman the first Sultan — Conquests of Nicomedia and Nicæa by Orkhan — Murad I. crosses the Hellespont and captures Adrianople, Philippopolis, and Rumelia — Bulgaria added to the Ottoman Empire — Reign of Bayezid I. — The interregnum — Murad II. and Mohammed I. — Mohammed II. and the conquest of Constantinople — Servia, Bosnia, Trebizond, and Karaman added to the empire — The rebellious Jem and the pious Knights of St. John — Selim the Grim and conquests in Persia, Kurdistan, Syria, and Egypt — Possession of the caliphate — Suleiman the Legislator and the acquisition of Belgrade, Rhodes, Tripoli, and Algiers — Selim the Drunkard and the war with Ivan the Terrible — Georgia taken from Persia — Ottoman Empire at the time of Mohammed III.

It is important for purposes of reference, if not directly interesting, to relate so much of Ottoman history as may be necessary for the comprehension of the rise and decline of the empire. This recital will be limited to historic facts touching the acquisition and loss of territory. Readers who wish a brief survey of the historical development of Turkey will find the same in Stanley Lane-Poole's attract-

Rise of the Ottoman Empire 13

ive summary, "The Story of Turkey," and those seeking an exhaustive treatment of the subject are referred to Von Hammer's comprehensive work in seventeen volumes, "History of the Ottoman Turks."

When it is recalled that at the beginning of the 13th century the Osmanli Turks were pastoral tribes living in tents and movable huts in central Asia, slightly fixed to the soil, holding the camp rather than the land as native country, and recognizing allegiance only to powerful chiefs; that at the beginning of the 14th century they had migrated into Asia Minor and had become somewhat fixed to a small tract of land in Anatolia; at the beginning of the 15th century they had acquired vast possessions in Anatolia and Rumelia, Bulgaria, Ragusa, Servia, and Wallachia in Europe; at the beginning of the 16th century they had added Trebizond, Karaman, and Armenia in Asia, and Greece (including Constantinople), Bosnia, Herzegovina, Albania, and the Crimea in Europe; and by the middle of that century Tunis, Egypt, Algiers, and Tripoli in Africa, Kurdistan, Arabia, Syria, and Bagdad in Asia, and Moldavia, Hungary, and Transylvania in Europe — when significant facts like these are recalled, it is obvious that a brief historical survey of the rise and decline of the Ottoman Empire will form a necessary introduction to a study of Turkey and the Turks.

The Osmanli Turks are of Mongolian stock and they originated in the plains of Sungaria near the desert of Gobi. In the 13th century they fled before the fierce Mongols into Persia and from thence into Armenia. They were loosely federated under the leadership of hereditary chiefs, but they acquired skill in the arts of war as they migrated from the east. By chance they came upon two contending armies; and, with the instincts of warriors, the marauding Tatars cast their lot with the weaker force, and won the day for a Seljuk sultan in Asia Minor. In compensation for their services, they were given a small tract of land on the Byzantine frontier which included the two unimportant towns of Sugut and Eski Shehr.

The Tatar chief, who thus won a permanent foothold in Asia Minor for his tribe, was Ertoghrul, the son of Suleiman, a member of the family of Turks; and there was born to him at Sugut in the year A. D. 1258 a son Osman, the recognized founder of the Turkish Empire, whose descendants took the name of Osmanlis,

Rise of the Ottoman Empire 15

or Ottomans, as we more generally designate them. Osman succeeded his father in the year 1300; and, adding to his heritage Kara Hissar and other Greek towns, which he took by conquest, the Seljuk sultan, at Konia, permitted him to assume princely rank and gave him as symbols of royal elevation the drum and the horse-tail standard.

The Greek Empire was in decay and unable to withstand the fierce raids of the Mongols; but the barbarian conquerors were wholly deficient in organizing ability, and eventually one by one the subdued Greek provinces were possessed by Osman and his warriors as parts of the Ottoman Empire. Brusa was captured and Osman removed his capital thence from Sugut. He assumed all the prerogatives of an independent sovereign — coined money in his own name, caused prayers to be said for the reigning monarch, appointed governors for the conquered cities — and when he died in 1326, he bequeathed to his son Orkhan (1326-1359), the auspicious beginnings of a powerful Ottoman Empire.

Orkhan took Nicomedia and Nicæa from the Greeks and important towns and villages from Turkish states; he laid the foundations for a military empire in the organization of the famous (and later infamous) corps of the Janissaries; and he distinguished his reign by the foundation of numerous mosques, colleges, and other public institutions.

Murad I. succeeded Orkhan (1359-1389). After taking Angora, he crossed the Hellespont and laid the foundations for an Ottoman Empire in Europe by the capture of Adrianople, Philippopolis, and a large part of Rumelia. The appearance of the Osmanli Turks in Europe was apprehensively regarded by the Christian powers, and the military forces of the kings of Hungary, Servia, and Bosnia accordingly marched against Adrianople; but Murad I. won a signal victory over the allied Christian forces, and he returned to Brusa to celebrate the marriage of his eldest son Bayezid to the daughter of the prince of Kerman, a large part of whose territory came to the Ottoman Empire as a dowry. Returning to Europe he subdued Bulgaria and added it to his empire; he advanced into Servia and was forced to fight the allied armies of Hungary, Bosnia, Albania, Wallachia, and Servia. He was victorious in the great battle at Kosova and added Servia to his dominions. The victory, however, cost him his life. As he rode from the battle-field, a Servian soldier, who

Rise of the Ottoman Empire

simulated death, sprang up and stabbed the conqueror.

Bayezid I. took the oath of office on the battle-field (1389); and, before crossing the Hellespont, he augmented the Ottoman Empire by the capture of a number of important towns in Rumelia which still remained in the hands of the Christians. Bayezid I. next turned his attention to the capture of the capital of Byzantium; but invading Tatar tribes in some of his provinces in eastern Asia Minor forced him to return to Brusa. He was captured just outside Angora and died a prisoner of war in the year 1403. Tatar tribes overran the Ottoman provinces in Asia Minor and restored to their former emirs vast tracts that had been annexed by the predecessors of Bayezid.

An interregnum of ten years (1403-1413) in the dynasty of the Ottoman sultans follows, during which period there was civil war occasioned by the strife of the four sons of Bayezid I. for his throne. Mohammed I. (1413-1421) subdued his brothers and turned his attention to the restoration of the provinces lost during the closing years of his father's reign and the decade of civil war.

Murad II. succeeded Mohammed (1421-1451). His first official act was to besiege Constantinople; but a revolt in Asia Minor, headed by his brother, made it necessary for him to recross the Hellespont. The revolution was quelled, and the Asiatic provinces which had been lost to the Ottoman Empire, since the days of his grandfather and the interregnum, were restored. Returning to Europe, he faced a humiliating defeat at the hands of the great Hungarian general, Hunyadi; he was forced to sign a ten-year peace-treaty and to give up Servia and Wallachia. Murad abdicated in favour of his young son; but the Huns, following Christian advice, that compacts with infidel powers were not binding, violated the treaty. Murad resumed the reins of government; he marched against the treacherous Christians, utterly routed them, and abdicated a second time in favour of his son. But the lad was no match for the mutinous Janissaries, and Murad again assumed office and ruled until his death in 1451.

Mohammed II. (1451-1481) ascended the throne for the third time; and, in spite of the manifest incompetency of his earlier efforts at government, he accomplished the most significant fact in the rise of the Ottoman Empire — the conquest of Constantinople. Early in the spring of 1453 he declared war, on some

Rise of the Ottoman Empire

pretext or other, against the Greek empire and led an immense army against the capital. The weak and dissolute occupant of the Byzantine throne was no match for his antagonist; and on the 29th of May, 1453, the proud city of Constantine passed under Ottoman rule. Great as was the capture of Constantinople, it was not the only conquest of Mohammed. He recaptured Servia and Bosnia; annexed Trebizond and Karaman in Asia; established a suzerainty over the Crimea, and captured a number of islands in the Greek archipelago from Venice and Genoa.

Bayezid II. (1481-1512) succeeded the conqueror; but he was scarcely on his throne before he was called upon to quell a rebellion headed by his ambitious and valorous brother Jemshid, familiarly known as Jem. Suffering defeat, the young pretender fled and sought the protection of the Knights of St. John at Rhodes. The astute and shameful master of the ancient order pretended to give him protection and promised to furnish the necessary military force to depose Bayezid. From Jem's desolate wife he accepted twenty thousand ducats to accomplish this purpose. Meanwhile, the pious Christian master of the Knights contracted with Bayezid to hold the young rebel a prisoner for an annual consideration of forty-five thousand Turkish ducats. After being detained for some time at Rhodes, Jem was successively transferred from one commandery of the knights to another — to Nice, Roussillon, Pau, and Sassenage. Meanwhile, the monarchs of Europe recognizing the profitable nature of the care of Jem, expressed the desire to share with the Christian knights the ducats which the Sublime Porte was so willing to pay for brotherly peace. Charles VIII. of France accordingly relieved the knights of their charge and transferred him to the care and keeping of Pope Innocent VIII. The Holy Father consented to care for the prince for the sum of forty thousand ducats a year. Innocent did not live long enough to enjoy the anticipated financial reward. This was reserved for his successor, Alexander Borgia, who, as Stanley Lane-Poole has so well remarked, "has so many crimes on the place where his conscience should have been." The conspirators got into a squabble over the booty; Charles demanded the release of Jem; and, to spare Bayezid further trouble from his rebellious brother, it was agreed to have him assassinated for the lump sum of three hundred thousand ducats. Thus, after thirteen years of captivity among professing Christians, the unfortunate Jem ended his days. The melancholy incident is mentioned in this connection, because, in our estimates of the numerous shortcomings of the Ottoman infidels, this episode should not be forgotten; and, as the authority above quoted has so truly said, "when we come to read of the heroism of the Knights of Rhodes and Malta, it may be well to recall the history of Prince Jem, and to weigh well the chivalry that could fatten on such treason." Aside from the painful relations with his brother, the chief perfidy of which falls to the dishonour of Christian kings, popes, and knights, Bayezid II. was peace-loving and unambitious. His only wars were for purposes of defence; and during his reign there was won the first great Turkish naval victory off Sapienza against the Venetians.

Selim I., known as Selim the Grim, because of his merciless cruelty, deposed and succeeded his father (1512-1520). He was one of the greatest monarchs who has occupied the Ottoman throne, — a man of fine literary attainments, keen political sagacity, and tireless vigour. The anxiety that his father had experienced he obviated by putting his brothers to death. He left the Christian nations at peace, and directed his vast energies to the south and east — Persia, Kurdistan, Syria, and Egypt, all of which he annexed to his dominions, thus doubling the area of the Ottoman Empire. Most important, he came into possession of the caliphate of Islam, and thus became the spiritual head of the Mohammedan world. The sacred banner and relics of the prophets were transferred from the spiritual Arabian princes at Cairo to St. Sophia in Constantinople.

Suleiman I., known as the Legislator, the Magnificent, and the Sublime, succeeded Selim (1520-1566). A war with Hungary was the first event of his reign; and the strongly fortified city of Belgrade was added to his empire as the result. The island of Rhodes was taken from the Knights of St. John, and Tripoli and Algiers in Africa were made tributary states. Suleiman, however, suffered two significant defeats in the siege of Vienna and the great naval battle at Malta. He is without doubt one of the most dominating figures in Ottoman history. One of his Christian biographers says of him: "His personal qualities were superb; his wisdom, justice, generosity, kindness, and courtesy were a proverb, and his in-

MOSQUE OF SULEIMAN THE MAGNIFICENT.
(See page 273)

Rise of the Ottoman Empire 23

tellectual gifts were the counterpart of his fine moral nature.'' The reign of Suleiman, the Magnificent, marks the climax in the rise of the Ottoman Empire; for, while Cyprus, Crete, Georgia, and Tunis were subsequently conquered, and the real downward turn in the road was not reached for nearly forty years, the Ottoman Empire, henceforth, in all that concerns power, wealth, and prosperity, must look to the past.

The mean and ignoble Selim II., known as the Drunkard, next came to the throne (1566-1579). His reign was inaugurated by the first of a long (and probably still unfinished) series of wars with Russia; for, in his efforts to annex Astrakhan to his dominions, he found the Muscovite Ivan the Terrible his match. He succeeded better with Tunis and Cyprus, both of which he conquered; but he suffered a humiliating defeat in 1571 just outside the Gulf of Lepanto at the hands of the allied Christian forces of Austria, Spain, Venice, and Malta.

The weak and dissolute Murad III. (1574-1595) succeeded Selim. The Janissaries mutinied and made exacting demands which the impotent ruler was forced to grant. Georgia was taken from Persia and the province of

Azerbijon was captured, but Murad was forced to maintain defensive wars in Transylvania, Moldavia, and Wallachia.

Murad died in 1595 when matters in the north were going much against Turkey, and he was followed by Mohammed III. (1595-1603), who succeeded temporarily in subduing the rebellious provinces and in defeating the allied Austrian and Hungarian armies. Mohammed III. was the last of the Ottoman rulers to come to the throne with any experience in governmental affairs, since his father was the last of the sultans to share the control of the empire with the prospective heir. With Mohammed III. was introduced into Turkey the vicious system of imprisoning all possible rival claimants to the throne. According to the Moslem law of succession, the legitimate heir to the throne is the sultan's oldest male relative — not necessarily his son, but sometimes his brother or nephew. Ottoman rulers have held that empire is a bride whose favours cannot be shared; and the Koran teaches that sedition is worse than slaughter; hence, successive sultans from the time of Osman, the Victorious, to Mohammed III. have averted civil strife and transmitted the crown to their own offspring by the simple device of putting

Rise of the Ottoman Empire

to death ambitious brothers. Mohammed III. was the last to follow this rule. He was one of a family of one hundred and two children, twenty of whom were boys; and his nineteen brothers were summarily despatched to another world upon his ascent to the throne.

The reign of Mohammed III. brings to a close the third century of Ottoman history, and it terminates the expansion of Ottoman dominions. Henceforth, as will be shown in the succeeding chapter, the road is downward. The empire which he bequeathed to his son Ahmed was about equally divided among the three continents of Europe, Asia, and Africa, and extended from Mecca to Budapest, from Algiers to Bagdad. It included ancient sites like Nineveh, Babylon, Tyre, Carthage, and Memphis; such historical cities as Damascus, Alexandria, Athens, Mecca, Philippi, and Jerusalem; and, among great commercial centres, Smyrna, Cairo, Belgrade, Medina, Bagdad, and Constantinople. The Nile, the Tigris, the Euphrates, the Jordan, and the Danube were Turkish rivers, and the Red, the Black, and the Caspian Seas, as well as the eastern half of the Mediterranean, were Turkish lakes.

CHAPTER III

DECLINE OF THE OTTOMAN EMPIRE: 1603-1876

Causes of decline — The reigns of Ahmed and Mustafa — Wars with Poland and Persia — Occupation of Crete — Unsuccessful war with Austria and loss of Transylvania, Hungary, Slavonia, Podolia, Dalmatia, Morea, and Azov — War with Peter the Great — Moldavia and Wallachia taken by Catherine of Russia — First European alliance for the maintenance of the balance of power — Napoleon's invasion of Egypt — Rebellion in Servia — Destruction of the Janissaries — The Crimean war — Abdul-Aziz deposed.

WHEN Ahmed I. (1603-1617) became sultan in 1603, the Ottoman Empire had reached the downward turn in the road. Territorially it was at its zenith and comprised Transylvania, Hungary, Moldavia, the Crimea, Albania, Herzegovina, Bosnia, Greece, Wallachia, Servia, Ragusa, Rumelia, and Adrianople in Europe; Bagdad, Syria, Arabia, Armenia, Kurdistan, Karaman, Anatolia, Trebizond, Georgia, and Bithnyia in Asia; Tunis, Tripoli, Egypt, and Algiers in Africa; and Cyprus, Crete, Malta, Rhodes, and Mitylene in the Mediterranean.

Decline of the Ottoman Empire

And it was fifty years before Algiers was lost to the deys and Tunis to the beys, and a hundred years before Hungary was lost to Austria. Still, symptoms of decline were apparent long before the dismemberment of the empire began, even though these symptoms were slow and insidious in development.

The causes of the decline of the Ottoman Empire are numerous and complex: The Osmanli Turks — the ruling class, at least — had grown effeminate, incompetent, and corrupt; sultans no longer placed themselves at the head of the imperial army in times of danger; they ceased to concern themselves directly with affairs of state, preferring instead to lead ignoble and luxurious lives in their palaces in Constantinople; the capricious Janissaries also lost their martial efficiency and likewise degenerated; troops were inadequately equipped; officers could not be trusted; military training was neglected, and Turkey no longer kept pace with modern improvements in weapons and military tactics. Most important, perhaps, was the appearance in European history at this time of the formidable and avaricious Russians who practised the methods of by-gone generations of heroic Osmanli Turks. Hence, the three subsequent centuries of Ottoman history are characterized by humiliation, defeat, loss of territory, and corrupt rule.

Mustafa I. succeeded Ahmed in 1617, but his short reign was uneventful; he proved to be an imbecile, and was succeeded by his brother, Osman II. (1618-1622), the next year. The latter had an inconsequential war with Poland and an unsuccessful war with Persia, which resulted in the loss of all the Persian territory acquired during the previous half-century. The Janissaries mutinied; and, in his efforts to discipline them, they deposed and murdered him and placed Murad IV. (1623-1640), a child of eleven years, on the throne in 1623. In spite of his youth, Murad proved the most courageous and efficient sultan since the days of Suleiman, the Magnificent. He disciplined the rebellious Janissaries by decapitating the ringleader; he recaptured Bagdad and other Persian provinces lost during the reign of his predecessor; and he reformed provincial administration by executing every official whom he suspected of dishonesty.

Ibrahim (1640-1648), a dissolute, dishonest, and vicious ruler, succeeded his brother Murad. He took Azov from the Russians, and in part occupied the island of Crete; but be-

Decline of the Ottoman Empire

cause of his tyranny he was forced to abdicate in 1648 in favour of his seven-year-old son Mohammed IV. (1648-1687). The young sultan completed the occupation in Crete; but the territorial losses in the wars with Austria, Poland, Russia, and Venice were so great that he was deposed, and was succeeded by his brother Suleiman II. (1687-1691).

Suleiman waged a successful war against Austria and Servia, and Belgrade was again garrisoned with Ottoman troops. His brother Ahmed II. (1691-1695) followed him in a brief and disastrous reign. Austria wrested from him several provinces, and his empire was decimated by pestilence and civil strife. Mustafa II. (1695-1703) came to the throne in 1695. At first successful against Austria and the allied Christian powers, he finally suffered a crushing defeat. England and Holland intervened and brought about the treaty of Carlowitz, by the conditions of which Austria was left in possession of Transylvania and most of Hungary and Slavonia; Poland got Podolia; Venice retained Dalmatia and Morea, and Peter the Great, of Russia, got Azov. Mustafa abdicated in favour of his brother Ahmed III. (1703-1730).

Henceforth Russia is a power that has to be

reckoned with, and Ahmed was soon called upon to wage a defensive war against the wily Muscovite. Peter the Great was overwhelmingly defeated; and, had Ahmed chosen to follow up his victory, Russia might have been crushed by the Ottoman forces. But the sultan was content with the restoration of the fortress of Azov and its dependencies, and the assurance that Peter would grant a safe escort to Charles XII., of Sweden, to his own possessions, the Swedish king after the battle of Poltava having taken refuge in Turkey. A later unsuccessful war with Austria resulted in the loss of the remaining Hungarian provinces, together with large portions of Servia and Wallachia. Ahmed abdicated in favour of his nephew, Mahmud I. (1730-1754). Russia invaded the Crimea and captured Azov. Turkey met the allied Russian and Austrian forces; and the latter sustained a crushing defeat near Belgrade, and was forced to sue for peace. Orsova and Belgrade were restored to the Turks, together with portions of Servia, Bosnia, and Wallachia. Russia, unable to continue the war single-handed, likewise sued for peace. Turkey required her to raze the fortifications at Azov, and to guarantee to keep no warships in the Black Sea and the Sea of Azov.

Decline of the Ottoman Empire 31

But this was the last advantageous peace made by Ottoman rulers without the aid of foreign allies.

Osman III. came to the throne in 1754; three years later he was followed by Mustafa III. (1757-1773). The astute and unscrupulous Catherine now occupied the Muscovite throne, and the decadent sultans were no match for her genius and treachery. She conquered Moldavia and Wallachia; invaded the Crimea and the Greek archipelago, and instigated the Egyptian bey to rebel against the Sublime Porte. Abdul-Hamid I. (1773-1789) succeeded Mustafa, and Catherine found it to her advantage to arrange an armistice with Turkey. Then she secretly sent a strong Russian force across the Danube and inflicted such heavy injuries that she was able to exact the most humiliating peace terms which an Ottoman ruler had hitherto signed. The most damaging clause to Turkey was the permission given Russia to erect a church in Constantinople. This alone would have been inconsequential, but the wily Catherine further exacted that " the Porte promises to protect the Christian religion and its churches; and it also allows the court of Russia to make upon all occasions representations as well in favour of the new church at Constantinople, as on behalf of its ministers, promising to take such representations into consideration." Upon the basis of this flimsy clause Russia has since claimed the right of protection over all the Christian subjects of the sultan; and most of the subsequent wars against Turkey have alleged violation of this treaty-right as a pretext. The treaty further stipulated that Russia might fortify the Black Sea, have free navigation for her merchant marine in all Turkish waters, and establish Russian consulates at all Turkish ports. The last clause was a significant factor in the ultimate dismemberment of European Turkey. Greek traders received the consular offices; they developed Greek commerce and a Greek navy while flying the Russian flag; and Catherine's far-reaching schemes bore their precious fruits in the next century. She arranged with the Emperor of Austria for the immediate partition of portions of European Turkey, and together they crossed the Danube and invaded Ottoman territory, but Mustafa outgeneralled and defeated Catherine, and she was forced to make an inglorious retreat to Hungary.

Selim III. (1789-1807) followed Mustafa. It was now apparent to some of the northern

Decline of the Ottoman Empire 33

powers of Europe that Catherine was determined to transfer the seat of her government from St. Petersburg to Constantinople. Accordingly England, Holland, and Prussia formed an alliance for the protection of Turkey and the maintenance of the balance of power. The alliance was inoperative because public opinion in England declared against it. Austria, however, was intimidated, and Catherine was forced to continue her war against Turkey single-handed. Troubles nearer home — in Poland — made peace with Turkey convenient, and she annexed Otchakov with its seaboard as far as the Dniester to her empire, and placed Tiflis and Kartalinia under Russian protection. Death relieved this Bonaparte in petticoats from the complete annihilation of the Ottoman power in Europe. Her son Paul did not find it convenient to continue the war against Turkey.

A Catherine in pantaloons in France, it will be recalled, was making matters rather lively for Europe at this time. Napoleon had invaded Egypt; and the destruction of his fleet by Nelson led to the transportation of a Turkish army from Rhodes to Egypt, which was defeated by the Corsican, in 1799, at the battle of Aboukir; but an English expedition ultimately wrested Egypt from the French and restored it to Turkey.

In his efforts at governmental reform Selim was deposed by the Janissaries in 1807, and they placed on the Ottoman throne a tool of their own, Mustafa IV. (1807-1808). Fourteen months later the adherents of the deposed Selim marched against Constantinople to restore him to his throne. He was murdered as they entered the city, and Mahmud II. (1808-1839), his only surviving brother, was made sultan. Servia, aided by Russia, had been in rebellion against Ottoman power during previous reigns; and, in 1817, single-handed she was able to force Mahmud to grant her autonomy. In spite of the fact that Mahmud was a reformer of character and intelligence, his forces were too disorganized to cope with his Muscovite adversary, his rebellious Danubian provinces, and his troublesome vassal Mehemet Ali of Egypt. His empire in consequence was irreparably dismembered. By the conditions of the treaty of Adrianople, Greece was declared an independent kingdom; Russia acquired Anapa and Pola on the Black Sea; her protectorate over the Danubian provinces was confirmed and extended; and the Bosporus

Decline of the Ottoman Empire 35

and Dardanelles were opened to the merchant ships of all nations.

Sultan Mahmud II. has a large place in Ottoman history for his courageous act of complete annihilation of the capricious, corrupt, and disobedient corps of Janissaries. Turkish history, as the reader will have noted, is entirely military; and, from the time of Orkhan the Victorious to Mahmud the Reformer, the military strength of the empire was vested in the corps of the Janissaries. From the days of Murad (1360), Christian villages and towns in the empire were required quadrennially to contribute one-fifth of their male population — the healthiest, most vigorous, and brightest fifth — between the ages of six and nine years, as recruits for the Janissaries. These Christian-born lads were completely separated from families and friends, and taken to Constantinople, where they were given a Mohammedan education and military training. They were not permitted to marry or engage in commerce, but were supported at state expense, and subject to the discipline of one of their number. A few, upon reaching adulthood, were given posts in the civil service; but nearly all were drafted into military service in one of the 165 companies of the Janissaries.

During the period described in the previous chapter on the Rise of the Ottoman Empire, the Janissaries doubtless constituted the most efficient and formidable military body that the world had thus far known. Both physically and mentally they were picked men; they were given the best secular and religious education open to Ottoman laymen; they were more completely divorced from family ties than Roman Catholic monks; they were trained to render unquestioned obedience to their superior officers; and so long as they used their ability and power for the glory of the Ottoman Empire, Turkey was the most formidable military nation of the world.

But the Janissaries ultimately changed their aims and character; their military efficiency departed; they grew selfish and despotic, and they deposed and beheaded sultans at their pleasure. Various causes brought about their deterioration. A century after the conquest they were given permission to marry and to admit their own children into the service; later they were allowed to engage in trade; and, in case of distant wars, to provide substitutes. With these changes virtue, morality, discipline, and patriotism departed from among them. Various sultans endeavoured to reform

Decline of the Ottoman Empire 37

them, but they customarily deposed or beheaded any ruler who had the temerity to attempt to reform or purify the service. They were avaricious, corrupt, dissolute, and disloyal, and Constantinople was repeatedly at their mercy; until finally Sultan Mahmud II., in 1826, summarily exterminated every one of them and burned the historic quarters where they had so long resided.

Abdul - Mejid (1839 - 1861) succeeded his father, and ruled for twenty-two years. The Crimean war was the great event of his reign. Nicholas of Russia asserted his rights of protection over all the adherents of the Greek Orthodox church in Turkey; Abdul-Mejid declined to recognize the claim; and Russia, with Austria as an ally, invaded the Danubian provinces. It was apparent to the powers of Europe that Russian greed of Constantinople was the cause of the war; accordingly England and France (and later Italy) intervened; and the dream of Nicholas to occupy the city of Constantine was dissipated. The treaty which concluded the awful Crimean war forced Russia to cede to Turkey the districts in Bessarabia adjacent to the mouth of the Danube, and her exclusive protectorate over the Danubian provinces was abolished. They were placed instead under the guarantee of all the powers. The Black Sea was neutralized, and both Russia and Turkey were denied the right to have warships or erect arsenals there. Turkey further guaranteed hitherto unrecognized rights to her non-Moslem subjects, and established (on paper) that equality between her Christian and Mohammedan subjects which she has ever since studiously violated.

Abdul-Aziz became sultan in 1861; but he placed himself so completely under Russian control and plunged the empire into such great indebtedness that he lost his crown in 1876. He was succeeded by Murad V., who, because of his liberal views, was deposed after a reign of but three months. He was succeeded by his brother Abdul-Hamid II., the present sultan, whose long and eventful reign is discussed in the next chapter.

TOMBS OF MAHMUD II. AND ABDUL AZIZ.

CHAPTER IV

THE OTTOMAN EMPIRE TO-DAY: 1876-1906

Brief reign of Murad — Abdul-Hamid II. on the throne — Rebellions in Herzegovina, Bulgaria, Montenegro, Servia, and Rumania — War with Russia — The treaty of Berlin and disintegration of the Ottoman Empire — Armenian troubles — Rebellion in Crete and war with Greece — Macedonian outbreaks — Work of the commission — Growing influence of Germany — The future of Turkey.

THE scandalously extravagant administration of Abdul-Aziz plunged Turkey into an indebtedness of more than $100,000,000, with nothing to show for it. About the only praiseworthy act of his reign of fifteen years was a visit to London, Paris, and other European capitals. It was regarded as a great state affair for a successor of the Prophet to quit the Ottoman dominions, except when on the warpath. In fact the Koran forbids it; and, as Abdul-Aziz was a zealous religious bigot, while on his European tour he caused the soles of his shoes to be daily powdered with earth from his own dominions. But subserviency to the interests of Russia and the prospective bankruptcy of the Ottoman Empire cost Abdul-Aziz his throne. He was deposed May 29, 1876, and was succeeded by Murad V., a son of Abdul-Mejid.

During the corrupt reign of Abdul-Aziz liberal political notions had gained a footing among a few progressive young men who were called the "Young Turks." They demanded the abrogation of absolutism and the promulgation of a constitution with a liberal form of government. The murder of the deposed sultan, contrary to the wishes of Murad, produced a nervous illness, which, coupled with the fact that he sympathized with the Young Turk party, caused great alarm with the Sheik-ul-Islam, the ministers, and the court officials. To be possessed of liberal political notions was accounted evidence of insanity; and for a sultan to suggest a constitution and a limited monarchy was diagnostic of an advanced state of paresis. Accordingly, August 31, 1876, after a reign of but three months, the Sheik-ul-Islam declared Murad mentally unfit to rule; he was deposed and Abdul-Hamid II., the present sultan, succeeded him.

Abdul-Hamid found the Ottoman Empire bankrupt and in a state of rebellion. Insurrections in Herzegovina, Bosnia, and Bulgaria had broken out during the last months of the reign of Abdul-Aziz; and Montenegro and Servia had declared war against Turkey during the short reign of Murad. The Servians were brutally subdued in October; and, in attempting to put down the rebellion in Bulgaria, in May that year, the Turkish soldiers slaughtered whole communities of men, women, and children. The atrocities aroused the indignation of Christian Europe; and in September Mr. Gladstone published his historic pamphlet which produced intense feelings against the Turks. The sultan was alarmed, and he called to his aid the liberal statesman, Midhat Pasha, as Grand Vizier. The new premier assured his sovereign that a constitution and a liberal form of government were necessary to save the Ottoman Empire from complete disruption; and Abdul-Hamid, unwillingly, promulgated a constitution December the 23d, 1876.

There were but two sessions of the Turkish parliament; and trustworthy contemporary authorities assert that it behaved itself in a manner that at once filled those who wished well to Turkish reform with admiration and surprise. But Abdul-Hamid was the *bête noir*. The constitution had been forced upon him; he was unwilling to play the rôle of a servant of his people; corrupt and powerful provincial pashas, against whom parliamentary reforms were aimed, sided with the Padishah; and, February the 5th, 1877, the constitution was abrogated, Midhat Pasha was dismissed, and Abdul-Hamid resumed his despotic powers.

Turkish cruelties in the Balkan provinces had grown so glaring that Russia asked England and the other Christian powers to force Turkey to grant some of the reforms demanded by the revolutionists, and to cease the brutal massacre of innocent men, women, and children. But England, as Turkey's friend, was unwilling to employ force, and suggested moral suasion, which she had ineffectively employed ever since the Crimean war. A congress was accordingly called at Constantinople; the Great Powers drew up certain reform measures, which they required Abdul-Hamid to put into effect, but the sultan promptly declined to give the reforms consideration. England was unwilling to employ force, and Russia withdrew from the concert and declared war against Turkey, April the 24th, 1877. Abdul-Hamid relied implicitly upon the aid of England in case of war with Russia; and but for the indignation among the English people, occasioned by Mr. Glad-

The Ottoman Empire To-day 43

stone's pamphlet, this aid doubtless would have been forthcoming.

Russia formed an alliance with Rumania, the latter declaring her independence of Turkey, and the Danubian provinces were invaded. Mukhtar Pasha retained Kars for a time against the siege of the Russians; but defeats soon began to come "thick and fast." Lootsk was stormed by the Russians September the 3d; Nikšič was won by the Montenegrins September the 8th; Plevna was stormed September the 11th; Mukhtar Pasha suffered a severe defeat at Aladja Duga October the 15th; Gurko, the leading Russian general, stormed Gorin-Dubrik October the 24th, and four days later he captured Telish; Kars was successfully stormed November the 18th; the army of Osman Pasha was nearly annihilated and forced to surrender at Plevna, December the 10th, and the same month Gurko crossed the Balkans to aid the Servians.

The year 1878 opened with the capture of Sofia by Gurko, January the 4th; Kartzoff forced his army through the Troyon Pass, and January the 7th he captured a large body of Turkish troops at Shipka; the Servians forced Nish to surrender January the 10th and the Montenegrins took Antivari the same day; the army of Suleiman was completely routed near Philippopolis January the 17th; three days later Adrianople fell; and within a week the Russian troops were marching toward the undefended capital. Turkey sued for peace; an armistice was declared; and the treaty of San Stefano, signed March the 3d, 1878, concluded the war. Both sides had lost heavily; for in the taking Plevna the Russians had sacrificed 50,000 men.

England, angered at the success of the Russians, declined to abide by the conditions of the treaty of San Stefano, and declared that the matter must be submitted to a congress of the Great Powers; and to this proposition Russia did not object. Accordingly a congress convened at Berlin June the 13th, 1878. It subsequently transpired that the queen's government had concluded a secret treaty with Turkey prior to the meeting of the congress at Berlin. The chief features of the treaty of San Stefano are given in a closing chapter on the Near-Eastern Question. The treaty of Berlin was signed July the 13th, 1878. It provided (1) that Bessarabia, taken from Russia after the Crimean war, should be returned to her and she was allowed to retain her Turkish conquests in Asia — Kars, Batum, and Ardahan; (2) Servia, Montenegro, and Rumania were declared independent kingdoms; (3) Bosnia and Herzegovina were placed under the protection of Austria; (4) the portion of Bulgaria north of the Balkans was organized into an autonomous principality; and (5) Greece was apportioned Thessaly, and her boundary lines were more exactly defined.

The treaty of Berlin was more damaging to Turkey than the treaty of San Stefano had been; and it denied the Armenians the protection of Russia. In the light of subsequent events, Lord Beaconsfield's "peace with honour" was dyed in hypocrisy. By the terms of the secret treaty which England made with Turkey she undertook to defend the sultan's Asiatic provinces by force of arms from any further conquests on the part of Russia, in return for which she received the island of Cyprus, presumably as a base for operations; and in a mysterious way she announced herself to the world as the protector of the Christian subjects of the sultan in Armenia. The fact that she has done nothing to end maladministration and oppression in Armenia and that, when called upon in the name of humanity to stop senseless Armenian pillage and slaughter, she has confessed herself powerless to interfere, makes the hollowness of her pretensions clearly apparent. And for Lord Beaconsfield to assert that the treaty of Berlin gave Turkey " peace with honour " shows him to have been a man entirely without a sense of humour. A more damaging treaty could not have been concocted; and, as an English historian has pointed out, the selfish Beaconsfield and his grasping Berlin congress " sounded the knell of Turkish dominion in Europe."

With the loss of Rumania, Servia, Montenegro, Bulgaria, Bosnia, Herzegovina, and Thessaly — to name only the provinces lost to the sultan in Europe — she was reduced in area 138,000 square miles and 12,000,000 souls in population. She has a little more than a third as many square miles of territory in Europe as she had before the enforcement of the treaty of Berlin and but half the population. The part which England played in this treaty, as before suggested, was altogether dishonourable, for she has not only failed to give expression to her pretended protectorate of Armenia, but she has prevented other Christian nations from moving in the matter.

Acute troubles in Armenia began in 1883, and have continued intermittently ever since. The sultan had represented to England, at the

The Ottoman Empire To-day

close of the last war with Russia, that administrative abuses in Armenia would be reformed, but he had done nothing to better matters; and the Armenians, looking to England and Russia for support, broke out in rebellion at Erzerum. The rebellion was promptly crushed and the insurgents mercilessly slaughtered. Crete during the same year rebelled against oppressive Turkish taxes, and the Cretan insurgents suffered a like fate. Abdul-Hamid attempted to nationalize the Ottoman Empire in 1884, and outbreaks among his Christian subjects took place in many provinces. Moslem fanatics in Macedonia and the Yemen complicated the problem by committing senseless and inhuman outrages.

The year 1888 marks the beginning of the Armenian trouble in its graver form. That year the Armenians were active in agitating for the reëstablishment of their ancient kingdom. The Turks retaliated by oppressing the Armenians more than ever. The latter appealed to England, but she refused aid on the ground that interference was forbidden by the treaty of Berlin. The Turkish outrages continued during 1889 and 1890. Whole villages were slaughtered; and the sultan justified the action of his savage soldiers on the pretext that they were simply putting down rebellion and restoring peace by armed force. A threatened insurrection in the Yemen in 1891 disturbed the amicable relations between England and the sultan, but the incident put him on friendly terms with Russia.

During the year 1893 Armenian publicists established committees in the chief cities of Europe and began the agitation of Armenian grievances against the barbarities of the Turks. The sultan was angered by the unfavourable criticism which the propaganda of the Armenian committee occasioned abroad, and a reign of terror broke out in Armenia in 1895 and continued for nearly two years. Presumably at the instigation of the Ottoman government, the Kurds destroyed more than forty Armenian villages and murdered thousands of people. It has not been clearly established that these massacres were directly ordered by the sultan, but there is a mass of damaging circumstantial evidence to that effect. The righteous indignation of Europe brought the stupid sultan to his senses; and temporarily, the slaughter of the Armenians ceased.

Georges Dorys, in his " Private Life of the Sultan," relates that when the London press, after the Armenian massacres, urged Europe

ARMENIAN PEASANTS.

The Ottoman Empire To-day 49

to depose Abdul-Hamid, and Admiral Seymour, with an English fleet, in a disquieting manner manœuvred the Archipelago, the sultan one night decided that flight abroad was his only means of safety. "He summoned his ministers in extraordinary council," says Dorys, "to deliberate on the situation, while his yacht *Izzeddin* was anchored off Bechiktach with steam up ready to take him to Odessa. One of his ministers suggested that the German embassy be consulted. The sultan immediately despatched his favourite Izzet Bey to the representative of Kaiser Wilhelm. During the absence of his envoy the sultan, his face the picture of anxiety and gloom, paced feverishly up and down the room. He had on his person all his jewels; and bonds for a considerable amount could be seen stuffed into the pockets of his belt. But when Izzet Bey brought back the promise that Wilhelm would stand by *his friend,* Abdul-Hamid so far forgot himself for joy that he almost knelt down before the favourite, so profuse was he in his assurances of his gratitude and affection." As an additional bit of evidence of the sultan's fear of the results of the Armenian massacres, William Eleroy Curtis[1] states that

[1] "The Turk and His Lost Provinces." Chicago, 1903.

he was informed by a high authority in Constantinople that after the Armenian massacre the sultan distributed more than $1,000,000 among the European newspapers that treated him kindly, and it must be remembered that Abdul-Hamid is not a spendthrift. A former correspondent of the London *Times* states that Abdul-Hamid tried to buy that paper; and Dorys asserts that, in addition to $1,000,000 paid from the Turkish treasury in allocation to certain European newspapers, something like six hundred and forty decorations were conferred.

Armenian barbarities, however, are liable to be renewed at any time. With strong race and religious animosities such outrages are always possible in a theocratic despotism like Turkey. The Duke of Argyll remarked in this connection concerning the Armenian massacres of 1894, that it was " one of those appalling outbreaks of brutality on the part of the Turks which always horrify but need not astonish the world. They are all according to what Bishop Butler would call ' the natural constitution and course of things; ' that is to say, they are the natural results of the nature and government of the Ottoman Turks. The cruelties of their rule are not accidental, but chronic and inherent. Their revenue system is, to the last degree, corrupt and oppressive. Their judicial system is not only corrupt, but involves besides an open denial of justice to their Christian subjects. Their executive system of armed ruffians, in the shape of Zapties or police, is still such as was described forty-five years ago by Sir Fenwick Williams. Thus in all great leading departments of administration the causes of oppression are as obvious as they are grinding and desolating in their effects."

The Cretans rebelled against Turkish oppression again in 1896, and a year later the Greeks attacked the Turks in behalf of their oppressed countrymen in Crete, but they were disastrously defeated. After long delays in the settlement of the claims of French contractors for the construction of the docks at Saloniki — claims aggregating something like $15,000,000 — France, on November the 5th, 1901, seized the island of Mitylene and took possessions of the customs. The sultan again appealed to his friend the German Kaiser; but the German Minister of Foreign Relations advised the Turkish ambassador at Berlin to pay the bill. A small payment was made and a mortgage, upon the future receipts of the

Turkish custom-house, was given. When the second instalment of the mortgage fell due in 1905, France had to send another fleet to Mitylene, and the same process will probably continue until the debt is paid.

In 1903 there were serious outbreaks in Macedonia. The vilayets of Saloniki, Monastir, and Adrianople, unable longer to bear the oppression of their Turkish masters, revolted. William E. Curtis, who visited the Macedonian provinces shortly after the outbreaks, says concerning the causes of the difficulties: " Human life and property have been held as worthless by the Turkish officials and military garrisons. No woman has been safe from their lust. No man has been allowed to accumulate property or to improve his condition without exciting the avarice of the tax-gatherer and the military commandant. It has been useless for the inhabitants to save money or to produce more than enough to supply their own wants, for the slightest surplus would attract attention and be stolen from the owner. The Christian population has had no standing in the courts and is often prohibited from practising its religion. The number of lives wantonly taken, the number of women ravished and the number of children butchered in the

The Ottoman Empire To-day

Turkish provinces of Europe, particularly in Rumelia, where the population is almost entirely Christian, would shock the world if the truth were known." Macedonia is simply a replica of Armenia, so far as her grievances are concerned; but, being under the eye of the European powers, slaughter and pillage have not been permitted to continue indefinitely unrebuked.

Shortly after the Macedonian disturbances of 1903, Emperor Francis Joseph of Austria-Hungary and Czar Nicholas of Russia held a conference for the purpose of putting a stop to the outrages. They asserted that their aim was the preservation of the Turkish territory in Europe and the pacification of the revolting provinces. They demanded (1) a special governor-general for Macedonia to be appointed by Turkey; (2) the appointment of two civil commissioners — one to be named by Austria-Hungary and the other by Russia — to be associated with the governor-general in the control of the disturbed provinces, and (3) the reorganization of the military forces, and the supervision of the same by an Italian officer as commander-in-chief and sixty officers chosen from the armies of the Great Powers of Europe. These measures it was hoped would end the revolts and relieve the Christian population of needless Moslem oppression. The sultan, after some delay, consented to the reform measures for a period of two years. Provision was made for the renewal of the measure at the end of the two-year period; and before its expiration the sultan asked for its prolongation.

Both Austria-Hungary and Russia were disappointed with the results of the measure, and they reached the conclusion that so long as Turkey controlled the finances of Macedonia efforts to maintain peace would be futile. Taxes, they alleged, were collected after established Ottoman customs — more than half the amount collected going to the private fortunes of the tax-farmers; and none of the tax was used for internal improvements in Macedonia. The Great Powers of Europe accordingly declined to continue the previous reform measure. They demanded instead (1) that wholesale robbery of the Macedonian peasants must cease; (2) that hereafter the collection of taxes in Macedonia must be controlled by a finance commission selected by the Great Powers, and (3) that customs duties and taxes must be used for the good of Macedonia.

They selected their commissioners and sent

The Ottoman Empire To-day

them to Macedonia. But the governor-general, following instructions from the sultan, refused to sanction their official labours. The interested Powers, through their ambassadors at Constantinople, demanded a joint conference with the sultan, but this was refused. It was accordingly decided by the Powers to make a joint naval demonstration; and, if necessary, to seize certain custom-houses and blockade the coast. But the sultan regarded the action of the Powers merely in the light of a threat. Russia had just been humiliated by Japan; Austria-Hungary had home vexations; the German Kaiser was his friend and would take no part in such a demonstration; and it was not likely that the remaining Powers would undertake the task single-handed. The astute Padishah, however, was mistaken. True, Germany did not participate in the demonstration, — much to her discredit, — but the international fleet — minus the German man-of-war — assembled in the Piræus under the chief command of Admiral Ripper of the Austrian navy; and when the sultan saw that the Powers were in earnest, he beat a hasty retreat and opened communication with the ambassadors. His reply was evasive and unsatisfactory. To permit the finance commission appointed by the Powers to act in Macedonia, he claimed, would be in direct opposition to his sovereign rights, it would result in a loss of his prestige, and debase him in the eyes of his subjects. In an unveiled threat of the massacre of the Christians in Macedonia, he said: "Should the ambassadors persist in carrying out their purpose of bringing greater pressure to bear, the Porte declined to assume any responsibility for all events which might result, as well as for the consequences of the discontent in the Ottoman public opinion following upon the infringement of the rights of the empire."

This was a stupid bit of diplomacy, and the Powers accordingly forced an immediate agreement to the conditions they thought necessary to impose. The finance commissioners are now (1907) in Macedonia and at work; and it is generally believed that both revolts and oppressions will cease. The pity is that the Armenian troubles cannot be handled by a similar commission.

After the Armenian and Macedonian troubles, the most significant fact in recent Turkish history is the growing influence of Germany with the Sublime Porte — an influence that has been alike mischievous to the sultan and his oppressed Christian subjects; for, as Mr. Curtis very properly says: "Germany is more culpable than any of the other nations, because its government sustains and protects the sultan in his atrocious policy of administration, not only in Macedonia, but in all parts of the Near East." It is commonly said in diplomatic circles at Constantinople that when the sultan has instigated a fresh slaughter of his Christian subjects and the result causes a serious situation that "he simply grants another profitable concession to some German syndicate as an additional policy of insurance against intervention." Germans enjoy greater privileges and suffer fewer annoyances than any other merchantmen in Turkey; and they hold most of the recently granted advantageous government concessions. No one would find fault with the legitimate commercial success of Germany in Turkey; but when it is recalled that this success is the direct result of questionable diplomacy, the culpability of Berlin is apparent.

At the present time there is no conspicuous bow of promise in the sky of Turkish history. "There are some," says Stanley Lane-Poole, "who believe in a great Mohammedan revival, with the Sultan Khalif at the head — a second epoch of Saracen prowess, and a return to the good days when Turks were simple, sober, honest men, who fought like lions. There is plenty of such stuff in the people still; but where are their leaders? Till Carlyle's great man comes the hero who can lead a nation back to paths of valour and righteousness, to dream of the regeneration of Turkey is but a bootless speculation."[1] But will the great man come?

[1] "The Story of Turkey." New York, 1888.

CHAPTER V

THE PEOPLE OF TURKEY: THE TURKS

Origin of the Osmanli Turks — Ethnic stock — Asiatic home — Race intermixture — The physical type — Mental characteristics of the Turks — Turkish women — Polygamy — Legal rights of Moslem women — Occupations and amusements — The Turkish home — Democratic social ideals — Dress and habits — Alterations in the Turkish character — Effect of contact with the Christians — The blindness of human beings.

THE Turks claim that they are descended from Japhet, son of Noah, who was the father of three sons; and that to his first-born, Aboul-Turk, he gave the sovereignty of Turkestan. Aboul-Turk prospered and increased his dominions, and at the ripe age of two hundred and forty years he died, dividing the augmented Turkestan equally among his five sons. These, in turn, prospered and enlarged their territories, and so the story runneth down through the long ages to Abdul-Hamid of our own day.

Ethnologists, on the other hand, tell us that the Turks belong to the Tataric group of the

Sibiric branch of the Asian race; that they are the immediate kith of the Turcomans, Yakouts, Kirghis, Cossacks, and Huns, and first cousins of the Mongols, Kalmucks, Lapps, Magyars, Japanese, and Koreans. Their ancestral home was in Turkestan, north of the Pamir Plateau, and in the immediate vicinity of the Persians. They early developed marauding and predatory instincts; and Chinese annals, two hundred years before the Christian era, mention their inroads into that empire. The story of the invasion of Asia Minor and Europe by the Osmanli Turks, during the thirteenth century of our era, has been told in a previous chapter. It is unnecessary to point out that in their wanderings and conquests the blood of the Osmanli Turks has undergone much admixture, and that the modern Turk one meets in Constantinople has more Semitic and Aryan than Tataric blood in his veins. He lacks most of the physical traits of the Sibiric branch of the Asian race; but his language, strange to say, has maintained a singular purity; and Mr. Brinton tells us that the diverse branches of the Tataric group have no difficulty in understanding its ordinary expressions.

In spite of the conquests of the Osmanli

The People of Turkey

Turks in Asia, Africa, and Europe during the past six centuries, they have done little to assimilate the people whom they have conquered and ruled, and they have been even less assimilated by them. In all the numerous provinces of the Ottoman Empire — with the possible exception of three or four vilayets in Asia Minor — the Osmanli Turks are in a minority. In the Armenian provinces, a third of the population is composed of Turks, a third of Armenians, and a third of Kurds. In Syria, Palestine, and Arabia, only the officials are Turks; and, in European Turkey, the Osmanli Turks form less than one-tenth of the population. There has been some fusion of Osmanli Turks with the Moslem Kurds, Arabs, and Albanians; and the system of polygamy, with the practice of augmenting the harems by the purchase of slaves and concubines, has done something to transform the physical and mental type.

Most Turkish men whom I met in Constantinople exhibited the Caucasian rather than the Mongolian type; although I was repeatedly told that I must go to the interior provinces of Asia Minor if I wished to discover the ethnic characteristics of the thoroughbred Osmanli Turks. The men are fine-looking fellows with well-proportioned bodies and of medium stature; the nose is aquiline; the eyes are large and expressive; the hair is dark or chestnut coloured; the complexion is fair, and the jawbone high and somewhat square — the only genuinely Mongolian trait that I remarked. They have a high degree of muscular power, but they are of an indolent and inactive disposition. Although they possess great capacity for doing nothing, and for wanting to do nothing, they can scarcely be called lazy. The static condition of inactivity of the race is due (1) to the fact that the Turk is too proud to be a labourer; (2) to the fact that he is too stupid to engage in any calling requiring marked ingenuity and inventiveness, and (3) to the fact that his religion inculcates a fatalism that is hostile to effort. He has, however, marked capacity for military discipline, and his readiness to endure hardships and privations is one of his redeeming features. His courage, uprightness, obedience, and temperance have won high praise from the Christians in Turkey. I was repeatedly told by business men in Constantinople that whenever they had to delegate business missions that required absolute honesty, they always engaged a Turk rather than a Greek, an Armenian, or a Jew.

The People of Turkey

The Turk is by instinct a gentleman, with dignified and courtly manners — born of the fact, doubtless, that he is a member of a ruling race. The Prophet taught his followers that they were born to conquer and to rule the world; and the Turk has taken this tenet of the faith literally. When he oppresses Christians he is simply exercising his spiritual authority and he assumes that he is doing the appointed work of God. Religious sanction, in no small measure, is directly responsible for many of his acts of cruelty and oppression toward non-Moslems. In religious matters he is vindicative, intolerant, and cruel; and as Henry M. Field once said, "when the Turk is not demonized by the excitement of war or by the frenzy of religious excitement, he is not a bad fellow — not worse than other men."[1] Kind, patient, and good natured; fond of children and of animals, and in civil life courteous and considerate, the nascent fighting instincts are strong and ferocious, and when once aroused he slaughters and burns without mercy.

In the range of his intellectual interests and the depth of his sympathies for the refined pleasures of life — music, drama, art, and the

[1] "The Greek Islands and Turkey after the War." New York, 1885.

like — the Turk is even more circumscribed than the average American business man — a mental state which suggests excessive stupidity. While possessing indomitable courage and great conquering power, the Turk is distinguished neither by the ability to construct nor create; and he does not imitate well. He simply borrows. He borrowed his religion from Arabia; his literature from Arabia and Persia; his arts from Persia and Byzantium; and most recently he has borrowed his clothes from Europe. Turkish trade and commerce are largely in the hands of Greeks, Armenians, and Jews; and the Turkish army is mainly officered by Germans, Frenchmen, or Englishmen. The static character of the Turkish people, although largely responsible for their failure to keep pace with the ages, is not without its compensations; for, as Sir Charles Norton Edgecomb Eliot has truly said, " they have perpetuated and preserved, as if in a museum, the strange medley which existed in southeastern Europe during the last years of the Byzantine Empire."[1]

My impressions of Turkish women are necessarily based upon derived data; although I found them much less secluded than my read-

[1] "Turkey in Europe," London, 1900.

A TURKISH WOMAN OF QUALITY.

The People of Turkey

ing had led me to suppose. They go practically where they please between sunrise and sunset — the aristocratic women accompanied by eunuchs, the middle class women by slaves, and the peasant women unescorted. No one molests them, for Turks never speak to women on the street — not even to their own wives; and no one stares at a woman, this custom being confined to the Christian countries of Europe. The women wear a thin gauze or tulle face-covering — the yashmak — and on the street they carry parasols to protect themselves from the observation of rude, staring Frenchmen and other Christians. They wear a loose shapeless tunic that hangs from the shoulders like a bag. In their locomotion on the street they have an ungainly and waddling movement; and I was told that their idle and inactive life develops a very poor physique. The mental type is as low as the physical. Few of them can read or write in the mother-tongue; and they add to their illiteracy superstition, vulgarity, and religious fanaticism. I marvelled with Mr. Ramsay that Turkey could produce so many good men from a motherhood so stunted and impoverished in strength and moral vigour.

Polygamy is much less common in Turkey

than is generally supposed; the Koran permits a man to have four wives and to be the owner of as many female slaves — all of whom stand in a wifely relation to their owner — as he can afford to buy and maintain. But polygamy is an expensive institution; wives must have separate apartments and their own servants; and an expense incurred for one wife must be incurred for all the wives, for all Mohammedan wives must be treated on a basis of equality. Only when the first wife is childless is it customary for the Turk to incur the running expense of three households — for he has his own establishment apart from his wife or wives — by taking a second wife, and only when his primary desire for offspring is strong will a Turk add this extra expense and risk his own domestic peace. The mother, rather than the wife, holds the highest place in the esteem of the Turk; she is respected, obeyed, and revered; and she — in the case of the reigning family — and not a wife — enjoys the title of Valideh Sultan. A Turk will tell you that his wives may die, but he can replace them; that his children may pass away, but others may be born to him; but he asks who shall restore to him his cherished mother when death has claimed her?

The People of Turkey

Turkish women possess larger legal and proprietary rights than their Christian sisters. They share with their brothers their father's estate; they retain entire control of the property that comes to them at the time of their marriage, or that they may afterward inherit; and they may dispose of the same as they choose. A Turkish woman may sue or be sued independently of her husband and she may even sue or be sued by him. She may plead her own cause before the law courts; and, as a matter of fact, often does. In the matter of divorce the husband has the vantage-ground; but even here, the women are safeguarded by religious and social prerogatives, which makes it less easy to separate from a vixen hanum in Turkey than in the United States.

During religious ceremonies in the mosques, the women are cooped in latticed pens in the galleries — much as in bygone years Protestant churches in New England used to coop their deacons in the amen corner, though without the latticed work, and prompted, of course, by other motives of piety. Several books on the Mohammedan religion that I have consulted state that women are regarded as soulless. This I suspect is an error, since the Koran extends the promise of future life and the joys of paradise to both men and women. It says, "God hath promised to all believers, men and women, gardens and goodly places to dwell in for ever." Again: "For all believing men and believing women, devout men and devout women, truthful men and truthful women, for all men and women who remember him, God hath prepared forgiveness and a great reward."

The Turks have a proverb, "Either marry or bury your daughter before she is sixteen," which is suggestive of the low social and mental status of women in the Ottoman Empire. They marry and are often the mothers of children before they reach fifteen; and premature marital obligation not only arrests their physical development, but abbreviates the period which should be devoted to mental and moral training. The Christian schools in Turkey have changed matters a bit, but the Turks themselves — both men and women — have no adequate conception of the viciousness of their system; and they sometimes oppose the Christian schools on the ground that they unduly emphasize the virtues of celibacy. Mr. Dwight has a less charitable explanation for Turkish opposition to girls' schools. He says: "The man of the east knows that if the woman is allowed to read and to think, facilities for gratifying his own tastes will be greatly diminished. So he obstructs efforts to open her mind, pointing out that any large view of education will teach her to sew instead."[1]

The Turkish women are even less active and more indolent than the men. An English woman, Miss Pardoe, writing of the domestic manners of the Turks in 1836 — and from all that I could learn they have changed little in three score and ten years — says: "Their habits are, generally speaking, luxurious and indolent, if I except their custom of early rising, which, did they occupy themselves in any useful manner would be undoubtedly very commendable; but as they only add by these means two or three hour of ennui to each day, I am at a loss how to classify it. Their time is spent in dressing themselves, and varying the positions of their ornaments, in the bath, and in sleep, which they appear to have as entirely at their beck as a draught of water; in winter they have but to nestle under the coverings of the tandour, or in summer to bury themselves among their cushions, and in five minutes they are in the land of dreams. Indeed, so extraordinarily are they gifted in this re-

[1] "Constantinople and Its Problems." Chicago, 1901.

spect, that they not unfrequently engage their guests to take a nap, with the same *sang-froid* with which a European lady would invite her friends to take a walk."[1]

The Turkish house divides closely along sex lines into selamlik and haremlik, separated only by a hallway or door, but really two distinct houses. The selamlik is the abode of the man and the boys over twelve years of age; and the haremlik the quarters for the women and girls. Both men and women, among the better classes, have their own households and servants; they seldom dine together and they take their amusements separately. Men friends are entertained in the selamlik, and women are received at the haremlik, but the sexes do not mingle socially. A Turk never enters the quarters of his women if there are shoes at the door — an indication that there are callers at the haremlik, as Turks are permitted social intercourse only with the women of their own harems. The Turkish house is furnished with primitive simplicity. There are no chairs, tables, or beds, because the Turks do not require them; they sit on the floor, eat from small trays or stands, and sleep on the floor, the bedding being stowed away

[1] "The City of the Sultan." Philadelphia, 1837.

The People of Turkey

in cupboards during the day. The Turkish bath is found in every house of importance; there are scores of public baths in all the cities and towns where the charges are moderate, and the mosques maintain free baths for the poor people. Public baths in fact serve the purposes of clubs in Turkey for both men and women — always separately, of course.

In spite of the fact that the Turks have grown proud and haughty because they have been so long a ruling people, aristocracy and hereditary rank count for very little. The humblest Turkish lad may rise to the first place in the empire, after that of the chief magistrate of the realm; and the poorest Turkish girl may become the mother of a future sultan. All Moslem subjects — slaves and freedmen — are on a level beneath the sultan. The sultan's own family does not form a privileged class, and his daughters may marry humble subjects, and in a few generations their genealogy and that of their descendants becomes altogether obscured.

In matters of costume (and probably also in character) the Turks have undergone marked changes during the last half-century. Native costumes have very generally been abandoned for ugly and ill-fitting European clothes. The hideous red fez has very generally superseded the rich and gorgeous turban of muslin or cashmere; and a crowd of fez-topped Turks in the distance looks for all the world like a field of red poppies. The flowing and graceful robes of silk and woollen have been laid aside for the stiff and angular European coat and trousers. And the traditional slippers of yellow morocco have been displaced by the conventional European and American boots. A few of the old Turks in Constantinople — and many more in the provinces — still wear the picturesque Turkish costume, — turban, caftan, and slippers; but the black frock coat and the cutaway have made rapid strides in Turkey in a score of years. The dress of the women too has undergone rapid and hideous transformations. A plumed hat is sometimes worn beneath the veil and the mantle frequently covers a Paris gown. Extraordinary variety and brilliancy in colours once gave the dress of the Turks character and distinction; but they are rapidly sinking to the dead and sombre mediocrity of European uniformity. Edmondo de Amicis mournfully notes in this connection: " Every year sees the fall of thousands of caftans and the rise of thousands of frock coats; every day dies an old Turk and a reformed Turk is born. Newspapers succeed to the rosary, cigars to the chibouk, wine takes the place of water; the coach displaces the araba; French grammar is studied instead of Arabian grammar; pianofortes and stone houses succeed to the timbur and the house of wood. Everything is changing and being transformed."[1]

The Turks have a highly amusing explanation of the origin of national costumes. The legend runs as follows: A sultan of the Ottoman Empire once shut up in the Castle of Seven Towers in Constantinople all the kings and emperors of the world. In a fit of generosity he decided to release them and return them to their respective countries; but in order that they might be distinguished, he ordered that each should be dressed in a different costume; and when they got back to their home countries, these kings and emperors required their subjects to adopt the style of dress which had been devised by the Sublime Porte; and thus, explains the Osmanli Turk, varieties in dress among the different nations of the world originated.

It seems also probable that the Turkish character as well as the Turkish costume has un-

[1] "Constantinople" [1896].

dergone marked changes in modern times. That prince of geographers, Elisée Reclus, in his monumental work says: "The Turk whom the use of power has not corrupted, whom oppression has not debased, is certainly one of those men who please most by a happy blending of good qualities. Never does he cheat you; honest and upright, he is true as steel to his own folk; extremely hospitable; respectful yet never servile; discreet, tolerant, and benevolent, and very kind to animals." The French geographer's judgment I found repeatedly confirmed by Americans and Englishmen who had lived for many years in Constantinople. I was told, however, that if I wished to know the Turk at his best that I must seek him in the provinces and not in the great cities; and this opinion is sustained by Kesnin Bey who says of the provincial Turk: "His sobriety is proverbial; no European peasant could stand such frugality, nor subsist upon such simple fare as coarse black bread and draughts of cold water. Upon this the Turkish peasant easily lives. The dram-shop for him does not exist. In his personal habits he is clean, for his religion exacts that he shall often perform his ablutions. For all that, he loftily ignores the simplest rules of health.

His home is a mere den that is dug out of the ground, without furniture and void of windows. In general, the Turkish peasant is a monogamist. If he takes a second wife it is because he wishes to have a second servant. But he treats this latter affectionately, and adores his children. One cannot too greatly praise his kindness to animals. In many of the provincial districts the donkey has the privilege of two days' holiday in the week. This sentiment of gentleness, which does such honour to a bellicose people like the Turks, is to be remarked throughout the entire nation."

It is not easy to point out the causes of the deterioration of the Turkish character in the larger cities and towns. An Irish humourist has asserted that "it is the Christians who have corrupted the Turk." Granted that the charge contains an element of truth, it should also be pointed out that the Turk corrupts the Christian. The juxtaposition of the two religions produces results subversive alike to the doctrines of the Man of Nazareth and the Prophet of Mecca. The authority already quoted on the probity of the provincial Turks says in this connection: "The worshippers of Christ, who live in the midst of the worshippers of Mohammed, are not of more immaculate morals nor of cleaner conscience than they. They look upon the Mussulman as an oppressor who may be duped and exploited without scruple." To what extent the mechanical mixture of races and religions in the Ottoman Empire has caused mutual demoralization, I am not prepared to say; but after a visit to Turkey and consultation with Christians who had been brought in intimate relations with the Osmanli Turks, together with a careful collation of practically all that has been written about the Turks, I conclude that Carlyle's drastic characterization of the " unspeakable Turk," which is widely accepted in England and America, is due to a certain blindness in human beings.

In one of his delightful psychological essays Professor William James remarks: " The blindness in human beings is the blindness with which we are all afflicted in regard to the feeling of creatures and peoples different from ourselves. We are practical beings — each of us with limited functions and duties to perform. Each is bound to feel intensely the importance of his own duties, and the significance of the situations that call these forth. But this feeling is in each of us a vital secret for sympathy with which we vainly look in others. The others are too much absorbed in their own vital secrets to take an interest in ours. Hence the stupidity and injustice of our opinions, so far as they deal with the significance of alien lives. Hence the falsity of our judgments, so far as they presume to decide in an absolute way on the value of other person's conditions or ideals.'' Carlyle's epigrammatic characterization of the Turk as an unspeakable creature, from my own observation and study, is a point in illustration of the blindness in human beings which Professor James has so aptly described; and in rejecting the Scotch essayist's wholesale condemnation of the Osmanli Turks, I am not unmindful of the awful butcheries they have committed, and continue to commit, and of their incurably barbarous and corrupt government — probably one of the most infamous forms of despotism in the world. But I am as little inclined to condemn the Turks, as individuals, for these awful barbarities as I am to hold the entire American nation responsible for not dissimilar acts in the Philippine Islands, the English people in South Africa, the Germans in the Kamerun, the Belgians in the Congo country, the French in Madagascar, and the Dutch in the East Indies. Turkish character is so very complex that with Joaquin Miller, the poet of the Sierras, I can say:

> "In men whom men condemn as ill,
> I find so much of goodness still;
> In men whom men pronounce divine,
> I find so much of mar and blot
> I hesitate to draw the line
> Between the two, where God has not."

CHAPTER VI

GREEKS, ARMENIANS, AND HEBREWS

Diversity of races in Turkey — Their relative moral worth — Greeks — Their numerical strength — Physical and mental characteristics — Deficiency in practical ethics — Religion and education — Armenians — Geographic limits of the province — The ethnic stock — Habits and character — Lack of personal courage — The Gregorian church — Intellectual progress of the Armenians — Hebrews — Their degraded condition in Turkey — Relation to Judaism.

LIKE the audience that listened to St. Paul on the day of Pentecost the inhabitants of the Ottoman Empire " are out of every nation under heaven." The empire includes — and in large numbers — besides the Osmanli Turks, Greeks, Armenians, Albanians, Jews, Kurds, Persians, Bulgarians, Wallachians, Circassians, Arabians, Gypsies, Ethiopians, to name but a few of the most numerous ethnic stocks. The heterogeneous nature of the population is the most striking fact of travel in Turkey. One meets, for example, in Constantinople representatives of all the races of Europe, most of the races of Asia, and some of the races of Africa — not chemically but mechanically mixed. They dislike one another even more than they dislike the Turks, their masters; and Europeans living among them esteem them less highly than they esteem the Turks. Curzon, after extended travels in the Ottoman Empire and much intercourse with its different peoples, reached the conclusion that it requires the wits of four Turks to overreach one European, two Europeans to cheat a Greek, two Greeks to cheat a Jew, and six Jews to cheat one Armenian. It is greatly to be regretted that this astute English traveller did not include the Albanians, Kurds, and Persians in his descending scale of moral worth.

The Greeks constitute not only the most numerous but the most intelligent people in the Ottoman Empire. They are more numerous than the Turks in European Turkey; they form one-fifth of the population of Constantinople and one-half of that of Smyrna; they constitute the element of greatest wealth and commercial power in the coast towns of both European and Asiatic Turkey; in Asia Minor they are most numerous in the vilayets of Trebizond and Aidin, and the district of Karaman; in such islands as Rhodes, Mitylene, Cyprus, and Crete they form the backbone of the population; and everywhere, in both commerce and agriculture, they are more intelligent and more enterprising than the Turks. Although few Greeks hold posts of honour or responsibility in the Ottoman government, they are the leading bankers, physicians, and traders, and they represent the largest element of wealth and progress, as well as the intelligence and culture of Turkey. Both physically and mentally they are the most active element of the mixed Ottoman Empire. Go where you will — to Constantinople, Saloniki, Smyrna, or Trebizond — you are pretty certain to find that the Greeks are the most efficient and successful carpenters, tailors, shoemakers, bakers, barbers, dressmakers, laundresses, grocers, restaurant and hotel keepers.

The Greeks are of medium stature, with a propensity for stoutness among the men and corpulency among the women. The skull is more globular than the classic type and the nose less straight and narrow, owing to the extended intermarriage with Slavic peoples. The complexion is brownish and the hair dark or black. The Greeks are a vivacious people, fond of display and position, and they possess great subtlety in monetary transactions. They have clung to their language with marvellous tenacity; the historic sense is strong in them, and they have great love for education and learning. Rich Greeks in Turkey send annually to their fatherland large sums for the foundation of schools and hospitals, the maintenance of museums, and the restoration of historic buildings. In Turkey they maintain more than two thousand elementary and secondary schools for the education of Greek children. Some of these — like the Zappion college, the Pallas school, the Hellenic lyceum, and the Phanar schools in Constantinople — have splendid buildings, large endowments, and strong corps of instructors.

The Greek, however, is markedly deficient in practical ethics; he is notably untrustworthy, and his word has little value. Honesty likewise is not one of his virtues; and his cunning — to quote from a writer friendly to the Greeks — "comes very near fraud, and he lies in the most impudent manner. He is noisy, blustering, familiar, obsequious, dissolute, a gamester, and a drunkard. The Greek is also charged with being quarrelsome, volatile, and presumptuous, and he is genuinely disliked by Franks and Turks because of his turbulence and unreliableness." The friendly writer already quoted adds: " He has never been able to cure himself from cheating. If he be a sharp, intelligent merchant, that is not to say he is an honest one. Too often he truly proves to be the *polumètis Odysseus* of antiquity. He would never scruple to break his word if it suited him; and in honesty he is far inferior to the Turk. If summoned to appear before the local tribunal, he changes his nationality with surprising quickness. Proteus-like, he is to-day a Mussulman and to-morrow a Hellene. Even the Greek consuls complain of the part they are compelled to play when forced to give protection to individuals whose nationality is as doubtful as their morals."[1] Mark Twain does not greatly exaggerate the Greek character in his "New Pilgrim's Progress," when he says that "in recommending his son to a merchant, a father does not say he is a nice, moral, upright boy, and that he goes to Sunday school and is honest; but he says ' this boy is worth his weight in broad pieces of a hundred — for, behold, he will cheat whomsoever hath dealings with him; and from the Euxine to the waters of the Marmora there abideth not so gifted a liar.' "

Among the Americans, English, Germans, and French in Turkey one constantly hears the

[1] "The Evils of the East, or Facts about Turkey." London, 1888.

expressions "cheat like a Greek" and "lie like a Greek" in characterizing moral obliquity. There may be a grain of truth in the defence of pro-Hellenic writers that the moral lapses of the Greeks in the Ottoman Empire are due to the microbes in the corrupting Turkish atmosphere; but it has been my experience in travelling in Greece, where the atmosphere has been regenerated by the exhilarating air of independence from the Ottoman yoke for nearly four score years, that one meets astonishingly often with like moral lapses. I recall that at such presumably trustworthy institutions in Greece as national banks and government railway offices I had to make careful reckoning of my coin after presenting my letter of credit or purchasing a railway ticket; and that in a majority of cases I discovered errors in favour of bank or railway, although errors never happened in my favour. I suspect that Greek historians are not far from the truth when they assert that falsehood and cheating antedate the conquest of Greece by the Turks, and that they reach back to and beyond the palmy days of Solon and Lycurgus.

The Greek is as strongly attached to his religion as to his language, and the followers of the Prophet do not have a monopoly of religious fanaticism. The Greek church is known as the Orthodox; and it is distinguished from the Roman Catholic church by the fact that the authority of the Pope at Rome is rejected, the doctrine that the Holy Spirit proceeds from the Son is denied, and the clergy are permitted to marry. The Orthodox church in Turkey enjoys religious autonomy, and it is ruled by the Patriarch and the Holy Synod of Constantinople, assisted by a national council composed of twelve lay members, with whom is sometimes associated an assembly of the most influential Greeks in Turkey. As a class, I did not find the Greek clergymen possessed of much culture; and I thought them intellectually inferior to the Greek physicians, bankers, and important traders whom I met in Turkey. The Orthodox church is accused by many of its more intelligent and progressive adherents of encouraging idleness among the common people by constantly adding to the number of religious festivals. In some places, I was told, no fewer than two hundred and eighty church festivals are observed yearly.

It is no easy task to indicate the geographic limits of Armenia since the sultan forbids the speaking or the writing of the word; and maps which give Armenia as a distinct province in

Asia Minor are promptly confiscated by the Ottoman government. Nevertheless, there is, or was, a distinct geographic unit of that name, now under the sovereignty of Persia, Turkey, and Russia. Turkey has christened her Armenian territory Kurdistan; although the Armenians themselves designate their territories east of the Euphrates River as Greater Armenia, and those on the west as Lesser Armenia. The Armenian population is most dense in the Turkish vilayets of Erzerum, Van, Harput, Sivas, Diarbekr, and Bitlis, with considerable numbers in the inland districts north of the Aleppo — Trebizond, Brusa, and Angora. There are about four million Armenians in Asia Minor. Smyrna has a large Armenian population, and there are 150,000 Armenians in Constantinople.

The Armenians belong to the Indo-Eranic group of Aryan stock, and they are racially near of kin to the Persians, Kurds, Hindus, Beluchis, and Gypsies. The complexion varies from light to olive; the beard is flaxen or chestnut coloured, the eyes are large and black or blue, and the nose is prominent, with an accentuated outline similar to that of the Jews. Indeed, several of the facial characteristics of the Armenians are distinctly Semitic. Many

Greeks, Armenians, Hebrews

of the Armenian traders and bankers one meets in Constantinople are short, solidly built, and thick-necked, while the Armenian porters (hamals) in Constantinople — all from the Van region in Asia Minor — are large, robust, and well-built fellows. They share with the Jews so many mental and physical characteristics, although linguistically of Aryan stock, that they are not infrequently referred to as "Christian Jews," or "Hebrews who have been baptized." They are, however, more adroit in monetary transactions than the sons of Israel, and one often hears it said in Turkey that no Jew can flourish within ten miles of an Armenian.

Lamartine once characterized the Armenians as the Swiss of the east. "They are laborious, peaceful, and regular in their habits," he said, "but calculating and rapacious. No heroism or spirit of resistance marks their character. Their genius shines in commerce, and they place it at the service of any one who is their master." This diagnosis touches the dominant element of strength and weakness in the Armenian character. As a race they are supple and flexible in commercial matters, and they possess financial talents of a high order. The richest bankers in Constantinople, for example, are Armenians; but, like the multimillionaires in the United States, their fortunes have often been made in violation of such well-established ethical laws as rectitude and probity. They take naturally to usury as a vocation, and their love for the filthy lucre is so intense that it dwarfs all higher spiritual aspirations. When an Armenian speaks of talents, he means talents of gold; hence, in spite of native mental alertness, marvellous power of application, and extraordinary scholastic excellence in schools and colleges, his literature has no great merit, he has little artistic feeling, and he has accomplished nothing distinctive in architecture.

The Armenian character, however, has an even greater weakness than sordid and inordinate love of gold. I refer to his lack of personal courage, his want of heroism, and his unwillingness to fight for his rights and to assert by forceful means, when necessary, his sense of self-respect. This ethical defect is widely recognized by those familiar with the Armenians. Writing of them more than fifty years ago the author of "Anadol, the Last Home of the Faithful," says: "More simple and abject than the ambidextrous and vainglorious Greek, possessing sounder sense, if

ARMENIANS WEAVING.

Greeks, Armenians, Hebrews 89

not more vivacity, and, above all, less imbued with national pride and ambition, the supple and self-interested Armenian humbles his brow in the dust of the lordly, pride-sowing and poverty-reaping Moslem; and, unfeared, becomes the master of his master's all." Mr. Ramsay, the Scotch archæologist, after twelve years' residence among the Armenians, concludes that they tend toward one type — " submissive to the verge of servility, accepting without attempting to resist ill-treatment and insult at which a worm would rebel." Friends in Constantinople, who were eye-witnesses of the awful massacres there ten years ago, told me that they did not observe a single instance of resistance, but that the Armenians permitted the Turks to hew them down like trees; and that a spark of courage and heroism might have spared many lives. G. Stanley Hall very appropriately says: " Non-resistance under all provocations is unmanly, craven, and cowardly. An able-bodied young man, who cannot fight physically, can hardly have a high and true sense of honour, and is generally a milksop, a lady-boy, or a sneak. He lacks virility, his masculinity does not ring true, and his honesty cannot be sound to the core."[1]

[1] "Adolescence." New York, 1904.

With bright intellects, industrious dispositions, large powers of forbearance, and frugal habits, the credit account of the Armenian character is more than offset by want of courage, dissimulation, craft, and greed for gain; and Europeans living in Turkey, and coming only in contact with rich and grasping mercantile Armenians, with Curzon, place them at the very foot of the ethical ladder. I have met in both America and Europe individual Armenians who measured up to all that was best in life, both in their ideals and practices; but such instances simply prove that the Armenian character is not a rule without exceptions. Lack of courage, heroism, and warlike disposition has influenced the history of the Armenian people as well as the Armenian character; for, at the appearance of succeeding invaders, to borrow an expression from Xenophon's "Cyropædia," "the Armenians, according to their habit, did not withstand the shock." Of the Turk it has been said that up to a certain point he works for the good of his country, but that the Armenian works always and only for no one but himself.

The Armenian church is divided into three branches or sects — the Gregorian or Orthodox Armenian church, the Roman Catholic

Armenian church, and the Protestant Armenian church. The great majority of Armenians are adherents of the Gregorian church, which, like the Greek Orthodox church, rejects the authority of the Pope at Rome. The head of the Gregorian church bears the title of Catholicos and resides at Etchmiadzin in Russian Armenia. He is represented in Turkey by a Partiarch at Constantinople, who is the civil and religious head of the Gregorian subjects of the sultan. The Gregorians are punctilious in the performances of church ordinances; they observe fasts and feasts with rigour; and they attach much importance to pilgrimages to the shrines of saints and martyrs. As in the Moslem and Greek Orthodox churches, the lower orders of Gregorian clergy marry and engage in secular vocations.

The Roman Catholic Armenian church dates from the time of the crusades when the Armenians came in contact with the Latin Christians. The number of adherents is not considerable and is confined mainly to Constantinople, Smyrna, and Erzerum. The authority of the Pope at Rome is recognized; certain forms of worship of the Gregorian church are retained; the ritual is given in Armenian and not Latin, but the clergy are subjected to celibacy. The Patriarch of the Roman Catholic Armenian church resides at Constantinople, and enjoys the same prerogatives as the Orthodox Greek and Gregorian Patriarchs. The Protestant Armenian church numbers about sixty thousand members, chiefly in Asia Minor. The organization and growth of the church are mainly due to the labours of American missionaries. The Protestant Armenian church has a head (Vekil) at Constantinople whose appointment is sanctioned by the sultan and who exercises certain powers on behalf of the church in Turkey.

The Armenians have done much in recent times to improve the intellectual condition of their people; and the system of national schools, supported entirely by voluntary contributions, has made an elementary education possible for a large number of poor Armenian children. Attention has also been given to secondary education, and there are several very good Armenian colleges at Constantinople. The Christian missionaries — Roman Catholic and Protestant — have rendered invaluable service in the secondary and higher education of Armenian youths. In the Protestant colleges at Rumili Hissar (Robert College), Scutari, Beirut, and Aintab the Armenian students represent the largest national element, and they are very generally the most apt and studious. As an evidence of the results of the national Armenian educational movement, it may be mentioned that those great strong street porters — originally from the wilds of Van and Trebizond — that one sees in Constantinople carrying trunks, bureaus, and pianos on their backs, nearly all of them can read. The ancient Armenian alphabet, with its thirty-six letters, reaching back to the time of the Phœnicians, has been preserved with great fidelity during the long centuries that Armenia has been without a country; and the recent national educational movement is doing much to restore the language and arouse an interest in the ancient literature.

There are in Turkey about 350,000 Hebrews, and about 50,000 in the city of Constantinople; and although they have been less persecuted in Turkey than in any other country of Europe — excepting England — nowhere does one find such indescribable degradation, filth, and squalor as in the Jewish quarters of Constantinople. They probably represent the very lowest physical, mental, and moral types of the Hebrew race. Edmondo de Amicis has well characterized them as "insignificant, sallow, and flabby; their vitality centred in their eyes, and trembling with avarice and cunning." This degraded condition he thinks less due to the political and civil oppression of their Turkish rulers than to their own "shameless uncleanliness, precocious marriages, and abstention from all laborious trades."[1] With the possible exception of the Gypsies, the Jews are the most backward and the most disliked people in Turkey. Miss Garnett says that all kinds of crimes, fictitious or real, are charged against the Jews in Turkey, from the obligation never to transact business with the Christians or Moslems without defrauding them, to the kidnapping of children for their passover sacrifice — a widespread vulgar belief common to both Turks and Christians. She adds: "The very mention of a Jew is prefaced by a Greek with an apology for naming the race, and the Moslems on their side treat this section of the subject population with unmitigated contempt, not manifested as a rule in acts of personal violence, but in scornful gestures and opprobrious epithets."[2]

The physical type, although of an inferior order, is in the main that of the Semitic race

[1] "Constantinople." New York [1896].
[2] "Turkish Life in Town and Country." London [n. d.].

Greeks, Armenians, Hebrews 95

— medium skull, oval face, thick lips, accentuated nose, soft eyes, full beard, and dark, wavy hair. The Hebrews of Turkey hail from two diverse geographic sections. A few came direct to Constantinople from Palestine after the fall of Jerusalem, but most of them are descendants of Jews who fled from Spain and Portugal during the fifteenth and sixteenth centuries to escape the Holy Inquisition. These latter speak a language that is a mixture of bad Spanish, corrupt Greek, and infamous Turkish, but in writing they use the Hebrew alphabet.

Leprosy is prevalent and hereditary among the Spanish Jews in Turkey. Many of the Jews are wealthy, but they conceal their wealth in their squalid hovels and they do little to elevate themselves and their degraded brethren. The Universal Israelitish Alliance has made heroic efforts of an educational sort; and most of the larger synagogues in Constantinople and the chief provincial cities have schools attached to them in which the Hebrew religion, the Greek and Turkish languages, and the elements of commercial science are taught. Most of the Jews in Turkey are engaged in the tobacco trade; in the great cities many are private bankers and money lenders; and many more, to quote from Mr. Davey, "are purveyors of the worst forms of vice."[1]

The Jews in Turkey represent a number of distinct sects of the Hebrew religion. The Karaites regard themselves as the most orthodox. They accept the Pentateuch but reject the Talmud, and they claim an origin that antedates the destruction of the first temple. They have their own synagogues and rabbis, and are represented at the Sublime Porte by a chief of their own. The Mamins or Mohammedan Jews are found chiefly in Saloniki. They practise certain ancient Hebrew rites secretly, but outwardly they affect the religious forms of Islam — attend mosque services, observe the fast of Ramazan, and marry out of their own sect. They are sometimes described as false Mohammedans. The Turkish Jews do not follow the law of monogamy which was promulgated by the Rabbi Gershom in the twelfth century, although, as with the Turks, polygamy is not common. Only when the first wife is childless, or is the mother of girls only, does the Turkish Jew incur increased household expenses and risk the disturbance of his domestic bliss by bringing to his home a second daughter of Israel as wife.

[1] "The Sultan and His Subjects." New York, 1892.

The Jewish rabbis, in Constantinople, concerning whom personal information was obtained, seemed unmistakably inferior to their colleagues in Europe and America; and I was quite ready to agree with Kesnin Bey that " the Jews of the east in no wise resemble those Israelitish bankers, who, with their millions, dazzle the world of Paris, London, and Vienna " and that " they differ even from the middle-class European Jews who make their living by usury on a modest scale. Nor have they anything in common with the handsome Hebrews of Algeria, notable for their stalwart form, resolute bearing, and noble mien. The Turkish Jew has something slovenly, ill-smelling, and unbuttoned about him. Persecuted, trodden down, as he has been for centuries, he has a servile, cringing, timid manner. While his coreligionists in the west have grown rich and respectable, he has remained in his poverty, a poverty that is only equalled by his ignorance. Such is the Jew of Constantinople."[1]

---

[1] "The Evil of the East, or Facts about Turkey." London, 1888.

CHAPTER VII

KURDS, ALBANIANS, PERSIANS, AND OTHER RACES

Kurds — Their origin and relation to the Mohammedan religion — Tribal life — Conflicts with the Armenians — Albanians — Strong muscular type — Low intellectual attainments — Occupations — Persians — Commercial enterprises — The Constantinople colony — Circassians — Emigration to Turkey — Beauty of their women — Wallachians — Connection with the Latin races — Physical and mental type — Bulgarians — Their Asiatic origin — Industries — Gypsies — Their degradation — Ethiopians — The eunuch type.

WHILE of Aryan stock and belonging to the same ethnic family as the Armenians and Persians, the Kurds have so frequently intermarried with Semitic and Mongolian races that their physical type does not possess the typical characteristics of the Indo-Eranic peoples. Mentally also they represent a more backward state of civilization than either Armenians or Persians. The forebears of the Kurds were the ancient Parthians; and their empire existed for five hundred years, — to A. D. 220. Since the conquest of Kurdistan by the Osmanli Turks, the Kurds have wavered between

Kurds, Albanians, Persians 99

the two warring sects of the faith of Islam, siding now with the Sunnites of Turkey, and now with the Shi'ites of Persia, and thus maintaining semi-independence of their Ottoman rulers. Three times during the last century — 1834, 1843, and 1847 — they endeavoured to throw off the Turkish yoke and reëstablish their nationality.

The Kurds number about 2,000,000 in Turkey and 750,000 in Persia. They are most numerous in the vilayets of Erzerum, Diarbekr, and Bitlis. Some are pastoral and migratory; others sedentary and agricultural; and all cling tenaciously to tribal forms of government, whether under the sovereignty of the sultans of Turkey or of the shahs of Persia. This has fostered pride of ancestry; and some of the powerful Kurdish chiefs claim an ancestry of at least five hundred years. Writing of them, Sir H. C. Rawlinson says: "There was up to a recent period no more picturesque or interesting scene to be witnessed in the east than the court of one of these great Kurdish chiefs, where, like another Saladin, the bey ruled in patriarchal state, surrounded by an hereditary nobility, regarded by his clansmen with reverence and affection, and attended by a bodyguard of young Kurdish warriors, clad in chain armour, with flaunting silken scarfs, and bearing javelin, lance, and sword as in the time of the crusades."

Both men and women among the Kurds are strong and well-built; they have dark hair, bristly whiskers, small eyes, and overhanging eyebrows; the mouth is wide; the complexion is dark, and they are harsh-featured and savage-looking. They have great powers of physical endurance; they are born horsemen, and they make splendid fighters with lance and sword. The Kurds of the mountains make the best Turkish foot-soldiers, and those of the plains the best cavalrymen. Naturally brave and hospitable, and possessed of a rude but strict sense of honour, they lead a semi-nomadic life, but they have a bad reputation as predatory thieves. They are largely engaged in the rearing of cattle, horses, sheep, and goats. Their horses are highly esteemed for their strength and their goats for their fleecy hair. In recent times the Turkish army has received large recruits from Kurdistan, and they are the finest-looking soldiers one sees at the great military functions at Constantinople.

While nominally Mohammedans, the Kurds hold lightly to the faith, and superstition plays a larger part in their religion than is war-

A KURD PEASANT.

ranted by the Koran. They are not, however, very fervent in their devotions, and it is a common saying in Turkey that no saint can come out of Kurdistan. They rove too much to observe the methodic religious ceremonies of the faith of Islam. Like the nomadic Arabs, the Kurds do not esteem highly the harem system; and their women, in consequence, mingle freely with the men. They display the male characteristics of firmness and decision; when the men are absent on wars they direct the economic and civil affairs of the tribe, and at all times they play a large part in tribal politics.

The Kurds have been charged with being the chief tools of Turkey in the oppression and the maltreatment of the Armenians; and the charge has an element of truth. For a thousand years the Armenians and Kurds have been in conflict. The Armenians of Asia Minor are a sedentary people; they make excellent farmers, tradesmen, and producers. The Kurds are primarily consumers; they manufacture little but carpet; and while they have splendid herds of horses, cattle, and sheep, they lack the business shrewdness to dispose of their products. With their keen business perceptions and subtlety in monetary transactions, the Armenians act as middlemen. They buy the carpets, hides, and wool from the Kurds for a trifle and sell them at handsome profits. The Armenians, in consequence, have ready money; the Kurds are poor; they borrow money at heavy usury. When the interest falls due and is unpaid the Kurds are prosecuted and squeezed. Usurers are no better liked in Asia Minor than in Russia and the United States; and when the Sublime Porte desires to have the Armenians maltreated and oppressed, the Kurds get the job, and they " pay back " in plunder, pillage, and massacre. In the recent cruel slaughter of more than a hundred thousand innocent Armenians, the Kurds were simply the tools of the Ottoman government.

It must also be remembered that a fierce race-war is in progress in Asia Minor; and that the Kurds are the rivals of the Armenians for the supremacy of the plateau. As in the recent race-war in South Africa, might and not right triumphs. The Kurds are nominally Moslems; and although they are outnumbered by the Armenians in the proportion of one to two, they have at their command the strong military arm of the Ottoman Empire. With their superior intellectual and numerical strength, the Armenians might be as inde-

A KURD WOMAN.

Kurds, Albanians, Persians 103

pendent to-day as the Greeks, or as autonomous as the Bulgarians, if they possessed a tithe of the courage, valour, and heroism of the militant Kurds; but, as already pointed out, these manly virtues are foreign to the Armenian character. Hence, the apparent triumphs of the Kurds.

The Albanians are mountain highlanders; they occupy the plateau formed by the Dinaric Alps in western Turkey, and number about 2,000,000. They are probably the lineal descendants of the ancient Illyrians and Epirotes. They are the tallest people in southern Europe; they have strong muscular bodies; their skulls are generally round; their faces are square, and the complexion varies from brunette in the north to blonde in the south. They are proud, independent, arrogant, turbulent, and predatory; and they have been little influenced by the successive civilizations under which they have lived — Hellenic, Latin, and Turkish. While brave and warlike, they are devoid of cohesion, national sentiments, and the capacity to form combinations and rule themselves. Their language, although of Aryan stock, has borrowed many words from the Latin and the Greek; and broad skulls and square faces would suggest that the race-type has been partly Slavonized by intermarriage with Servians and Croatians.

The Albanians have little creative power and they have borrowed their civilization, their customs, and their religion from their masters and neighbours. Originally Greek Orthodox Catholics, many of the tribal chiefs, for the advancement of their own material interests, adopted the faith of Islam at the time of the Ottoman conquest. During the reign of Sultan Murad II. (1421-1452), the Sublime Porte, incensed by the apostasy of the Albanian hero Scanderbeg from the Mohammedan religion, caused the Albanian churches to be converted into mosques, and commanded the people on pain of death to confess that " there is no God but God and Mohammed is his Prophet." At the present time, about half the Albanians adhere to the Greek Orthodox church; a few are Roman Catholics and the others Mohammedans. But the Albanians do not cling very tenaciously to religion, and it forms no barrier to social intercourse. Miss Garnett, who has lived in the Albanian highland, says: " Christian men wed Moslem maids and *vice versâ*, the sons being brought up in the faith of their fathers and the daughters in that of their mothers. Moslems revere the Virgin Mary and

Kurds, Albanians, Persians 105

the Christian saints, and make pilgrimages to their shrines. Christians reciprocally resort to the tombs of Moslem saints, for the cure of ailments or the fulfilment of vows; while Christians and Moslems alike mingle with their culture beliefs the ancient pagan rites and superstitious usages which both creeds have proved powerless to eradicate."[1]

Agriculture, in a primitive way, is carried on by the old men, the women, and the children. The able-bodied Albanian men prefer to follow such callings as soldier, trader, sheep-herder, and brigand. As with all clannish and tribal races, blood-feuds are very common among the Albanians, and they maintain ancient codes of tribal honour very punctiliously. The Moslem Albanians are highly valued as soldiers by the Turks because of their great power of physical endurance, their rapidity of motion, their ability as marksmen, and their carelessness of danger; but they object to conscription and much prefer predatory and feudal wars in their own mountain highlands to regular military service.

The Albanians are swaggerers and braggarts, and their self-assurance knows no bounds; but their splendid stature and pic-

[1] "Turkish Life in Town and Country." London [n. d.].

turesque national costume make them objects of keen and abiding interest to travellers in Turkey (and Greece). They still wear starched accordion-plaited white cotton petticoats or kilts, about the length and the fulness of the skirt of a ballet-dancer, the long white leggings, the curiously embroidered gold vests, jackets with long flowing sleeves, and belts that are a perfect arsenal of small arms.

The Persians, although not a numerous race in Turkey, are the most picturesque, and historically the most important of the Indo-Eranic group of Aryan subjects of the sultan. With their lofty astrakhan head-dress and their long caftans of dove-coloured stuff, tied at the waist by a broad band of silk, they form the most picturesque element of the diversified population of the Ottoman Empire. Symmetrical in corporeal proportions, with slender but finely formed bodies, oval faces and regular features, abundant hair, and beard of a dark chestnut colour, they are a handsome people, and preserve some of the best physical characteristics of the ancient Eranic ethnic type. Unlike the Turks, they are active, laborious, and clever business men. They adhere to the Shi'ite branch of the Mohammedan religion; and in Turkey they are non-conformists and

Kurds, Albanians, Persians

their commercial enterprises are not looked upon with favour by zealous Sunnites.

About twelve thousand Persians are settled in Constantinople near the mosque of St. Sophia; they have a bazaar of their own, and they sell carpets, embroidered stuffs, astrakhan, tea, spices, tobacco for narghilés, arms, and choicely wrought metal goods. They occupy three monster khans which look like mammoth cloisters or huge fortresses. One of these, the Valideh Khan, houses from five to six thousand Persian merchants, and it looks much like a mediæval fortress. It has a great inner court which is surrounded by a double row of galleries. Rows of cells or small rooms lead from the galleries, and these are used as shops, offices, and private apartments. The great massive stone building, with its granite walls and iron-barred windows, is, in truth, a stronghold in troublous times for Persian merchants, and a storehouse for their goods.

The Circassians, since the conquest of the western Caucasus by Russia, have been an important element in the Ottoman Empire. They are Mohammedans; and their new masters governed them so badly that about a half million have voluntarily migrated to Turkey since the Russian conquest of Circassia in

1864. They came in such great numbers that it was not easy to provide for so large a host; and Turkey forced her Christian subjects to share their lands with the Circassian emigrants and to aid them in getting a start in their adopted country. Hunger, sickness, and change of climate caused them to perish by thousands; and their young girls and children — famed since the days of the Byzantine Empire for their physical beauty — were sold to procure bread. Turkish harems were filled with Circassian girls; and at Constantinople they became a drug on the market, and they had to be shipped to the slave markets in Egypt and Syria.

The Circassians are of Caucasic stock, and they are ethnically related to the Georgians, the Avars, and the Kurins. In spite of their long seclusion in the defiles and fastnesses of the Caucasus mountains, they exhibit astonishing diversity in physical and mental characteristics. After the Georgians, the Circassians have always been accounted the handsomest women of the white race, and the men have been equally famed for their noble features. The Circassians have well-formed and graceful bodies, handsome and regular features, dark hair, black eyes, with a variation in complexion

A CIRCASSIAN.

Kurds, Albanians, Persians

from brunette to brownish. They have always been known for their hospitality to strangers, their implacable vindictiveness in tribal feuds, and their warlike and intrepid natures; but they have never engaged in commerce, and they have not cultivated the arts of peace or taken intellectually a high rank among the races of the western Caucasus. The Christians in Turkey, among whom they live, regard them as turbulent and lazy; and the waning power of polygamy has greatly lessened the demand for Circassian girls among the Moslems.

Five hundred thousand Wallachians occupy the hill country of Macedonia, Thessaly, and Albania, and they are to be found in large numbers in Constantinople and the other important towns in European Turkey. The origin of these Latin-speaking Wallachians is shrouded in mystery. Some ethnologists assert that they are Latinized Dacians; others claim that they are descended from Italian legionaries and Roman soldiers brought hither by Trajan; but whatever their origin, it seems probable that they represent a strong admixture of Slav and Illyrian blood. Their language was for a long time regarded as a Slavic dialect; and the Slavonian was for many years used in their churches and courts of law.

Since the independence of the Wallachians in Rumania from Turkish rule and the organization of schools and universities in the new kingdom, Rumanian patriots and scholars have laboured assiduously to bring their language within the Romanic fold. They have abandoned the Russian for the Latin characters, and they have sought to purge their language of Servian, Greek, and Turkish words and expressions, and to substitute therefor words and idioms derived from the Latin.

The Wallachians have sunburnt features, finely shaped mouths, fair hair, and expressive eyes. They are graceful in their movements, and have great power of physical endurance. Although not subjected to formal scholastic discipline, they possess no mean order of intellectual power, and are distinguished by such valued mental traits as quickness of perception, gay spirit, and rare gifts of repartee. They are industrious tillers of the soil, excellent horticulturists, and enterprising traders. They are shrewd and thrifty, but sly and servile. They belong to the Orthodox church, but their social relations with the Greeks are unimportant; and while it is said that a Wallachian may sometimes wed a Greek girl, no Wallachian maiden would ever marry outside of her community. An English traveller in writing of the Wallachians, who live in the mountainous parts of European Turkey, says: "Even in these high altitudes the thrift and industry of the Vlachs are conspicuous. Cornfields and vineyards clothe the hillsides, and the terraced and well-irrigated gardens produce an abundance of fruits and vegetables. The houses are for the most part small, and, like those of Greek mountain villages, roofed with broad limestone slabs, which require, in addition to their other fastenings, heavy stones to keep them from being displaced by the furious winds to which these regions are exposed." The Wallachian women still wear the picturesque national dress — embroidered chemisettes, loose floating vests, coloured aprons, golden nets, and golden sequins in the hair.

Although Bulgaria now sustains an autonomous relation to Turkey, the majority of the inhabitants of the vilayet of Adrianople are Bulgarians; there are scattered Bulgarian communities in the Macedonian provinces and about 5,000 Bulgarians live in Constantinople. Like the Osmanli Turks, the Bulgarians are of Asiatic origin. Originally they came from the Finnic group of the Sibiric branch of the Asian race; but, like the Servians and the Russians, they have been converted into Slavs. Somewhat below medium in stature, they are broad-shouldered and strongly built. Less vivacious than the Wallachians and less supple than the Greeks, they are not deficient in intelligence, and they make thrifty agriculturists and laborious husbandmen. Miss Garnett says of them: " The salient characteristic of the Bulgarian peasantry [in Turkey] is their industry. The frequent church festivals and holidays observed by the Bulgarians, in common with the Greeks, make it necessary for them to work doubly hard on the other days in order to accomplish the year's work in twelve months. And during the spring and summer the whole family labour assiduously from sunrise to sunset, the women and girls as soon as their household duties are finished going out to assist the men and boys in the fields. The spinning, weaving, and other home manufactures are carried on chiefly in the winter, when the female portion of the family is less called upon for outdoor work than in other seasons."[1] The Bulgarians adhere to the Orthodox Greek church, although since 1870, in consequence of its demand for religious autonomy, the Bulgarian church has been outside the Orthodox

[1] "Turkish Life in Town and Country." London [n. d.].

Kurds, Albanians, Persians 113

Greek communion. It is governed by a synod of bishops and an Exarch, resident at Constantinople, chosen by the bishops with the approval of the sultan. A few Bulgarians have embraced the faith of Islam and there is a small Roman Catholic contingent among the Bulgarians in European Turkey.

Some of the minor races in European Turkey must be passed unnoticed; but in closing the subject, brief mention must be made of the Gypsies and the Ethiopians. Neither race is numerically strong in Constantinople and European Turkey, but both appeal to the interest of the traveller. The ubiquitous Gypsies are a branch of the Indo-Eranic peoples, who left India so late as the twelfth or the thirteenth century, and they have been roving over Europe ever since. Like the Jews, they are a race without a country, but unlike the Jews they have never disbanded tribally. The physical Gypsy type is not unlike that observed in eastern Europe, and particularly in Transylvania. They are unquestionably the filthiest race in Turkey; and in Constantinople they live about the inner circle of the walls of Stambul in squalid hovels and in the most promiscuous fashion. Kesnin Bey says of them: " Each tribe recognizes the authority of a chief whose power appears to be absolute. Children get no education whatever, but learn to beg as soon as they can walk; when they grow older, they add yet other accomplishments, such as the adroit theft of fruit from orchards or of pullets from farmyards. Take them all in all, they are marauders, unpleasant, disagreeable if you will, but not dangerous criminals. Then, in a picture, how effective they are!"[1]

The Gypsies have no history, no written language, and no religion. A tradition is current in Turkey that when God distributed religions to the various races of the world, the recipients engraved their respective creeds on wood, stone, metal, or in books; but that the thriftless and improvident Gypsies wrote their creed on cabbage leaves which were soon found and eaten by a donkey; and hence the Gypsies have no religion of their own. The Gypsy men in Constantinople are chiefly engaged in horse-breeding and horse hire; and the women sell lavender and herbs, tell fortunes, make excruciating vocal utterances to the accompaniment of tambourines, and sell their charms for Turkish piastres, English shillings, or French francs.

[1] "The Evils of the East, or Facts about Turkey." London, 1888.

A GYPSY GIRL.

Kurds, Albanians, Persians 115

Not all the Ethiopians one sees in Constantinople are eunuchs, but all the eunuchs are Ethiopians; and, of the nineteen subject races of the Sublime Porte, they insidiously make their appearance most often in the pages of Ottoman history. The Kislar-Agassi, or chief of the guard of eunuchs, after the sultan, ranks with the Sheik-ul-Islam and Grand Vizier as one of the three most powerful statesmen in the empire. The Ethiopians in Turkey belong to the Abyssinian group of the Semitic stock of the Eurafrican race. Their skin is dark brown, their hair crisp, and they have some of the negro features, but they are not true negroes but negroids, and represent a mixture of Arabic, Hebrew, and negro blood. The surgical operation, to which the eunuchs are subjected in infancy, modifies greatly both the physical and the mental Ethiopian type. Those seen in Constantinople are tall, fat, and flabby, and suggest fattened swine. They have short bodies, long arms and legs, and beardless, withered faces. Mentally they are cunning, sly, cowardly, stupidly faithful, and astutely treacherous.

The operation which produces the eunuch is performed in early childhood by mercenary parents, but only one castrate in every three survives to reach adulthood; and, as thousands are required every year, the wanton immolation of Ethiopian youths must be enormous. The iniquitous traffic lessens a bit with the decline of polygamy, but large numbers are still required in Turkey as harem guards, companions to women, and confidential messengers and servants to sultans and high officials. The sentiment of the author is well voiced by Edmondo de Amicis in the plea, " O philanthropists, public men, ministers, ambassadors, and you deputies to the parliament of Stambul, and senators of the Crescent, raise your voices in the name of God against this bloody infamy, this horrid blot upon the honour of humanity, that in the twentieth century it may become like the slaughter in Bulgaria, only a painful recollection." [1]

[1] "Constantinople." New York [1896].

AN ETHIOPIAN EUNUCH.

CHAPTER VIII

THE FAITH OF ISLAM

Theocratic nature of the Ottoman government and its relation to the Mohammedan religion — Beginnings of the faith of Islam — Life of the founder — Effect of the flight from Mecca — Conflict of spiritual ideals and temporal power — Pathological mental condition of the Prophet — Factors in the spread of Islamism — Nature of the religion — Mohammedan creed — Sunnites and Shi'ites, the two great sects — Their differences.

THE institutions and civilization of Turkey are so interwoven with the faith of Islam that a brief chapter on the Mohammedan religion is called for at this point. Readers seeking a fuller treatment of the subject will find the same in James Freeman Clarke's "Ten Great Religions," or the excellent articles by Professors Wellhausen, A. Müller, Nöldeke, Wilhelm Spitta-Bey, and Stanislas Guyard in the "Encyclopædia Britannica," and for an exhaustive treatment see the larger works by Muir and Sprenger.

The Ottoman Empire is a theocracy; its chief magistrate claims to be a representative of God; and by the largest branch of the Mohammedan church — the Sunnites — this claim is recognized as valid. The Shi'ites, it is true, deny the claim on the ground that the caliph of the faith of Islam must be a lineal descendant of the Prophet, and they do not in consequence recognize the sultans of Turkey as commanders of the faithful.

Dr. Samuel Johnson once said that there are but two religions that are objects of curiosity and interest — the Christian and the Mohammedan; all the others he regarded as barbarous and devoid of interest. It is well to recall in this connection that Mohammedanism is the only religion that has ever succeeded in displacing Christianity, and that the faith of Islam has always been a real and profound barrier to the spread of the gospel of Christ. James Freeman Clarke has remarked that of all the great religions of the world the faith of Islam is the only one " whose origin is in the broad daylight of history and its author is the only one among the great men of the world who has at the same time founded a religion, formed a people, and established an empire."

The founder of the faith of Islam was born in the city of Mecca in the year 570, of poor but honest Arabic parents. They died when

The Faith of Islam

he was a child and he grew up in the family of an uncle. He won esteem from his relatives and associates; and when still a young man he engaged to take charge of the camels and the trade of a rich Arabic widow whom he afterward married. He was always of a profoundly religious cast of mind; and, on the numerous trips which his business required him to make in the surrounding country, he was keenly impressed with the absence of spirituality in the divers forms of polytheism practised by the people.

He regarded the current religions as low forms of idolatry, and he began to preach a more sublime idea of one God, eternal, immense, almighty. He advocated so vehemently the destruction of the idols in the temples of Mecca that he aroused the bitter opposition of the temple priests and they resolved upon his ruin. After facing numerous persecutions, he fled with some of his followers to Medina in the year 631 of the Christian era, and the first year of the Mohammedan. His doctrines spread rapidly after his permanent settlement in Medina. For thirteen years he had faced persecution with humility; now he decided to advance his cause by means of arms. An army was organized; numerous battles were fought, and eight years after his flight from his native city, he reëntered Mecca as a conqueror, at the head of 10,000 soldiers. He threw down the idols and the statues; he established in the temples his own forms of worship; and he forced the inhabitants to accept his faith.

Once master of Mecca, he extended his religion and dominion over neighbouring provinces; and when he died in 641 and was succeeded by his faithful friend Abu-Bekr as caliph — for he left no heir — he had conquered more than two-thirds of the peninsula of Arabia and compelled the people to adopt his religion. The first three caliphs who succeeded Mohammed completed the evangelization of Arabia and extended his religion to Syria, Armenia, western Persia, and northern Africa as far west as Kairwan, including Egypt, Tripoli, and eastern Tunis. The Saracens extended the Mohammedan boundaries westward from Kairwan through Tunis, Algiers, and Morocco, and across the Strait of Gibraltar into Spain; to the islands of the Mediterranean — Sicily, Cyprus, Crete, Corsica, and Sardinia; to central and western Asia Minor and northern and eastern Persia. It was reserved for the Osmanli Turks to complete the evangelization of

The Faith of Islam

Asia Minor and carry the faith over the Hellespont into the Greek Empire in Europe.

Moslem scholars regard the faith of Islam as the fulfilment of Biblical prophecies. They refer to the prediction of Moses in the eighteenth chapter of Deuteronomy (verses 15 and 18) " that the Lord will raise up a prophet for the Jews from among their brethren," as fulfilled in Mohammed; and they call attention to the fact that the Ishmaelites — the Prophet's people — were the only brethren of the Jews. Certain it is that, in its early stages, Islamism was simply regarded as a sect of Christianity. Henry Otis Dwight says in this connection: " When Islam became a danger to the Christian world, the theologians of the east accepted Mohammed at his own valuation, as a believer in the religion revealed to Moses and Jesus. They did not see in his doctrine a new religion. They regarded the Prophet of Mecca as a Christian gone astray like the Gnostics of earlier periods." In its inception it certainly was no easy task to differentiate Islamism from Christianity when it is recalled that " the Mohammedan believes in one God, uses psalms of praise derived from the Hebrew hymnal, promulgates a code of morals virtually the same as that of Sinai, and admits the miraculous birth and the unique character of Jesus Christ." [1]

It is the opinion of James Freeman Clarke that up to the flight from Mecca the religion of Mohammed could not have differed essentially from that of Jesus; and he calls attention to the fact that before the flight, the Prophet had borne adversity and opposition with a patience almost sublime; he had been a prophet teaching God's truth to those who would receive it; and, by the manifestation of that truth, commending himself to every man's conscience; he had accepted all the essential truths of the Old and the New Testament and had recognized Moses and Christ as true teachers; he had taught that there was one universal religion, the substance of which was faith in one supreme being, submission to his will, trust in his providence, and good-will toward his creatures; and during the thirteen years of his preaching a body of men and women had arisen who rejected idolatry, worshipped the one great God, lived lives of prayer, practised chastity, benevolence, and justice, and stood ready to do and to bear everything for the truth. But when Mohammed added to the duties of a prophet and re-

[1] "Constantinople and Its Problems." Chicago, 1901.

ligious teacher those of a warrior and statesman, according to Mr. Clarke, Islamism ceased to be a sect of Christianity and became an independent religion.

Carlyle, it will be remembered, while admitting that Mohammed triumphed by the sword, insists that his sword was the reward of thirteen years of patient and enduring faith; and he very truly adds that religious sects are not founded by politicians but by men of faith, by men to whom ideas are realities, by men who are willing to die for them. Such a faith is certain of ultimate triumph. It thus seems evident that after the flight from Mecca worldly success and the acquisition of temporal power not only weakened the spirituality of the Prophet but as well that of his followers. Renan says that the Mohammedan leaders who continued the Prophet's cause after his death were " men almost without religious faith."

In the same tenor Professor Wellhausen remarks: " With the flight to Medina a new period in the life of the Prophet begins; seldom does so great a revolution occur in the circumstances of any man. Had he remained in Mecca he would in the best event have died for his doctrine, and its triumph would not have come until after his death. The flight brought it about that he, the founder of a new religion, lived also to see its complete victory, — that in his case was united all that in Christendom is separated by the enormous interval between Christ and Constantine. He knew how to utilize Islam as a means of founding the Arabian commonwealth; hence the rapidity of its success. That this was no advantage for the religion is easily understood. It soon lost the ideality of its beginnings; for almost from the first it became mixed up with the dross of practical considerations. In reaching its goal so soon, its capability of development was checked for all time to come."

The viewpoint of Goethe concerning the character and sincerity of Mohammed was not dissimilar. Before the flight he thinks the Prophet was a really great spiritual leader; but he adds that, during the ten years devoted to the organization of a fanatical army that was to conquer the world, " what in his character was earthly increased and developed, and what was divine retired and became obscure, and his doctrine became a means rather than an end." Goethe once told Lewes, his English biographer, that he had hoped to write a drama upon Mohammed to illustrate the sad fact that every man who attempts to realize a great idea comes in contact with the lower world, must place himself on its level to influence it, and thus often compromises his higher aims, and at last forfeits them.

Mental pathologists, on the other hand, have explained the contradictions in the life of the Prophet by theories of epilepsy and hallucination. Dr. William W. Ireland, an eminent Scotch alienist, believes that Mohammed was subject to some nervous disease accompanied by hallucinations. Theophanes, Honoras, and contemporary Greeks assert that he was afflicted with epilepsy. After a careful examination of all the evidence touching the mental health of the Prophet Doctor Ireland concludes that " it seems likely that Mohammed at the commencement of his mission was subject to hallucinations of hearing and sight, which, taking the tone of his deeply religious feelings, and his dislike to the idolatry and polytheism of the people of Mecca, were interpreted by him as messages from God. In this belief he was prompted by his wife Kadija, and some of his relations, and was thus induced to commence his remarkable course of apostleship. How far these hallucinations accompanied the remaining twenty-one years of his life, it would be difficult to say. There are some reasons to believe that they became less frequent after the flight to Medina; but it is evident that after his claim to divine inspiration was fairly settled by himself and admitted by others, he would be disposed to regard his dreams and omens, and the impulses of his own thoughts and feelings, as so many signs from Allah, whose messenger he believed himself to be."[1]

Whatever the explanation of the origin of the inspiration of Mohammed or the causes which operated so strikingly to change his character after the flight from Mecca, the fact nevertheless remains that, in a surprisingly brief historic period, his faith made unprecedented conquests among the Caucasian, Mongolian, Malayan, and African races; and, from the latter, large additions continue to be made. It is not enough to say — as historians have said — that the faith of Islam was spread by the sword. The extraordinary military achievements of the Prophet doubtless gained proselytes; and his appeal to the latent hereditary martial instincts of barbarism was consequential. Other causes were operative; and one of these — and an important one from the viewpoint of the author — was the distortion and exaggeration of the teachings and prac-

[1] "The Blot upon the Brain." New York, 1886.

tices of the Man of Galilee from the second to the fifth centuries of his era. The social effect of nunneries and monasteries and the ascetic character of the celibate life, whatever their influence for good or evil, had come squarely in conflict with the strong natural instinct for the propagation and perpetuation of the species. A well-known psychologist, Doctor Ireland, has stated the matter so much better than I am able to put it that I quote his words: " From an early time in the Christian church the love of women had been proscribed as something inconsistent with the highest virtue, a species of stain, if not of defilement to the saintly ideal. At the commencement of the Hegira, Syria and Egypt were full of monks and nuns and hermits who exalted an incomplete life as the highest fulfilment of duty, and assumed a superiority over those who handed down the lamp of life to other generations. Against such asceticism Islam came with the full force of a reaction in favour of nature."

The Moslem religion has no mysteries, no sacraments, no intermediate persons between God and man, no altars, no images, no ornaments. God is invisible; the heart of man is his altar, and every Moslem is a priest. There are religious teachers and preachers, but no priests in the technical sense of that term. Islam teaches that no man can intervene between a human soul and God; and Mohammedans repudiate the doctrines of those Christian sects holding the priest as a necessary agent in communion with God. Every Mohammedan mosque has an Imam, or leader of the congregation; but he merely directs the devotions of his parishoners, conducts marriage ceremonies, assists at burial services, and performs minor judicial and notarial functions. He is a married man and he customarily has a stated occupation as artisan, clerk, or trader. A lecturer (muderris) is connected with each of the larger mosques. His duty is to expound the Koran and give lectures on religion and morals. He receives a definite salary from the government and is a member of the Ulema, or higher ecclesiastical body. A brief extract from Mr. Dwight's "Constantinople" will give a notion of the nature of his service: "He sits cross-legged in his pulpit or on a raised dais on the floor of the mosque, and there he dogmatizes without fear of rejoinder or question from the people who sit cross-legged in a circle about him. Turks will tell you that the man's influence is solely the influence of education, and that the possession of knowledge is what the people respect. At the same time these Ulema do claim the sole right of expounding the way of salvation, and to narrow the uses of intellectual gifts to defence of their ancient sources of revenue in gold or in power. Here at least they show the external signs of priestcraft."[1]

The Ulema, or association of wise men, is composed of the higher religious teachers and the chief functionaries of the law, and is presided over by the Sheik-ul-Islam, a layman. One section of the Ulema — the mufti — interprets the Koran. The Ulema includes all the great theologians, jurists, teachers, and savants, and is a sort of a Moslem French Academy.

The creed of Mohammedanism is fivefold: (1) Confession of the unity of God; (2) prayers at stated times; (3) almsgiving; (4) observance of the fast of Ramazan, and (5) the festival of Mecca. There is no god but God (la Ilah illa Allah) is the corner-stone of Islam monotheism. The doctrine of one personal God, without any obscuring distinction of his manifold nature, appealed strongly to the simple-minded Arabs, Persians, and Turks. The Athanasian creed, it will be recalled, has

[1] "Constantinople and Its Problems." Chicago, 1901.

always been a stumbling-block to the advance of Christianity among primitive people. The prayers are five in number — at sunrise, noon, afternoon, sunset, and evening, with the additional attendance at a prayer service at midday on Friday. Originally each prayer required two prostrations of the body, but the number was increased to four. Almsgiving is intended to awaken a feeling of fellowship among the faithful; but it has grown to be a sort of tithe and has furnished the basis of the Moslem fiscal system. The fast of Ramazan comes the ninth month of the Moslem year and lasts for thirty days. It is rigidly observed from dawn to sunset, when all restrictions are removed and feasting may continue until sunrise. The fast is followed by a three days' feast known as the lesser Bairam. Moslems are enjoined to observe the feast of sacrifice on the day of the Meccan festival even if they cannot be present on the spot.

The Mohammedan church is divided into two great branches — the Sunnites and the Shi'ites; and they are as widely separated by sectarian animosities as the three great branches of the Christian church — the Roman Catholics, the Orthodox Greeks, and the Protestants. The Sunnites stand for the established and his-

The Faith of Islam

toric forms of Islam orthodoxy, and they discourage the spirit of inquiry, rationalistic tendencies, and freedom of religious thought. So late as the fourth quarter of the nineteenth century a professor in the Azhar mosque college at Cairo attempted to read Avicenna with his students; and for purposes of illustration he brought a globe to his lecture-room. The innovation met with such stout opposition from his colleagues that it procured his exile on the pretext that his methods of teaching were socialistic and democratic! The Sunnites adhere to a collection of prophetic laws which includes the remarks and counsels of the Prophet, his deeds and silences — it being considered that what he abstained from doing or saying fully indicates his opinion, and hence the duties of his followers. The Sunnites are divided into four sects — the Hannbelites, the Hanefites, the Malekites, and the Schafiyites — according to their ritual, and they include from 130,000,000 to 150,000,000 followers in Turkey, Arabia, Turkestan, Afghanistan, Egypt, Tripoli, Tunis, Algiers, and Morocco.

The Shi'ites are considered an heretical branch of the Mohammedan religion. They reject *in toto* the teachings of the Sunna, but they attach great importance to the religious utterances and practices of Ali, the son-in-law of the Prophet and the fourth caliph. The first three caliphs they regard as usurpers and repudiate their teachings accordingly. They are more zealous in the worship of saints than the Sunnites, and they place more emphasis upon religious festivals and ceremonials. But they hold less tenaciously to the exclusive inspirational character of the Koran, and they make quite as much use of the ethical teachings of great writers like Hafiz and Sadi as they do of the precepts of the Prophet. The Shi'ites number not more than 20,000,000 persons; and they are to be found chiefly in Persia, India, and among the Tatars in Asia.

CHAPTER IX

HOW TURKEY IS GOVERNED

Nature of the Ottoman theocracy — The Sultan's ministry — Grand Vizier — Sheik-ul-Islam — Political divisions of the empire — Local administration — Basis of Turkish law — Rights of foreigners — The army — Military reforms — War strength — Navy — Finance — Imperial taxes — Revenues and expenditures — National debt — Turkey an irredeemably corrupt despotism.

TURKEY is a theocratic, absolute monarchy subject to the personal control of the sultan. He is the temporal autocrat of the empire and the assumed caliph or spiritual head of the Moslem world. He is "by the Grace of the Almighty Creator, Lord of Lords, Dominant Sovereign in Arabia, Persia, and Greece, Invincible and always Victorious, Emperor of Constantinople, Distributor of Crowns to the Great Princes of the Earth, Sovereign Master of the two seas and of the adjacent countries, Protector of the Sacred and August Cities of Mecca and Medina and of endless other countries, kingdoms, empires, isles, and peoples," together with sundry honorary titles such as

"Shadow of God," "Refuge of the World," and "Slayer of Infidels." The late Hon. Wm. E. Gladstone suggested "the Great Assassin" as an additional honorary title for the present sultan.

The absolutism of the sultan is tempered by the supposed opinions and sayings of the Prophet, the interpretation of the spiritual precepts of the Koran (made by the Ulema, an ecclesiastical body), and the direct and indirect pressure of the Great Powers of Europe.[1] While the sultan concentrates all power within his person, he is assisted in the direction of the legislative and executive administration by a Grand Vizier, or prime minister, who takes direct charge of the civil administration, and a Sheik-ul-Islam who superintends the worship of the Mohammedan religion and the administration of justice according to Moslem canon law. Both these officials act under the authority of the sultan. He selects, in addition, ten subordinate ministers, who — with the Grand Vizier and the Sheik-ul-Islam — form a council of state. The subordinate ministers are entrusted with special branches

---

[1] Two efforts have been made to give Turkey a constitution, during the reign of Abdul-Mejid, in 1856, and twenty years later at the beginning of the reign of Abdul-Hamid II., but both miscarried.

How Turkey Is Governed

of administration, not unlike the cabinet posts in England and the United States. They are as follows: President of the Council of State, Minister of War and Master of Artillery, Minister of the Navy, Minister of the Interior, Minister of Justice, Minister of Foreign Affairs, Minister of Finance and the Civil List, Minister of Religious Endowments and Charitable Bequests, Minister of Public Works, Commerce, and Agriculture, and Minister of Public Instruction.

Associated with the various ministries are certain legal advisers called mufti and a great army of hangers-on. All important appointments are made by the sultan, and many of the minor offices are filled by the ministers, subject to the sultan's approval. Influence, pull, and backsheesh, however, play an even larger rôle in the selection of civil servants in Turkey than in the United States. The leading civil functionaries bear such titles as Effendi, Bey, and Pasha, the latter title being given only to civil and military officials of the highest rank.

The Sheik-ul-Islam, although not a priest himself, is the president of the Ulema or ecclesiastical council, which deals with all matters touching the Mohammedan religion. The

Kislar Agassi, or chief of the black eunuchs, forms a connecting link between the civil and ecclesiastical government on the one hand and the personnel of the imperial palace on the other. His rank is that of Marshal of the Palace, but his influence is unlimited and his power over the sultan exceeds that of either the Grand Vizier or the Sheik-ul-Islam. Kesnin Bey says of the grand eunuch: " After the sultan, this gelding counts as the first person in the empire; he stands above the law, and, if so minded, may fearlessly box a recalcitrant minister's ears. He goes by the pretty name of Europeanophagus, or devourer of all that is European; and he poses as the rabid defender of Asiatic barbarism."

For administrative purposes the Ottoman Empire is divided into thirty-seven states or vilayets — eight in Europe, eleven in Asia Minor, five in Armenia, three in Mesopotamia, six in Syria, two in Arabia, and two in Africa. A governor-general (vali), who is the personal representative of the sultan, is at the head of each vilayet. He is supposed to be assisted in the government of his state by a council composed of leading publicists selected from both Moslems and non-conformists; but as he has absolute power to appoint and dismiss mem-

How Turkey Is Governed

bers of his council, his government is often a worse form of despotism than that of the Sublime Porte at Constantinople. The vilayets are divided into provinces, subject to the authority of inferior governors appointed by the governor-general, and these again subdivided into districts and communities.

In theory all nationalities in the Ottoman Empire are equal before the law; without regard to ethnic stock or religion, all may be admitted to the civil service; and all subjects, however humble their origin, are eligible to the highest offices of the state. In practice, however, civil officers are chosen almost exclusively from among the Moslem subjects, for a despotic government like Turkey finds it easier to attain its ends with civil servants who have a common religious belief. Fortunately, however, as Reclus has remarked, " the despotism of the Turks is not the despotism of learning based upon a knowledge of human nature and directed to its debasement. The Osmanli ignores the art of ' oppressing wisely,' which the Dutch governors of the Sunda Islands were required to practise in former times, and which is not quite unknown in other countries. The pashas allow things to take their course as long as they are able to enrich themselves and their favourites, to sell justice and their favours at a fair price, and to bastinade now and then some unlucky wight. They do not inquire into the private concerns of their subjects, and they do not call for confidential reports on families and individuals. Their government, no doubt, is frequently violent and oppressive; but all this only touches externals. Such a government may not be favourable to the development of public spirit, but it does not interfere with individuals; and powerful national institutions — such as the Greek commune, the Mirdit tribe, and the Slav community — have been able to survive under it. Self-government is, in fact, more widely practised in Turkey than in the most advanced countries of western Europe. It would be difficult to force these various national elements under a uniform discipline, and the lazy Turkish functionaries generally leave things alone."

Turkish law is based upon (1) the Koran; (2) traditions derived from the first four caliphs; (3) decisions made by celebrated Imams during the first century of Islamism; (4) formal decisions on questions proposed to the Sheik-ul-Islam, and (5) custom, which is equal in authority to positive law. In a theocratic government canon law necessarily plays a leading rôle; but the Turkish law recognizes among Ottoman subjects the broad distinction of Moslems and non-Moslems. Besides the free exercise of their religion, and the management of their own monasteries, schools, hospitals, and charitable foundations, the Ottoman government grants to the heads of non-Moslem religious communities a certain amount of judicial power. Non-Moslem religious communities enjoying such power include the Orthodox Greek church, the Roman Catholic church, the Gregorian Armenian church, the Roman Catholic Armenian church, the Protestant Armenian church, and the Hebrew church.

Foreigners residing in Turkey are under the laws of their respective countries; and in all matters in which Turkish subjects are not concerned, they are amenable to a tribunal presided over by the consul of their country. In questions which relate to landed property, foreigners are amenable to the Ottoman civil courts; but in all cases between foreign and Turkish subjects, a dragoman of the foreign consul must be present to see that the trial proceeds according to law. When two foreigners of different nationalities have legal differences, the case is tried in the court of the defendant.

Turkey recognizes the passports issued by foreign governments when these passports have been duly countersigned by a Turkish consul or minister; but she does not recognize the passports of foreigners of Turkish origin. Hence foreign consuls are unable to extend protection to naturalized Turkish citizens. This unfair discrimination has been the cause of no end of strife with countries to which large numbers of Armenians and Greeks have emigrated; Great Britain and the United States have suffered most; and it is much to be desired that each of these countries should exact a naturalization treaty from Turkey that will place all its citizens on a basis of equality with the Sublime Porte.

Absolute and despotic governments generally rest upon military foundations. The Ottoman Empire claims a war strength of 1,500,000 men, including permanent and territorial reserves, and an effective combatant service of 700,000 men, distributed as follows: Infantry, 648 battalions, 583,200 men; cavalry, 202 squadrons, 55,300 men; artillery, 1,356 guns, 54,720 men; and engineers, thirty-nine companies, 7,400 men. This is the paper war

AN OFFICER IN THE TURKISH ARMY.

strength of the Turkish army, but it is probable that the active army does not have more than 200,000 men. The empire is divided into seven army corps and stationed as follows: at Constantinople, Adrianople, and Monastir in Europe, and Erzingan, Damascus, Bagdad, and Sana (the Yemen) in Asia.

The Turkish army is composed of (1) the regular army and its reserves, (2) the Landwehr, and (3) the Landsturm. All Ottoman subjects over twenty years of age who are Moslems are liable to military service, and this liability continues for twenty years. Non-Moslem males pay an annual exemption tax of about $1.50. The nomadic Kurds and Arabs, although liable to service, generally evade it. Conscripts are divided into first and second levies. The former serve six years in the regular army, eight years in the Landwehr, and six years in the Landsturm. The second levy consists of those not drawn for the contingent; they constitute a part of the reserve and undergo from six to nine months' drill in the first year of their service, and thirty days' drill at their homes in subsequent years.

In a previous chapter it was pointed out that one of the causes in the decline of the Ottoman Empire was the degeneration in the Turkish army. Successive sultans have endeavoured to reform the army and for this purpose have secured the best available military instructors in England, France, and Germany; but all to no purpose. Concerning the failures in Turkish military reforms, Sir Charles Norton Edgcumbe Eliot writes: " The Turkish reformer and the Christian reformer have nothing in common, and the mass of the Turks mistrust the reformer. Even in such matters as military reform, where there can be no doubt that improvements are in the interest of the Moslem and the Moslem only, the Turk will not take the view which his friends think he obviously ought to take. Foreign military instructors have again and again presented recommendations, and again and again they have been rejected, sometimes openly, sometimes with a pretence of acceptance, but always quite firmly. The Turk has a dim perception that even in military matters he cannot understand and practise European methods. If he tries to do so the control will pass out of his hands into those of people who are cleverer than himself. But though he may think them cleverer, he does not on that account feel any respect for them. He regards them as conjurers who can perform a variety of tricks which may be,

TURKISH WAR-SHIPS IN THE GOLDEN HORN.

How Turkey Is Governed 143

according to circumstances, useful, amusing, or dangerous; but for all Christendom he has a brutal, unreasoning contempt — the contempt of the sword for everything that can be cut, and to-day the stupid contempt of the blunt sword."[1]

The military strength of Turkey is in her army and not in her navy. Three times she has built up a powerful navy, but each time it has been destroyed by the combined fleets of European nations — at Lepanto in 1571 by the united navies of Spain, Malta, Genoa, Venice, and Pius V.; at the passage of Scio in 1770 by Russia and England, and at Navarino in 1827 by England, Russia, and France. To-day the Turkish navy is of little or no value. It is composed largely of rebuilt old ironclads; and the few modern war-ships that have been built for Turkey at Philadelphia and Elswick have been stripped of everything portable and sold as old iron by unpaid naval officers. Hardly any of her war-vessels can be used, because their engines, boilers, and machinery have not been kept in repair. A handsome marble building in Constantinople serves as headquarters for the admiralty and more than three million dollars are annually appropriated for the

[1] "Turkey in Europe." London, 1900.

navy; but the Ottoman admiralty, as Mr. Curtis has well said, is the most extraordinary marine morgue in existence. Hassan Pasha, the secretary of the navy, is one of the richest men in Turkey, and he is also probably one of the most corrupt men in the empire. The navy is recruited in the same way as the army, partly by conscription and partly by voluntary enlistment, the time of service being twelve years. The nominal strength of the Ottoman navy (on paper) is six vice-admirals, eleven rear-admirals, 208 captains, 289 commanders, 228 lieutenants, 187 ensigns, 30,000 sailors, besides about 9,000 marines.

The sultan of Turkey is as absolute in matters of finance as in other governmental affairs. He holds the purse-strings of the imperial exchequer, spends the revenues as he pleases, and makes no report of expenditures. In the absence of a budget, accurate financial information is not available; but I have relied upon the facts given in the "Statesman's Year-Book," and a report on Turkish finance made by Sir Edgar Vincent. The revenue of the Ottoman government is about $85,000,000 a year and the expenditure $95,000,000. The annual deficit of $10,000,000 is met, after the manner of Bret Harte's "Plain Language from Truthful James," by "ways that are dark and tricks that are vain."

The largest single item of revenue is the tithe, or tenth, which is levied on all products of the soil — cereals, vegetables, fruits, cotton, opium, honey, oil, charcoal, etc., sometimes collected in kind and sometimes in money. The method of collecting the tithe is one of the standing evils in Turkey. Crops are valued in the spring; but when the grain has been cut, it cannot be removed from the field, no matter what may be the condition of the weather, until the tax-gatherer has again seen it. He may be in a distant part of the province, and the weather or marauding flocks of birds may in the meantime have made profit for the farmer impossible. The finest and heaviest sheaves are always selected for the government, and these must be threshed separately. The farmer must in addition give the bailiff six measures of wheat and barley for every head of cattle that he possesses. The oppressed tillers of the soil must thus not only pay the ten per cent. required for government revenue, but they must in addition bear the burden of gathering the tax which varies anywhere from five to ten per cent., according to the rapaciousness of the tithe collector.

Imperial lands pay no tax, and most of the lands of Turkey belong to the crown; but private landowners must pay a property tax on all lands which they occupy, and an additional tax on all houses and lands which they lease — four per cent. in each case. The government realizes $12,000,000 a year from this source. There is a three per cent. income tax on profits and incomes of all kinds, and this yields $3,800,000 a year. A military exemption tax is levied on all non-Moslem subjects which amounts to $4,500,000. Sheep and goats are taxed from thirty to eighty cents a head, yielding about $8,700,000 a year. Since 1883 the tobacco monopoly of Turkey has been in the hands of Austrian and Turkish bankers, and the government's share of the profits amounts to about $260,000 a year. There are in addition tribute duties on tobacco, salt, spirits, silk, and fish, yielding $5,700,000. The tribute duties are now assigned directly to the Ottoman Debt Administration for the payment of the interest on national debts. There is besides an import duty of eight per cent. on all articles brought into Turkey, and an export duty of one per cent. on all articles sent from the country. The import and export duties together yield $11,000,000 a year.

The largest single item of expenditure is the public debt, $32,400,000; but the combined military departments — war, gendarmerie, marine, and artillery — require $39,000,000 a year. The sultan of Turkey is the best paid monarch of Europe. His income, in spite of the poverty of the country, reaches $6,000,000 a year, about $4,000,000 from government revenues and $2,000,000 from his immense estates; but he is required to pay his numerous items of personal expense from this fund. This does not, however, include the interest which he receives on funds invested in foreign banks, and his foreign investments are said to be not less than $18,000,000. With the possible exception of the figureheads of American trusts and insurance companies, there is probably nowhere else on this planet such disproportion between remuneration and service as in the case of the successor of the Prophet. In the matter of salaries of government officials on the other hand — to except, of course, heads of departments who augment their incomes by plunder and boodle — there is no country in Europe where civil servants are paid such mean salaries; and the chronic state of impecuniosity of the imperial exchequer renders the regular payment of even low salaries impossible.

Minor officials go unpaid; but servants of the government who occupy posts of power and honour simply plunder, oppress, and fleece the common people, and the non-Moslem subjects of the sultan very naturally suffer most.

The public debt of Turkey is something enormous — amounting to more than $700,000,000 — and the government revenues scarcely pay the interest on the principal. There is still due Russia a considerable balance of war indemnity, together with special indemnities to Russian subjects, and an indemnity to the Damascus-Serghis Railway. As Turkey is practically in bankruptcy, the finances are supervised by a council of administration which represents the domestic and foreign bondholders. The council takes charge of certain tribute revenues on tobacco, salt, spirits, stamps, fisheries, silks, etc., and distributes the same each month among the various creditors.

The irredeemably corrupt and cruel nature of the autocratic despotism of Turkey cannot be too strongly stated. A despotism that oppresses and slaughters, as the Ottoman despotism has oppressed and slaughtered in Armenia and Macedonia in recent years, and in Greece and the Balkan provinces in former times, is its own condemnation. General Fenwick Williams, the able English defender of Kars during the Crimean war — when England was Turkey's ally — denounced the whole machinery of the Ottoman government as "an engine of tyranny perhaps unequalled in the world;" and concerning the provincial police system of Turkey he wrote Lord Clarendon, "It is needless for me to assure your lordship that no language can portray the infamy which characterizes the life and character of this body of men." And I have no reason to believe that these matters have improved a whit since the close of the Crimean war. Under the cunning Abdul-Hamid they have probably grown worse.

CHAPTER X

AGRICULTURE, INDUSTRY, AND COMMERCE

Agriculture the mainstay of the people — How the lands are held — Chief agricultural products — Forests — Fisheries — Industries — Their primitive nature — Commerce — Foreign trade — Exports and imports — Customs duties — Commercial importance of Constantinople — Mercantile navy — Turkish railways — Postal service.

AGRICULTURE, although the mainstay of the people of Turkey, is in a very backward state. The soil is of excellent quality and the whole country is well fitted to make Turkey a great agricultural nation; but only a small proportion of the tillable land is under cultivation; the taxes are burdensome and the system of tax-collection is unfair; there are oppressive customs duties which cripple the exportation of produce from one province to another, and there are no good roads and few railways. While the great mass of the people live by agriculture and cattle-rearing, these are carried on by the most primitive methods.

Land is held under four different forms of

A TURKISH PEASANT.

Agriculture, Industry, Commerce 151

tenure: (1) Crown lands, which form the largest part of the tillable area, held by the sultan, the right to cultivate the same being granted by the government upon the payment of fees; (2) pious lands, those held by mosques, schools, or other Moslem foundations, most of which in recent times have been seized by the crown; (3) crown grants, or landed property given to army officers by previous sultans in recompense for military services, and now hereditary and exempt from taxation, and (4) freehold property which does not exist in mentionable quantities, since this is the only form of real estate subject to taxation. The agricultural lands for the most part belong to the Sublime Porte, the Mohammedan church, and a few large proprietors, and the taxes come from the products of the soil rather than from the land itself.

The chief agricultural products are grain, maize, flax, cotton, hemp, tobacco, opium, silk, wine, and olives. There is an export duty of one per cent. on all agricultural products sent abroad, except cereals, and a duty of eight per cent. if the products are sent from one part of Turkey to another. European Turkey is rich in forest lands,— something like three and a half million acres,— but the forest laws are not enforced and this source of agricultural wealth is rapidly diminishing. The most valuable woods are the pine, fir, larch, oak, and cedar. Oxen and buffaloes are the chief beasts of burden in farm work, and the wooden plough is still in general use. Angora, the goat that grows the mohair wool, and the acorn cups of the Valonia oak, used for dyeing and tanning, add materially to the agricultural wealth of the Ottoman Empire.

The fisheries of Turkey are important, those of the Bosporus alone representing an annual value of more than a million dollars; and the Mediterranean produces excellent sponges, the Persian Gulf pearls and the Red Sea the valuable mother of pearl. The ranges of crystalline schist in Europe yield iron, lead, and copper ore, and Asia Minor is rich in minerals — chrome, silver, coal, zinc, antimony, manganese, lignite, emery, asphalt, lithographic stone, meerschaum, and petroleum; but owing to the difficulties in obtaining concessions from the government, very little mining is done. All exported minerals pay a royalty of from five to fifteen per cent. In late years something has been done by the Ottoman government to develop the coal industry, but it is of an inferior quality, and its sale would be

Agriculture, Industry, Commerce 153

limited but for the fact that all vessels flying the Ottoman flag and all railways in the empire are obliged to purchase seventy-five per cent. of their entire consumption of coal from Turkish mines.

Turkey is almost entirely without industries of any kind, and she is now an important market for foreign manufacturers. Formerly she led in the manufacture of carpets, silk textiles, and morocco leather; but she is no longer able to compete with the progressive countries of Europe. Even the fez, the emblem of Turkish nationality, is now largely manufactured abroad. There are a few cotton, silk, and woollen mills at Constantinople and Saloniki; attar of roses, carpets, and silks in considerable quantities are manufactured at Adrianople; and a few house industries are carried on in a primitive way in some of the smaller towns. The government has recently granted concessions for the manufacture of glass and paper and there is a good deal of brass turning and beating of copper into utensils for household purposes.

There are some industries in the Asiatic provinces of Turkey. Damascus has five thousand hand looms and employs more than ten thousand workmen in weaving silk, cotton, and woollen fabrics. Silk textiles are also manufactured at Brusa, Diarbekr, Bagdad, and Beirut; carpets and rugs at Bitlis, Sivas, and Smyrna; leather goods at Aintab, Erzerum, and Bagdad; and there are waning muslin industries at Mosul.

In spite of her exceptionally favourable geographic conditions, the transit and shipping trade of Turkey is very slight. Her total foreign commerce is about that of the unimportant republic of Mexico, and one-tenth that of the little kingdom of the Netherlands; and two-thirds of her foreign trade consists of imports. The chief imports in the order of their monetary value are cotton cloth, sugar, quilting, cotton yarn, coffee, petroleum, flour, rice, hides, madapolams, woollen goods, kerseymeres, hardware, iron, carpets, and coal; and the chief exports, in the same order, grapes, silk, wheat, opium, cocoons, wool, valonia, mohair, hides and skins, ores, coffee, figs, olive-oil, carpets, bones, and nuts.

Great Britain has thirty-four per cent. of the Turkish import trade and thirty-five per cent. of the export trade; France has twelve per cent. of the import trade and thirty-one per cent. of the export trade; Austria-Hungary has nineteen per cent. of the import trade and

Agriculture, Industry, Commerce 155

ten per cent. of the export, and Italy five per cent. each of the export and import trade. Less than four per cent. of Turkey's export trade is to the United States and her import trade is a small fraction of one per cent. As before noted, customs duties are levied at the uniform rate of eight per cent., except certain government monopolies — salt and tobacco — which pay seventy-five per cent. Turkey protects her citizens against one of the great humbugs of modern commerce — patent medicine — by prohibiting its importation. She also puts gunpowder and rifled arms in the prohibitive list with patent medicine. Recent harbour improvements at Constantinople, Smyrna, and Saloniki have improved shipping facilities, but they have increased tariff charges. The addition of the quay dues to the eight per cent. ad valorem on imported goods has diverted the transit trade of Constantinople from the interior of Asia Minor to other ports.

Constantinople, with one of the finest harbours in the world, has an insignificant trade; and it is indicative of the backward state of Turkish civilization and the defective form of the Ottoman government that the chief exports are of Asiatic origin — mohair, cereals, and gums from Anatolia, and carpets, rugs, and hand-made textiles from Armenia, Persia, and the Caucasus region. Saloniki has a large railway trade with northern Europe and steamer trade with the Mediterranean countries in wheat, barley, raw silk, maize, wool, timber, sponges, and tobacco; but two-thirds of the Saloniki trade is in the hands of the Hebrews. Dedeagatch, near the mouth of the Maritza River, has a considerable export trade in Bulgarian wheat, and Adrianople, which is now connected with Constantinople and Budapest and Vienna, has considerable domestic traffic with interior towns. The commerce of European Turkey is confined to these four cities.

The value of the trade at the various Turkish cities in Asia Minor is much greater. Smyrna leads with an annual export trade of more than $22,000,000 and an import trade of $12,000,000. Smyrna has a good harbour, excellent steamer connections, and a railway line east to Afion Kara-hissar on the line of the Anatolian Railway which connects the city by rail with Constantinople. The Smyrna and Kassaba Railway also has branch lines connecting Smyrna with Soma and Burnabat. Aleppo, with Alexandretta, its seaport, has the second largest trade of the Asiatic cities. Its chief articles of commerce are cot-

Agriculture, Industry, Commerce 157

ton and silk stuffs, tobacco, wine, oil, and indigo. Aleppo has a large caravan trade with Bagdad, Diarbekr, Mosul, and Armenia. Bagdad, on the banks of the Tigris, and formerly the capital of the empire of the caliphs, ranks third. It has a large trade in silk and cotton cloth and leather goods. Trebizond, on the southeastern coast of the Black Sea, is the fourth commercial town of Asia Minor. It is the centre of the Anatolian trade and the transit trade from Persia. Its commerce includes such articles as wool, mohair, skins, wax, gall nuts, gums, and shawls. Trebizond exports a half-million dollars worth of goatskins yearly.

Beirut, the seaport for Damascus and Syria, is fifth. Its chief exports are madder, silk, wool, olive-oil, and gums. Hodeida in the Yemen on the Red Sea has a large trade in choice Mocha coffee, and Bassora at the head of the Persian Gulf exports quantities of grain, dates, and gum arabic.

Turkey has a mercantile navy of 107 steamers and 916 sailing vessels, — all small boats, — but forty per cent. of her exports and imports are carried in English bottoms. Greece comes second with ten per cent.

Caravan routes are still much used for the

camel trade in Asia Minor, and roads everywhere in the Ottoman Empire are poor.

In European Turkey there are only 1,269 miles of railway. The Oriental Railway connects Constantinople with Budapest and Vienna, and passes through Adrianople and Philippopolis. It has branches from Tirnova to Burgas in eastern Rumelia, and to Dedeagatch on the Ægean Sea. Another branch from Üskup and Mitrovitza connects Saloniki with the Oriental Railway. Constantinople is connected with Saloniki by a line that extends from Dedeagatch, connecting the two main lines of the preceding railway. There is also a short line — 137 miles — from Saloniki to Monastir.

In Asia Minor 1,667 miles of railway have already been built, and many more are contemplated. The Anatolian Railway, 642 miles, and built mainly by German capital, is the most important. It extends from Haidar-Pasha, on the Bosporus opposite Constantinople, eastward to Angora, with a short branch to Adabazar. A longer branch extends from Eski Shehr, midway between Constantinople and Angora, southeasterly to Konia. The continuation of this branch will form the Bagdad Railway which the present sultan is so anxious to see completed. The Smyrna and Kassaba

Agriculture, Industry, Commerce 159

Railway which connects with the Anatolian Railway and has branches to Soma and Burnabat (321 miles) has already been mentioned. The Aidin Railway, constructed with English capital, connects Smyrna with Ayasoluk (and Ephesus), Aidin, and Dinair. With its branches it covers 320 miles. The Damascus and Hama Railway extends from Beirut to Damascus and southward from Damascus to Muzrib. It was built by French capital and covers 150 miles. There are in addition three short narrow-gauge railways in Asia Minor — the Mudania and Brusa Railway, connecting the city of Brusa with the Sea of Marmora; the Jaffa and Jerusalem Railway, connecting the holy city with the Mediterranean, and the Mersina and Adana Railway, connecting Adana and Tarsus, two important interior towns, with the seaport of Mersina on the southeastern coast of Asia Minor.

The inadequacy of the Turkish postal and telegraph service has also crippled the development of the economic interests of the Ottoman Empire. There are only 1,297 post-offices and 907 telegraph offices in the whole country; and the postal service is so badly administered that the European nations find it necessary to maintain their own services in Turkey. In Constantinople, for example, one may patronize the imperial Ottoman postal service, the British, German, Russian, Austrian, or French post-offices. All but Germany maintain both head and branch offices at the capital; and most of these nations have found it necessary to extend their postal service to Smyrna and other important towns. The Turkish postal service is characteristically inexpeditious and unreliable, and the foreign post-offices are much patronized even by Turkish subjects.

CHAPTER XI

EDUCATION IN TURKEY

Place of education in the Koran — Education and the state — Mosque schools and their courses of study — A Moslem child's first day at school — The mosque colleges — Nature of the college instruction — Special and technical schools — The paper university at Constantinople — Schools maintained by the Greeks — Schools of the Christian missions — Robert College — Other American institutions — Roman Catholic schools — Newspapers — Press censorship — Publication of books — Index expurgatorius.

EDUCATION and culture are highly esteemed in Moslem countries, popular opinion to the contrary notwithstanding. The Koran maintains that " the ink of the learned and the blood of the martyrs are of equal value in the sight of heaven," and it regards as the four cardinal virtues " the science of the learned, the justice of princes, the prayers of the faithful, and the valour of the brave." Miss Garnett is entirely right in maintaining that there is " no country in Europe in which primary education was provided for at so early a date as in Turkey, or so many inducements held out to poor parents to allow their children to participate in its benefits."

There are three agencies in the direction of elementary and secondary education in Turkey — the mosques, the state, and the various religious communities. Up to sixty years ago, elementary education was entirely in the hands of religious authorities and free from supervision or interference from the government. From the time of the conquest elementary schools were organized as dependencies of the mosques; and Moslem children were given the rudiments of an education. This system is still in vogue. In 1846 an effort was made to secularize elementary education, but the measure was only partial, and singularly defective as an educational code. In 1869, however, Abdul-Aziz promulgated one of the most comprehensive and exemplary state educational codes in existence. It provided for a complete system of elementary, secondary, and higher schools, school supervision and inspection, the training of teachers, and compulsory attendance. It required that primary schools for both sexes should be organized in all towns and villages, and it made school attendance compulsory for boys from six to eleven and girls from six to ten. The course of study in the elementary schools included the alphabet according to the new method, the Koran, the Tedjvid and books of morals, the catechism, writing, arithmetic, Turkish history, geography, and the elements of practical knowledge. In wards or villages with mixed population, the law required the establishment of separate schools for Moslem and non-Moslem children, but it required that non-Moslem children be instructed in the catechism and rites of their respective religions under the direction of their pastors or priests and in the language of their particular nationalities.

It was an excellent scheme for a national system of state-supported schools, but it has remained practically a dead letter. There are, it is true, a few state-supported schools in Constantinople and the other large cities; but they do not exist in mentionable numbers, when the entire Ottoman Empire is taken into consideration. The mosque schools (mektebs) continue to give the rudiments of education to the Moslem boys of Turkey; and they are both more numerous and more efficient than similar educational agencies in Spain and several other Christian countries in Europe.

The Koran forms the basis of the course of study in the mosque schools, with the addition of reading, writing, and arithmetic. The teacher sits cross-legged at a low desk and the children squat in rows about him on the matted floor and recite their lessons after him in concert. The Koran is expounded in Arabic, and it is probably as little apprehended by the Turkish lads as the Latin in the schools of the Humanists and Jesuits from the time of the Renaissance down to the beginning of the nineteenth century. The mosque schoolmaster, in the smaller towns and villages, like his New England colleague of an earlier date, is jack-of-all-trades. Besides teaching the boys' and girls' classes — when girls' classes actually exist — he leads the prayers at religious services, conducts funerals, acts as legal adviser and conveyancer, and he may even practise medicine in the shape of charms. Most mosques have small endowments for educational uses, but the remuneration of the Turkish schoolmaster is even smaller than in the United States. He depends largely on the optional fees of his pupils — about fifty cents a child for the school year — although no Moslem child can be excluded from school because of poverty.

The first day of a Moslem child at the mosque school is one of the events of his life

Education in Turkey

and it is exalted to the dignity of a great family function. Miss Garnett gives this interesting pen-picture of the ceremony which she witnessed: " Dressed in his holiday suit, and bedecked with all the jewels and personal ornaments which his parents possess or can borrow for the occasion, his little fez almost concealed with strings of gold coins, pendants, pearl tassels, and various little objects worn as charms against ' the evil eye,' and his finger-tips tinged with henna, he is mounted on a superbly caparisoned horse, and led in pompous procession through the streets of the neighbourhood. In front of him his future instructors walk backwards, slowly and gravely, as if to prolong the ceremony. Behind him one boy carries on a silken cushion a copy of the Koran, to know which holy book by heart entitles a youth or maiden to the honourable title of *Hafiz;* another bears his folding book-stand of walnut-wood inlaid with mother-of-pearl, on which the sacred volume is placed when open; a third holds his *chanta,* or writing-case of velvet, embroidered with stars and crescents in gold thread. Behind these come all his future schoolfellows, walking two and two, chanting verses said to have been composed by the Prophet extolling the pleasures of knowledge, exhorting to love of one's neighbour, inciting to industry, and concluding with good wishes for their new companion, eulogies of his parents and teachers, and finally glorification of the sultan, all the bystanders loyally joining in the refrain *Amin! Amin!* On returning to the boy's home, his father distributes coppers to his schoolfellows, and also to all the poor folk sure to be collected round the gateway."[1]

Higher schools or colleges, of the sort which existed in Europe during the mediæval period, are connected with all the larger mosques. They are essentially theological seminaries and take the place of the famous universities at Damascus, Cairo, Kairwan, Bagdad, Nishapur, and Cordova, which existed during the brilliant days of Mohammedan supremacy. Besides being theological seminaries, the mosque colleges are schools of languages and jurisprudence. As pointed out in the chapter on "The Faith of Islam," the Mohammedan religion has no priesthood standing between God and the congregation; but the Koran and the Sunna being so full of minute and complex details for the regulation of private and civil life, their interpretation falls to the lot of theolo-

[1] "Turkish Life in Town and Country," London [n. d.].

gians, known as Ulema, who are trained in the mosque colleges.

In former days the mosque colleges were well endowed; and students received, in addition to free instruction, free quarters, free rations, and oil for their lamps. But recent sultans have confiscated these pious foundations; and to-day only the more favoured get free sleeping-places within the mosque, a chest for their things, and a daily ration of bread. The less favoured shift for themselves or depend upon Moslem charity, which is always considerate of college students. The students' quarters surround a courtyard in the form of a quadrangle, and several students occupy one room which serves as study, kitchen, and chamber.

There are about one hundred mosque colleges in Constantinople (with six thousand students) and one or more in each of the provincial cities. The students are recruited from the lower and middle classes of society, and when admitted they must be able to read in the Arabic, to write and count, and know the Koran by heart. Professors and students gather each morning for prayers, after which the professors take their seats about the pillars in the great court of the mosque, and the students crouch on mats at their feet. There are few books and the instruction is mainly oral. During the first collegiate year the chief work is the mastery of the grammar of the classical Arabic. The rules are read out in the memorial verses of the Ajrumiya, and the instructor adds an exposition which is generally read from a commentary. The second year is devoted to dogmatics, demonstrated by scholastic dialectics. The dogmas of Islam not being numerous, the attributes of God form the basis of the year's instruction. The study of canon law, based upon the Koran and tradition, is taken up the third and fourth years. The Koran having previously been memorized, the sense of its words is now explained. Compendiums are learned by heart and explanations are given from commentaries and noted down by the students word for word. The professors are not permitted to add anything of their own. The recognized books of jurisprudence, some of them covering more than twenty folio volumes, are thus memorized. Other studies in the collegiate course include rhetoric, logic, prosody, and the doctrine of the correct pronunciation of the Koran. At the end of the three or four years of study, the young collegians enter upon their duties in the law courts or become

Education in Turkey

teachers and preachers in town or village mosques. Only graduates of the mosque colleges are admitted to the Ulema, the great ecclesiastical council of Moslem Turkey. As graduation from the mosque colleges is an exemption for life from military service, many young men pursue the prescribed course of study with no thought of adopting an ecclesiastical career.

In addition to the schools and colleges conducted by the mosques, there are a few secondary and collegiate institutions at the capital and in the larger provincial cities that are maintained by the government and that are secular in character. They are patterned more or less after the French lycées and they offer a wider range of studies than the mosque colleges. Languages — French, German, and Turkish, as well as Arabic — and mathematics are emphasized in these schools. One of their purposes is to fit boys for the special and technical government schools of medicine, law, civil service, war, and the like. The Imperial Ottoman Lyceum at Constantinople, the Ottoman Commercial School at Halki, the Idadiye School, and the Rushdiye School in Constantinople belong to this class; but the reactionary nature of the present sultan has greatly crippled the usefulness of these higher preparatory schools as feeders of the technical schools. The Ashiret School at the capital is the foundation of Abdul-Hamid II. It is for the education of the sons of distinguished Arabs and Kurds from such remote sections of the Ottoman Empire as Kurdistan, Mesopotamia, Syria, and Tripoli. It has something like ninety boys, but the Arab contingent surpasses all the others in intelligence and aptitude for work.

Turkey has a reasonably well developed system of special and technical schools, including the School of Mines and Forests, the Imperial School of Medicine, the Superior Military School, Civil Service School, School of Languages, Veterinary School, Artillery and Engineer School, and School of Fine Arts in Constantinople, and the Naval College on the island of Halki. The Superior Military School has from six hundred to seven hundred cadets, and the Imperial School of Fine Arts in the garden of the old Seraglio has rather good courses in drawing, painting, modelling, architecture, the history of art and kindred subjects. Among other institutions at the capital of a more or less direct educational nature are the Imperial Meteorological Observatory, the Russian Archæological Institute, the libraries of

A TURKISH SCHOOL.

the mosques of St. Sophia, Sultan Bayezid, Noori-Osmaniye, the Sultan Mahmud, the Abdul-Hamid Mosque Library, the Atif Effendi Library, and the Greek libraries in the Phanar and at Pera.

After his tour of visitation to the capitals of Europe, Abdul-Aziz dreamed of consolidating all the higher educational agencies of his capital into a great University of Constantinople after the pattern of similar institutions at Paris, Vienna, and Berlin; but he was deposed before his dream was realized. Abdul-Hamid II. in 1900 conceived a similar scheme of a great Ottoman university to commemorate the twenty-fifth anniversary of his accession to the throne, and Professor Vambéry of Budapest was invited to assist the sultan in the work of unification. There is on paper a University of Constantinople; and, according to the *Minerva,* it has full faculties of law, medicine, philosophy, mathematics, and natural science. But I have not been able to learn that the university *as such* had any students.

In a report on the relative condition of the different races of Turkey in respect to schools and illiteracy, made by M. Monier of Paris forty years ago, the Arabs were accounted the best educated; they were reported a reading people, and they furnished more schoolmasters than any other race in the Ottoman Empire. In education and reading propensities the Turks were given second place. The Greeks came third. He found the masses of the Armenians very ignorant, but he observed an awakened interest in education among the Armenians of the western districts — particularly in such cities as Constantinople, Smyrna, and Brusa. The Kurds he did not find at all well read or well taught. The Albanians, Bulgarians, and Bosnians seldom read or wrote, and they did not speak any language decently. The Jews were regarded as the most illiterate. Their schools were ill-constructed and dirty and few of the people could read or write in the Hebrew or any other language. Educational conditions among the subject races of Turkey have not changed greatly during the four decades that have elapsed since the publication of the Frenchman's report.

The Greeks in Turkey have long been most active in the matter of education. Their great National Training School at Phanar, founded 1453, with its fine library and excellent secondary schools, enrolls more than five hundred students each year. The theological seminary at Halki, on one of the islands in the Sea of

Marmora, has been in existence since 1844, and it trains more than eighty Orthodox Greek clergymen every year. There are also numerous private schools — like the Pallas and the Zappion in Constantinople — that have been munificently endowed by wealthy Greeks. The Armenians have done something for themselves in the matter of providing educational facilities and they have had many schools provided for them by the Christian missions — Protestant and Roman Catholic. The Bulgarians and Bosnians, since their virtual liberation from Turkey, have made extraordinary strides in education and culture. The Kurds are probably about where they were forty years ago; and the Jews, of Constantinople at least, cling as tenaciously as ever to their filth and ignorance.

Perhaps the most striking factor in Turkish education during the past forty years has been the progress of the schools and colleges under the auspices of the Protestant and Roman Catholic missions. The Protestant missions alone have 527 schools with 23,572 pupils and forty-five colleges with 3,004 students in the Ottoman Empire. Robert College at Rumili Hissar on the Bosporus, established in 1863, with a gift of $400,000 from Christopher R.

Robert of New York, is one of the most unique collegiate institutions in the world. The aim of its founder was to give Turkey and her dependent provinces a non-sectarian Christian college after the pattern of the small colleges of New England; and to make it possible for young men of all creeds and nationalities to obtain a collegiate education at moderate cost. The college is organized under the laws of the state of New York, and is administered by the president and his associate teachers. It has an endowment fund of $250,000, fifteen acres of land, three large stone buildings, a gymnasium, a president's house, and two professors' houses. It has a faculty of thirty-six instructors, fifteen of whom are Americans. About three hundred students are enrolled each year in the preparatory and collegiate departments. Most of the nationalities of the east are represented, the Armenians, Bulgarians, and Greeks leading. Eleven languages are taught in the college. Cyrus Hamlin, its organizer, was president from 1863 to 1877; he was succeeded by George Washburn, his son-in-law, who continued in service until 1903, and C. Frank Gates has been the president of the college since. Robert College has rendered splendid service for education and culture in

ROBERT COLLEGE, AT RUMILI HISSAR.

Turkey. At both Belgrade and Sofia I was told that several of the most efficient Servian and Bulgarian statesmen and publicists had been trained in this institution. Wherever the traveller meets enlightened men in the Ottoman Empire, of whatever creed or nationality, if education is the subject discussed, Robert College is certain to be warmly praised. Americans may be justly proud of its superb service in the war of intellectual emancipation in the Near East.

Another excellent American educational institution is the Syrian Protestant College at Beirut. It was established in 1866, and is also chartered under the laws of New York; and, like Robert College, it is Christian but not sectarian. It draws its students from the Christian races of the east — from the Black Sea to the Sudan, and from Greece to Persia. It has preparatory, commercial, collegiate, and medical departments, and enrolls about 650 students a year. Euphrates College at Harput was organized 1878. It has both preparatory and collegiate departments for boys and girls — under separate management — and enrolls about a thousand students, one hundred of whom are in the collegiate department. During the recent Armenian outrages, Kurds and Turks burned the college buildings, but they have been rebuilt in part, at least, from indemnity funds paid by the Turkish government. Two other Protestant colleges in Turkey are the Anatolia College at Marsovan and the Central Turkey College at Aintab. Anatolia College was founded in 1886 and has 246 students. The Central Turkey College at Aintab was founded in 1874 and has 140 students. The constituency of both institutions is mainly Armenian and Greek.

There are also several good Protestant colleges and secondary schools for girls in Turkey. The American College for Women at Scutari, the Asiatic ward of the city of Constantinople, was opened as a secondary school for girls in 1871 and incorporated under the laws of Massachusetts as a college in 1890. Its students — about 160 each year — come from all parts of the Ottoman Empire, including Egypt, Syria, and the Greek islands which belong to Turkey. They are in the main, if not entirely, non-Moslems, and are chiefly Armenians, Greeks, and Bulgarians. English is the academic language, although eight or ten other languages are taught. Under the able presidency of Dr. Mary Mills Patrick the college has done strong, vigorous work and it has

Education in Turkey

trained a number of exceptionally fine teachers. The Central Turkey College for Girls at Marash was organized in 1884, and has about fifty students. There is also a high grade secondary school for girls at Aintab, and, as already mentioned, Euphrates College at Harput has a girls' department.

The Roman Catholics — and particularly the Jesuits — have many excellent schools and colleges in Turkey. The College of St. Joseph at Beirut, the College of St. Pulcheria at Constantinople, the College of St. Benoit at Galata, the school of the Augustine Fathers at Kum-Kapu, and the Armenian schools of the Immaculate Conception are a few of the well-known institutions directed by the Jesuits and other teaching orders. One may seriously question the utility of the Protestant and Roman Catholic missions in Turkey as proselyting agencies; but no one familiar with the facts will doubt the value of the non-sectarian educational work accomplished during the past forty years by these two great branches of the Christian church.

If the intellectual activity of a country is to be measured by the quality of its newspapers and journals, Turkey must take low rank; for as Kesnin Bey has quite truly said, the Ottoman press thermometer has remained stationary at zero for more than a quarter of a century. The press censorship under the reign of Abdul-Hamid II. has become both rigorous and absurd; and its influence has been as harmful to the political as to the intellectual life of the country. A French writer well states the case when he says: "Public opinion thus being gagged, the high are free to commit the most flagrant acts of injustice, while the low become indifferent like fatalists, and even lose all sense of their rights. The government is thus able to wallow in its corruption, for it has nothing to fear from the wrath of the masses."

No newspaper in Turkey is allowed to have its own telegraph service, and every item that is printed must be approved by government censors. And the list of prohibited subjects is legion, including matters touching the Mohammedan religion, the acts of the sultan and his ministers, all matters bearing on the relations of Turkey with foreign nations, insurrections or revolutions in Turkey or abroad, the army, finance, and the like. When King Humbert of Italy and President McKinley of the United States were assassinated, the newspapers were permitted only to state that these sovereigns had died. The press censors are frequently

Education in Turkey 179

dunderheads or men of inferior mental parts; and their invariable rule with items and articles they do not understand is, "when in doubt, strike it out." One who is in position to know the journalist's side of the matter asserts that " the unfortunate newspapers do not even pretend to fill their pockets, but only try to fill their columns without drawing down upon themselves a bastinado from the government. The government forbids them to deal with the higher subjects, so they must stop on the ground floor and interest themselves in the tittle-tattle of the servants' hall." [1]

Many newspapers are published at the capital in many different languages. The two leading Anglo-French newspapers are the *Oriental Advertiser* and the *Levant Herald;* the three leading papers published entirely in French are the *Stamboul,* the *Turquie,* and the *Phare du Bosphore;* the leading Turkish papers are the *Tarik,* the official organ of the Ottoman government, and the *Terjuman Hakikat;* the most important Greek papers the *Neologos* and the *Constantinopolis;* and the foremost Armenian papers the *Arevelk,* printed with Armenian characters but in the Turkish language, and the *Terdjuman-i-Efkiar.* There are also

[1] "The Evils of the East, or Facts about Turkey." London, 1888.

papers published in Hebrew, Arabic, Persian, Italian, Spanish, and a half-dozen other languages.

The censorship of books is even more stringent than that of newspapers. The manuscript of the most inconsequential pamphlet must be submitted to the Ulema, the ecclesiastical court; and if it should not happen to please the pillars of the faith of Islam, the necessary authorization to print is refused. But even when printed, an author is not certain that his book will be allowed to circulate. Recently the Turkish translator of Molière brought out in Constantinople an edition of "L'Avare" (The Miser). Abdul-Hamid, it would seem, in his childhood was nicknamed "the miser" by his brothers and sisters because of his juvenile greed; and nothing could convince him that the Turkish translation of Molière's comedy was not intended as an insult to the occupant of the Ottoman throne, and the edition was confiscated and the translator banished.

Another serious difficulty is the censorship of books on entering and leaving the country. Even such colourless publications as guide-books are seized by the customs' officials and held for days and sometimes weeks; and when returned they are reasonably certain to be minus their maps, if not otherwise mutilated. All books alluding to the Ottoman government or the faith of Islam are liable to seizure; and the " Index Expurgatorius " is something stupendous. It includes such harmless books as geographies, dramas, and poems. The poems of Lord Byron are not permitted to enter Turkey, presumably because of the poet's pro-Hellenic sympathies, and Dante is shut out, because in a part of the " Divine Comedy " he has put Mohammed into hell! Schiller's drama, " Don Carlos," and Verdi's opera, the " Masked Ball," are not allowed to be performed because they contain a conspiracy and the murder of a prince; likewise Shakespeare's " Macbeth " and Meyerbeer's " Huguenots." The extent to which the present sultan has pushed the matter of censorship is highly ridiculous, and its influence on education and culture has been unmistakably harmful.

CHAPTER XII

CONSTANTINOPLE: THE IMPERIAL CITY

Constantinople the continuous seat of empire for nearly sixteen hundred years — As rebuilt by Constantine — The seven hills — Its unrivalled geographic position — Natural divisions — The land-walls — Prison of the Seven Towers — At Meidan, the ancient Hippodrome — The Serpent Column — The Egyptian obelisk — The Burnt Column — Column of Constantine — Columns of Marcian and Arcadius — The Imperial Museum of Antiquities — The Cisterns.

CONSTANTINOPLE is the only city in Europe that has been the continuous seat of empire for nearly sixteen hundred years. The Delphic oracle told the men of Megara and Argos, under the navigator Byzas, to found a city that would be abiding "opposite the land of the blind." The "land of the blind," presumably, was Chalcedon on the Asiatic shore opposite the point where Byzas founded his imperishable city 657 years before the Christian era. The history of that city, under the changes of race, institutions, customs, and religions during more than twenty-five and a half centuries,

Constantinople: The Imperial City 183

is too exhaustive to attempt to summarize in this connection. Sufficient to note that Byzantium was the first city in Europe to fall into the hands of Darius; that it was burned by the Persians; rebuilt by Pausanias; besieged by Philip of Macedon, and saved by the Athenians; early allied with Rome, and destroyed by Septimius Severus in the year of our Lord 196.

It remained for Constantine the Great, a hundred years later, to rebuild it on a magnificent scale and make it henceforth the continuous seat of empire. He dedicated his new Rome the 11th of May, A. D. 330. "Throned in the Hippodrome, ever to be the centre of Byzantine life," wrote St. Augustine, "Constantine gave thanks to God for the birth of this fair city, the daughter, as it were, of Rome herself." It was his aim to make his city the most beautiful in the world; and to this end he ravished Rome, Syracuse, Athens, Antioch, and Delphi of their treasures.

The seven hills of his new city recalled to Constantine the western metropolis; and these seven hills and their intervening valleys may still be traced in spite of the pronounced changes in the topography of the imperial city, during the past fifteen centuries. The first, or most easterly hill, is to-day occupied by the Seraglio Palace, St. Sophia, the church of St. Irene, the imperial mint, the At Meidan, and the mosque of Sultan Ahmed; the second hill contains the Burnt Column and the mosque of Osman; the war office, Serasker Tower, and the mosque of Suleiman are on the third hill; the fourth hill is crowned by the mosque of Mohammed the Conqueror; the mosque of Selim is on the top of the fifth hill, and the Phanar, or Greek quarter, covers its northern declivity; Balat, the Jews' quarters, and Eyub, the sacred quarters of the Moslems, cover the sixth hill, and the fortress of the Seven Towers, or political prison, is on the seventh hill.

During the nine hundred years — from the accession of Constantine the Great (306) to the capture of the imperial city by the Latin robbers of the west (1204) — seventy-three rulers occupied the Byzantine throne; and during this long period, although it faced many sieges, the city was captured but once. Six Latin kings occupied the throne of the imperial city from 1204 to 1261; ten sovereigns succeeded during the period of the restored empire (1261-1453), and twenty-eight successors of the Prophet have ruled the city of Constantine since Mohammed the Conqueror

THE SECOND HILL OF CONSTANTINOPLE.

Constantinople: The Imperial City

waged the second successful siege of the imperial city in 1453.

From Herodotus and Polybius down to Gibbon and Freeman, historians have not wearied of extolling the unrivalled geographic position of Constantinople. It is the meeting-point of two seas and two continents — "stands in Europe, looks upon Asia, and is within easy reach of Egypt and the Levant on the south." Frederic Harrison remarks in this connection: "Of all cities in the world she stands foremost in beauty of situation, in the marvel of her geographic position, as the eternal link between the east and the west. We may almost add that she is foremost in the vast continuity and gorgeous multiplicity of her historic interests. For if Constantinople can present us with nothing that can vie in simplicity and pathos with the memories of Rome, Athens, and Jerusalem, it has for the historic mind a peculiar fascination of its own, in the enormous persistence of imperial power concentrated under varied forms in one unique spot of our earthly globe."

Constantinople is in reality three distinct cities — Stambul, the old city and the ancient Byzantium; Galata-Pera on the north side of the Golden Horn, and Scutari on the Asiatic shores of the Bosporus. The city is surrounded by water on all sides, except the west, and has a sea-front of more than eight miles. Stambul is on a tongue of land which projects into the Sea of Marmora, with the Bosporus for its eastern apex, and the Golden Horn on the north. The Golden Horn is an arm of the sea extending inland four and a half miles to the Sweet Waters of Europe. It forms one of the finest harbours in the world, varying in width from one-eighth to one-half mile, and deep enough to float ships of the largest size. The triangular promontory on which Stambul is located was defended on the land side by huge walls four miles long, now going to decay. These walls have encountered more than twenty sieges during the last fifteen centuries. The storming and sacking of Constantinople in the thirteenth century, by a mixed band of Christian vandals, Frederic Harrison has called " one of the most wanton crimes against civilization committed by feudal lawlessness and religious bigotry." He adds: " It is a dark spot on the record of the church and on the memory of Innocent III., and a standing monument of the anarchy and rapacity to which feudalism was liable to degenerate."

The land walls have not been touched since the Turkish conquest; and the breach, through

THE SEVEN TOWERS.

Constantinople: The Imperial City 187

which Dandolo and his fanatic crusaders poured like locusts, may still be seen. The crumbling walls and towers stand in solitude amid orchards and fields of the dead, and no populous suburbs have grown up round them as at Rome and other European cities. The historic citadel, the Seven Towers, formerly used as a state prison, but now quite dismantled, stands at the southern extremity of the land-wall where the latter meets the sea-wall. It was a sort of a Bastille and London Tower, and recalls the worst epochs of tyranny of the Ottoman sultans. One of the towers was the ambassadors' prison. Instead of politely receiving their passports, when their home governments were embroiled in war with Turkey, foreign ambassadors were locked up in the tower and treated as prisoners of war. Hither the Janissaries, in the days of their supremacy, brought recalcitrant sultans and grand viziers whom they wished to decapitate or torture; and here, likewise, offending officials were executed or condemned to suffer for years in wretched dungeons. "The place of heads," "the well of blood," and "the rocky cavern" are some of the gruesome divisions of the imperial prison still to be seen, although earthquakes and the ravages of time are hastening the destruction of the Seven Towers.

In spite of the antiquity of the city, Stambul is far less rich in monuments and relics, that have a visible connection with the past, than many younger European cities. Most of the memorials are buried deep under the ground; and, when the city is once uncovered by archæologists, rich treasures are certain to be found. The level of the At Meidan, the Hippodrome of Byzantine days, around which clustered many of the choicest monuments of the old city, is now more than ten feet above the original pavement. The Hippodrome was the great forum of the city; it seated 120,000 persons, and here the emperors were proclaimed, victorious generals rewarded, heretics burned, and criminals executed. The races, athletic sports, and exhibitions of wild beasts also took place in the Hippodrome. The bronze horses of Lysippus, now at Venice, were once here; a beautiful statue of Helen of Troy, a gilded statue of Jupiter, a Venus by Praxiteles, and an Apollo by Phidias — all pulverized by the godless and fanatic crusaders — once adorned the ancient square.

Of the ancient monuments of the Hippodrome only three are now visible — the Ser-

HIPPODROME. — EGYPTIAN OBELISK, SERPENT COLUMN, AND MOSQUE OF SULTAN AHMED.

pent Column from Delphi, the syenite Egyptian obelisk from Heliopolis, and the Burnt Column. The Serpent Column of bronze is eight centuries older than Constantinople. It was set up by the Greeks in the Temple of Apollo at Delphi, 2,386 years ago, as the base for the golden tripod that commemorated the final defeat of Xerxes; and it is one of the most precious metal relics of the ancient world. The column is wreathed around with three serpents, and the cities which participated in the battle of Platæa are inscribed on the coils; but the heads of the serpents have been cut off — tradition says by the Conqueror the day he took Constantinople — but one of them may still be seen in the museum of the city. The column is twenty feet high, and up to the Crimean war (1856) it was so deeply imbedded in the earth that its inscriptions could not be traced. At that time Sir C. Newton and the British soldiers cleared away the earth and restored it to view.

The Egyptian obelisk is sixty feet high and was brought from Heliopolis by Theodosius. The column is of syenite and its pedestal is of marble and granite. Bas-reliefs, representing scenes in the Hippodrome during the fourth century, adorn the pedestal. One of these represents the obelisk being dragged through the great square, and another shows the workmen placing it in position; the emperor and his sons, courtiers, guards, musicians, dancers, and spectators are represented with great minuteness; and the details of official garb and costume lend historical interest to the monument. A Greek inscription records the difficulty of its erection, and on the opposite side is a corresponding Latin inscription which reads:

> "To raise this four square pillar to its height,
> And fix it steady on its solid base,
> Great Theodosius tried, but tried in vain.
> In two and thirty days, by Proclus' skill
> The toilsome work, with great applause, was done."

There is a pillar or obelisk of masonry, near the Serpent Column, upon which once stood the bronze horses of Lysippus, now in St. Mark's Square at Venice. The horses were brought hither from Scio by Theodosius and taken to Venice by Dandolo in 1204. The pillar was covered with bronze plates which made it "gleam like a column of light." The column of Constantine, now familiarly known as the Burnt Column, stands in a prominent position on the second hill near the Hippodrome. It was the memorial which the great emperor erected to commemorate his rebuilding of the city; and it was annually the scene of a service of thanksgiving conducted by the patriarch in the emperor's honour. It is said to have been brought from Rome by Constantine; and, when first erected, consisted of eight drums of porphyry resting upon a pedestal of marble. It was surmounted by a bronze statue of the emperor, and its entire height was one hundred and twenty feet. The column early suffered injury and was bound together by bronze rings; and in view of the injury that has come to it by fires, it has been rechristened the Burnt Column.

The column of Marcian, near the mosque of Sultan Mohammed II., is a fine granite pillar thirty-three feet high, and surmounted by a Corinthian capital of marble bearing a cippus with an eagle at each corner. Only the colossal pedestal of the column of Arcadius, on the seventh hill, exists. A superb and highly ornamented fragment of the column is at the Avret Bazaar. The column, when in place, rose to a height of one hundred and fifty-nine feet. It was hollow and contained a spiral staircase that led to the summit. Like the column of Trajan at Rome, its exterior recorded in bas-reliefs the career and victories of Arcadius.

The Imperial Museum of Antiquities contains a splendid collection of ancient relics. Begun more than fifty years ago, the museum has been made, under the able curatorship of the eminent Turkish archæologist Hamdy Bey, a choice collection of antiquities. Among its treasures are the glorious sarcophagus of Alexander, one of the finest examples of ancient art; the tomb of Tabnith, one of the kings of Sidon; Assyrian and Babylonian cones and Hittite inscriptions, including the famous record of Sennacherib's expedition against Hezekiah; a head of Minerva from Tripolis; the Parian marble sarcophagus of a satrap found near Sidon, together with ancient Byzantine and Persian pottery, glass, etc. But the magnificent sarcophagus of Alexander the Great is the museum's choicest relic of the past.

In a city where rainfall was unequal and springs were almost entirely wanting, cisterns were as necessary to the ancients as fortresses. There were nineteen of these great underground lakes constructed in Constantinople by the Greek emperors, and several of them are still in use. They were built of stone or brick and the vaulted roofs rested upon pillars or columns. During the best periods of Byzantine art, grace and beauty were added to util-

SARCOPHAGUS OF ALEXANDER THE GREAT (END VIEW).

Constantinople: The Imperial City

ity. The Cistern Basilica, sometimes called the Underground Palace, is the largest in Constantinople; and it is still used as a storage water supply. It is 336 feet long, 182 feet wide, and its vaulted roof rests upon 336 columns. The columns are thirty-nine feet high. The Cistern of the 1,001 Columns is perhaps best known through the "Arabian Nights" and other eastern literature. It is 195 feet long, and 167 feet broad, and its roof is supported by 224 columns, each composed of three shafts placed one above the other and joined by sleeves. It was long used as a spinning factory; but after the recent Armenian massacres at the capital, the task of burying so many bodies was solved by throwing them into this cistern and closing the entrances.

CHAPTER XIII

QUARTERS OF CONSTANTINOPLE

Nature of the population — Beauty and wonders of the site — Characteristic quarters — The Phanar, the Greek quarter — Balat, the Hebrew quarter — Eyub, the sacred suburb of the Turks — Sweet Waters of Europe — Pera and Galata — Scutari — Cemeteries — Princes' Islands — Prinkipo and Halki.

CONSTANTINOPLE is a city of a million and a quarter people. No census has ever been taken, but this estimate is probably not far from correct. Less than a third of the inhabitants are Osmanli Turks; a fifth are Greeks, and nearly the same number are Armenians; one-twentieth are Jews, and the balance are Bulgarians, Persians, Kurds, Circassians, Gypsies, Albanians, Ethiopians, Italians, and other Europeans. When approached by water, the city presents a truly handsome picture — domes and minarets and the vast array of houses and mosques that swell upward from the water's edge invest the capital with a truly beautiful aspect.

William Holden Hutton thus describes the beauty and the wonder of its site: "Whether you pass rapidly down the Bosporus, between banks crowned with houses and towers and mosques, that stretch away hither and thither to distant hills, now bleak, now crowned with dark cypress groves; or up from the Sea of Marmora, watching the dome of St. Sophia that glitters above the closely packed houses, till you turn the point which brings you to the Golden Horn, crowded with shipping and bright with the flags of many nations; or even if you come overland by the sandy wastes along the shore, looking across the deep blue of the sea to the islands and the snow-crowned mountains of Asia, till you break through the crumbling wall within sight of the Golden Horn, and find yourself at a step deep in the relics of the Middle Ages; you cannot fail to wonder at the splendour of the view which meets your eyes. Sun, sea-light, the quaint houses that stand upon the water's edge, the white palaces, the crowded quays, and the crowning glory of the eastern domes and the mediæval walls — these are the elements that combine to impress, and the impression is never lost."[1]

[1] "Constantinople: The Story of the Old Capital of the Empire." London, 1900.

As already pointed out, Constantinople is made up of three quite distinct cities; and each of these cities has its peculiar and characteristic quarters. Among the quarters in Stambul that are of special interest are Phanar, the Greek quarter, Balat, the Hebrew quarter, Eyub, the sacred quarter of the Turks, and the Sweet Waters of Europe, the picnic grounds of all classes and the recreation quarter of Turkish women. After the conquest of Constantinople by the Turks many noble Greek families, that had left the city during the siege, returned and settled in the quarter now known as the Phanar. Finding themselves impoverished by the loss of their lands and the confiscation of their property, they engaged in commerce and grew exceedingly rich. They were exclusive in their social and marital relations; and after they had attained wealth and commercial power, they formed themselves into an aristocracy and claimed descent from Byzantine emperors, through the female line, and traced their heritage back to the first families of the old dynasty. They arrogated to themselves certain political and spiritual rights over the Greeks of the city; built sumptuous mansions; organized schools and colleges, and for several centuries the Phanariotes, as these select families were called, dominated the Hellenic life of the city. While the glory of the Greek aristocracy has faded, the quarter is still the residence of the Greek patriarch; here are located the large Greek national schools for both boys and girls; and the Greek library in the Phanar has many valuable manuscripts, including some rare Christian documents which date back to apostolic times.

Constantinople is certainly a very dirty city; but in a picturesque background much of the dirt loses its repulsiveness. This cannot be said of Balat, the Hebrew quarter, which is indescribably, nay, inconceivably dirty and filthy. I have seen at its worst Chinatown in San Francisco, the Whitechapel district in London, and the filthiest slums in Naples, but I have never seen anything comparable to the nastiness of Balat. Théophile Gautier characterizes it as " the squalid residue of four hundred years of oppression and exaction — the filth beneath which these people, everywhere proscribed, sought, like certain insects, to escape from their persecutors. They endeavour to save themselves from pursuit by the disgust which they inspire; they live in the mire and acquire its colour. It were almost impossible to imagine anything more impure or more thoroughly infected. Scurvy, scrofula, leprosy, and all the Biblical impurities and diseases, of which they have never been cured or cleansed since the days of Moses, devour them without a seeming effort on their part to oppose their ravages. Money and gain seem their sole idea; they do not shirk from even the plague, if they can make a small profit upon the garments of the dead. In this hideous region roll, pell-mell, Aaron and Isaac, Abraham and Jacob; and these unfortunates, some of whom are millionaires, live chiefly upon the heads of fish, which are cut off as poisonous; and which induces among the Jews certain dreadful disorders. This filthy diet has for them the paramount advantage of costing them nothing.''

It is not true that the Hebrews of Constantinople have been more oppressed by their rulers than the other non-Moslem residents. As a matter of fact they have felt the hand of oppression less than the Armenians and some of the other Christian communities. Neither is it true that they are poor; for while they live in filth and squalor, many of them are the possessors of great fortunes. While generally very ignorant, a number of the leading physicians in Constantinople are Hebrews and were born in the Balat quarter; and the famous

Kiamil Pasha, who renounced Judaism and became a Mohammedan to advance his personal interests, came from the same section. An explanation of the causes which produce the disgusting conditions at Balat is offered by Richard Davey, an English traveller. He says: "It is almost impossible to conceive of anything more terrible than the condition into which the Jews in the capital have fallen, and this, notwithstanding that they are, as a rule, a sober and law-abiding people. They marry exceedingly young, the lads at eighteen, the girls even under fifteen. The consequences of these early marriages are most disastrous. Large families are born, before the parents have acquired sufficient experience of life to bring them up properly. The houses are generally built of wood, and without any sort of drainage — unless we accept the open sewer, which runs along the centre of the street and which sends up the vilest stench, as a 'sanitary improvement.'"[1]

Eyub, the beautiful suburb of Stambul, is the sacred quarter of the Moslems. Here is located the only mosque in Constantinople which may not be entered by Christians, and I believe that it is the only quarter in Constanti-

[1] "The Sultan and His Subjects." New York, 1892.

nople where those not professing the faith of Islam are not permitted to live. It is surrounded by pretty gardens and Fields of the Dead, thickly planted with dark cypresses; for, next to Scutari, Eyub is the favourite burial-place in Constantinople. Most of the chief functionaries of the sultan — sheiks-ul-Islam, grand viziers, and chief eunuchs — are buried at Eyub; also several mothers of the sultans. Here also are manufactured the fezes worn by the Turkish soldiers.

The Sweet Waters of Europe, a village at the head of the Golden Horn and between the Kiaghad-Khane and Ali-Bey Rivers, is the recreation quarter of Constantinople. Besides the kiosk of the sultan, rich pashas and important government officials have pretty villas here. All about are splendid groves and fine meadows; and all classes of society during late spring and summer come here for picnics and outings. It is the chief recreation ground of Turkish women; and an English writer says concerning their Friday afternoon visits to the Sweet Waters of Europe: "The gaudily dressed Turkish women come and cluster on the sward, and spread their carpets and bask in the sunshine; and through the windows of the broughams drawn in line under the great plane-

CASCADES AT THE SWEET WATERS OF EUROPE.

Quarters of Constantinople 201

trees, the fair ladies of the imperial harem peep at the passing crowd from the folds of their snowy yashmaks. Alas! only thirty years ago, instead of sitting in those broughams, their highnesses and excellencies displayed themselves on the embroidered cushions of their arabas, and eunuchs in full Oriental costumes rode backward and forward on the finest of Arab horses, jealously guarding or making believe to guard the fair forbidden fruit these monstrous ugly wretches have in charge! Now the eunuch sits on the box like any other footman, white or coloured, save that he wears a fez instead of a cockaded hat, and your friends assure you, regardless of the shock to your feelings they inflict, that the ladies wear Redfern's tailor-made gowns, and sport the latest Paris fashion under their feridjés."[1]

Pera and Galata are on the north side of the Golden Horn and are reached from Stambul by two bridges of boats. Pera, which is on a hill overlooking both the Bosporus and the Golden Horn, is the aristocratic quarter of the Europeans. The foreign ambassadors and consuls have their quarters here; the gorgeous palaces of successful Greek, Armenian, and

[1] Richard Davey: "The Sultan and His Subjects." New York, 1892.

Hebrew financiers are also here; and most of the hotels for Europeans and Americans are in Pera. The streets are as narrow and badly paved as in Stambul; but the slopes of the hills and the wealth and position of the inhabitants tend to give the place a hygienic aspect not discerned in other parts of Constantinople.

Galata is at the base of the hill on which Pera is located and it fronts on both the Golden Horn and the Bosporus. It is the business and shipping centre for the Europeans. F. Marion Crawford has well characterized Galata as the fermenting vat of the scum of the earth. "It is doubtful," says Mr. Crawford, "whether in any city in the globe such an iniquitous population could be found as that which is huddled together by the water's edge from Kassim Pasha to Tophane. It is indeed an interesting region to the student of criminal physiognomy, for the lowest types of what must necessarily be called the civilized criminal classes fill the filthy streets, the poisonous lanes, and the reeking liquor shops, the terror of the Europeans above [at Pera] and the object of righteous hatred and loathing to the Turks on the other side. The Greeks and Armenians, who lead a sort of underground exist-

PERA AND GALATA.

ence, here make a good living, and by no means a precarious one, by a great variety of evil practises. Being all Christians they all claim the protection of one or the other of the European embassies, and the political situation of Turkey renders it practically impossible for the Ottoman authorities to arrest or punish one of these malefactors, the slightest interference with whose liberty might at once be made a *casus belli* by the foreign government whose protection he would claim."[1]

On the Asiatic side of the Bosporus is the third great division of Constantinople — Scutari, the ancient Chrysopolis. According to legend it was founded by Chryses, a son of Agamemnon; and the city played a leading part in the history of antiquity. It has a beautiful situation on a promontory, but its streets are tortuous and badly kept, its houses are shabby huts painted a dirty red colour, and the place is in a state of ruin that does not appeal to the sense of the picturesque. The jealous latticed windows everywhere suggest the nature of the population. Scutari is the metropolis of the Islam faith, and its soil is considered holy. The city has many mosques, eight of which are imperial foundations, numerous mosque colleges

[1] "Constantinople." New York, 1895.

and schools; and it is the headquarters for several orders of dervishes. The chief Field of the Dead in Constantinople is at Scutari. It is more than three miles long and is intersected by broad alleys. It is the largest Field of the Dead in Turkey — if not in the world — and wealthy Moslems, who wish to give evidence of their devotion to the faith of Islam, select this cemetery as the final resting-place for themselves and their families.

Another burying-ground in Scutari, which has a pathetic interest for Europeans, is the English cemetery, where eight thousand British soldiers, who met death by wounds or sickness during the Crimean war, sleep their last sleep. Here also are buried many Englishmen and some Americans who have died while residing in or near Constantinople. A large granite shaft commemorates the sacrifice of British soldiers during the Crimean war. A colossal angel, with drooping wings and pen in hand, is represented at each corner; and the sides of the monument contain memorial inscriptions in English, French, Italian, and Turkish — the languages of the four nations allied against Russia in that awful war. Not distant is the hospital where Florence Nightingale laboured with such heroism and devo-

ENGLISH CEMETERY AT SCUTARI.

tion to care for sick and wounded soldiers during this war.

The primeval ox-cart is one of the characteristic street scenes in Scutari. "Low, long-bodied conveyances upon clumsy wheels," as aptly described by F. Marion Crawford, "any one of them big enough to transport a whole family," and one often sees such family parties. "Women and children, the former more closely veiled than in Stambul, sit close together side by side from end to end, the paterfamilias generally squatting himself at the tail end of the cart; his expression resembles that of the European father under the same circumstances — a combination of anxiety, weariness, and shyness by no means becoming to the solemn Oriental face; the women, on the other hand, are intensely interested in the sights and incidents of the journey and look longingly at your light carriage as you drive swiftly by."

The Princes' Islands in the Sea of Marmora form a distinct quarter of the city of Constantinople. They are nine in number, but only two are now of special significance — Prinkipo and Halki. During the Byzantine period these islands served as asylums for deposed sovereigns and troublesome princes, hence the generic name. Prinkipo, once the chief resort of exiled royalties, is now a favourite bathing-place during the summer months. It is two miles long and less than a mile wide, and two peaks, separated by a deep pass, rise from its surface. Rich Europeans, Greeks, and Armenians of Constantinople have villas surrounded by pretty gardens on the slopes of the hills. Monasteries crown each of the hills — that of St. George on the south hill, 655 feet above sea-level, and that of Christ on the north hill. Both are old foundations. Halki, the second most important of the group, has a diversified topography, and is the seat of a number of important educational institutions, including the Imperial Commercial School, with 150 students, the Ottoman Naval School, and the Greek Orthodox Theological Seminary. The Monastery of St. George, belonging to the monks of the Holy Sepulchre of Jerusalem, is located here; also the Monastery of the Trinity, founded by Photius, the patriarch of Constantinople, who proclaimed the great schism of 857. Halki is the favourite burying-place for the patriarchs of the Orthodox church. The island of Platy still contains the subterranean vaults of the ancient Byzantine prisons where ecclesiastical and political offenders were deprived of their liberty. On this island also are the ruins of the Church of the Forty Martyrs built in 860. The island of Oxia contains the ruins and cisterns of the ancient monastery of St. Michael.

CHAPTER XIV

STREET SCENES IN CONSTANTINOPLE

Characteristic street scenes — Mark Twain quoted — The bridges of boats — Bridge of Valideh Sultan an open air salon — The dogs — Hamals or porters — Sedan chairs, caïques, and barcas — Fields of the Dead — Fires and fire brigades — Cafés — Turkish coffee.

THE streets of Constantinople are very narrow, crooked, steep, and dirty; and, when paved at all, badly paved. The city has no sewerage system, so that the public highways serve the added purpose of garbage drains. But they are withal singularly picturesque. Most of the races of Europe, many of the races of Asia, and some of the races of Africa may be seen at any hour of the day in their curious and variegated costumes, and heard speaking a diversity of tongues. From sunrise to sunset the city is a medley of human curios — peddlers hawking their wares, veiled women with their eunuchs or slaves, porters carrying huge dry goods boxes, trunks, or pianos, pilgrim bands just

TURKISH WATER-PEDDLER.

Street Scenes in Constantinople

starting for Mecca, donkeys, asses, saddle-horses, and dogs.

Mark Twain gives this characteristic account of a Constantinople street scene: "It was an eternal circus. People were thicker than bees in those narrow streets, and the men were dressed in all the outrageous, outlandish, idolatrous, extravagant, thunder-and-lightning costumes that ever a tailor with the delirium and seven devils could conceive of. There was no freak in dress too crazy to be indulged in; no absurdity too absurd to be tolerated; no frenzy in ragged diabolism too fantastic to be attempted. No two men were dressed alike. It was a wild masquerade of all the imaginable costumes — every struggling throng in every street was a dissolving view of stunning contrasts. Some patriarchs wore awful turbans, but the grand mass of the infidel horde wore the fiery red skull-cap they call a fez. All the remainder of the raiment they indulged in was utterly indescribable. The shops are mere hencoops, mere boxes, bath-rooms, closets — anything you please to call them — on the first floor. The Turks sit cross-legged in them and work, and smoke long pipes, and smell like — like Turks. That covers the ground. Crowding the narrow streets in front of them are beggars who beg for ever, yet never collect anything; wonderful cripples distorted out of all semblance of humanity, almost; vagabonds driving laden asses; porters carrying dry goods boxes as large as cottages on their backs; peddlers of grapes, hot corn, pumpkin seeds, and a hundred other things, yelling like fiends; and sleeping happily, comfortably, serenely, among the hurrying feet, are the famed dogs of Constantinople."

Two bridges have been thrown across the Golden Horn and connect Galata-Pera with Stambul. Both are pontoon bridges — strips of plank laid upon iron floats. There are sidewalks for foot-passengers and an arrangement in the middle of the bridges by which two of the floats may be detached so as to allow the passage of vessels. The bridges are open to passenger traffic from six o'clock in the morning until late at night. Toll-gatherers in long white tunics stand at the entrances; and foot-passengers pay one cent, mounted persons two cents, and carriages ten cents. Only fat pashas, government officials, and dogs pay no toll. The two bridges produce not less than two thousand dollars a day, but less than one hundred dollars reach the public treasury. "The rest," says William E. Curtis, "is stolen by people who

Street Scenes in Constantinople 211

have charge of the collection. Everybody gets his ' squeeze,' from the general manager down to the Turks with white aprons who stand at the entrances and take the money. Curious people have taken the trouble to stand at the approaches to the bridges and count the number of passengers within a certain time, as a basis for an estimate of the revenues, and assert that $2,000 a day is a low calculation."[1]

The outer bridge — sometimes called the New Bridge and the Bridge of Valideh Sultan — is the more centrally located. Here traffic is greatest and more than a hundred thousand people — not counting the pashas, government officials, and the dogs — cross this bridge during the day. It is the most picturesque street scene in Constantinople — a sort of an open-air saloon, combining many of the features of the Pincio at Rome, the Grand Boulevards at Paris, Hyde Park at London, and the Horse Show and Metropolitan Opera House in New York. The enthusiastic Italian traveller Edmondo de Amicis gives this vivid account: " Whatever can be imagined that is most extravagant in type, costume, and social class may there be seen within the space of twenty paces and ten minutes of time. Behind a throng of

[1] " The Turk and His Lost Provinces." Chicago, 1903.

Turkish porters, who pass running and bending under enormous burdens, advances a sedan-chair inlaid with ivory and mother-of-pearl, and bearing an Armenian lady; and at either side of it a Bedouin wrapped in a white mantle, and a Turk in a muslin turban and sky-blue caftan, beside whom canters a young Greek gentleman followed by his dragoman in embroidered vest, and a dervish with his tall conical hat and tunic of camel's hair, who makes way for the carriage of a European ambassador, preceded by his running footman in gorgeous livery. All this is only seen in a glimpse, and the next moment you find yourself in the midst of a crowd of Persians, in pyramidal bonnets of Astrakhan fur, who are followed by a Hebrew in a long yellow coat opened at the sides, a frowsy-headed Gypsy woman with her child in a bag at her back, a Catholic priest with his breviary staff, while in the midst of a confused throng of Greeks, Turks, and Armenians comes a big eunuch on horseback crying out, 'Make way,' and preceding a Turkish carriage painted with flowers and birds and filled with the ladies of a harem, dressed in green and violet and wrapped in large white veils; behind a Sister of Charity from the hospital at Pera, an African slave carrying a

THE NEW BRIDGE.

monkey, and a professional story-teller in a necromancer's habit; and, what is quite natural, but appears strange to the newcomer, all these diverse people pass each other without a look, and not one single countenance wears a smile. The Albanian in his white petticoat and his pistols in his sash, beside the Tatar dressed in sheepskins; the Turk astride of his caparisoned ass threads pompously two long strings of camels; behind the adjutant of an imperial prince, mounted upon his Arab steed, clatters a cart filled with all the odd domestic rubbish of a Turkish household, the Mahommedan woman afoot, the veiled slave woman, the Greek with her red cap and her hair on her shoulders, the Maltese hooded by her black faldetta, the Hebrew woman dressed in the antique costume of India, the negress wrapped in a many-coloured shawl from Cairo, the Armenian from Trebizond, all veiled in black like a funeral apparition, are seen in single file, as if placed there on purpose, to be contrasted with each other."[1]

The dogs of Constantinople constitute an important part of the capital's polyglot population. The city in fact is one huge dog kennel. The dogs are without masters, collars, or

[1] "Constantinople." New York [1896].

homes. They are born in the streets, and in the streets they are reared; here also they live and die. They have apparently districted the city, and a dog born in one ward is inhumanely treated by the canines of another bailiwick if he ventures out of his precinct. Christians, therefore, cannot keep dogs, because the Moslem republic of freebooters has no apparent provision in its constitution for the pampered curs not legitimately born in the streets of a given ward; and Christian dogs in consequence are the common targets of the entire canine Moslem population. Laziness comes as naturally to the dogs of Constantinople as to the other Orientals of the city; they sleep in the street all day and they howl and bark all night. Some one has truly said from nightfall until daybreak the imperial city is one continuous volley of canine musketry. The dogs of Constantinople are not, as has often been asserted, the city's scavengers; they produce infinitely more filth than they remove; and they are heartily disliked by the Christians. But the Koran, while pronouncing the dog an unclean beast, commands kindness to all animals; and while the Turks will not allow dogs in their houses, they treat them kindly, provide them with food, and sometimes leave legacies for

THE DOGS OF CONSTANTINOPLE.

their maintenance. The forebears of the present dog population followed the Conqueror into the city in 1453. They are not handsome creatures — tawny in colour, pointed ears, bushy tail, furry coat, and about the size of the collie; but they are not aggressive, and hydrophobia is almost unknown among them — due, probably, to the free lives they lead. Two sultans — Mahmud the Reformer and Abdul-Mejid — endeavoured to rid the city of the dogs by removing them to islands in the Marmora, but both efforts were strenuously opposed by the Turks. Greeks and Armenians secretly poison the dogs; and since the introduction of carriages in the city the decrease in the canine population has been marked, for the dogs never get out of the way of any one — people always step over or go around the dogs.

An object of constant amazement to the visitor of the capital is the hamal, or street porter; the prodigious weight which he is able to carry on his back ranges all the way from a well-loaded Saratoga trunk to a grand piano. He is thus defined by Gautier: " The hamal is a species peculiar to Constantinople; a sort of a camel with two legs and no hump. He lives on cucumbers and water, and carries the most enormous weights, up the most perpendicular streets, under a sun literally burning."[1] He carries a stuffed cushion on his shoulders, on which he places his burden, stooping gently beneath the weight, and bearing the strain upon his neck. Individual hamals carry burdens of eight hundred pounds weight on the back; and heavier burdens are borne by two, four, or six porters provided with poles, the ends resting on the shoulders, and the load suspended in the centre. The hamals of Constantinople are Armenians; they come from the vicinity of Lake Van; and they are organized into a union and monopolize the carrying trade of the city.

Cabs are little used in Constantinople because of the narrow, uneven, and crowded condition of the streets. Sedan-chairs are still used, particularly by women. They are carried by the strong hamals and are much more practicable on the steeper slopes than cabs. But, as the three main divisions of the capital are so nearly surrounded by water, caïques and barcas are the favourite public conveyances. Caïques are long narrow boats, tapering to a point at each end, decked at the stern and stem, and standing considerably above the water. They glide over the surface with mar-

[1] "Constantinople." New York, 1875.

THE FIELDS OF THE DEAD, IN THE HEART OF THE CITY.

vellous swiftness and they are as graceful as swans. It is necessary to sit very quietly in the caïques, and strict caution is required in embarking and disembarking, as they upset very easily. Caïques are generally rowed by Turks, and this is the most unique and expeditious form of conveyance. The barcas are broader bottomed; they founder less easily; and for the open Sea of Marmora, where the waves are sometimes strong, they are considered safer than the caïques. Barcas are generally rowed by Greeks, Armenians, or Italians.

The Fields of the Dead are not only the cemeteries but also the public parks and gardens of Turkish cities; for the Moslems bury their dead in the sunniest and choicest spots where they may mingle freely with the departed. When a body is laid at rest a cypress-tree is planted and a new grave is made for every person that dies; a coffin once deposited in the earth is never disturbed; hence, Constantinople is encircled and dotted with scores of cypress-forested Fields of the Dead. Head and foot stones mark the final resting-place of the poorer classes; to the graves of the better circumstanced a flat gravestone is added, and the wealthy often have imposing mausoleums of masonry. The tombs are columns of white marble, on the tops of which are sculptured turbans or fezes for the men and flower-pots or roses for the women. When the turban leans to one side, it indicates that the deceased met his death by decapitation by order of the sultan. Simple and touching inscriptions are cut in the marble columns. Here are the inscriptions on the tombs of two children: on the one, " A flower that had scarcely blossomed torn prematurely from its stem," and on the other, " Here lies one who has passed to those bowers where roses never fade, for they are moistened by a mother's tears." Beside the children the mother is buried.

The Turks place little vessels containing water on the graves of their dead for the benefit of the birds; sometimes these are chiselled out of the gravestone; they hold that birds carry messages from the living to the dead. Cemeteries are in consequence common places of resort and the best lands in the most populous parts of the city are devoted to their use. Miss Julia Pardoe says in this connection: " The Turk smokes his chibouk with his back resting against a turban-crested gravestone; the women sit in groups and talk of their homes and their little ones on the graves of their ancestors, and the children gather wild flowers that grow amid the graves, as gaily as though death had never entered there."[1] And Gautier in the same vein remarks: "In the east, life is not so carefully separated from death as with us; but they jostle each other familiarly like old friends. To sit, sleep, smoke, eat, or make love upon a tomb carries with it no idea of sacrilege or profanation; cows and horses feed in the cemeteries or traverse them at will; and people promenade or make appointments there, absolutely as if the dead were not lying around and beneath at the distance of a few feet or inches, stiff or mouldering in their coffins of larch."[2]

To the mind of the Turk, a Field of the Dead is a pleasure-ground rather than a place of melancholy or sadness. It has for him no associations of gloom or horror, for his Koran inculcates a doctrine of fatalism that makes him indifferent to death; hence it has no repugnance for him, because it has none of those gloomy attributes with which the Christian mind is wont to invest it. Numerous as are the Fields of the Dead in Stambul, the great cemetery at Scutari is the favourite final resting-place of the most devout followers of the

---

[1] City of the Sultan." Philadelphia, 1837.
[2] "Constantinople." New York, 1875.

Prophet; for according to an old legend, the Turks are ultimately to be expelled from Europe, and no devout Moslem wishes to subject his ashes to the possible sacrilege of unbelievers.

Fires are so frequent and destructive in Constantinople that it has been necessary to rebuild it from its foundations more than thirty times since it became an imperial city, or on an average of once in every fifty years. A single fire may consume as many as a thousand houses and shops in a few hours. The buildings for the most part are constructed of light inflammable material; the narrow and winding streets are easily obstructed; and the fire department is both inadequate and archaic. Watchmen are constantly on the lookout at Galata Tower in Galata-Pera, Serasker Tower in Stambul, and at Kandili in Scutari. As soon as a fire is observed red flags by day and red lanterns by night, from the two former towers, indicate the quarter of the fire; and in Scutari cannons are fired. Fast runners are sent at once to inform the firemen who are quartered in the various districts of the city. The fire brigade is a diminutive affair and the fire-engine is carried on the backs of four men. But as fires are extinguished at the expense of the

A TURKISH CAFÉ.

Street Scenes in Constantinople 221

owners of the property, and as there is no fixed price in Constantinople for putting out fires, the eternal parley ensues; and buildings are often in flames before the interested parties come to terms.

Cafés in Constantinople are not very cheerful affairs, less so, in fact than the Fields of the Dead; and the Turkish baths largely supersede them as social institutions. Cafés in Turkish cities are chiefly places for smoking and drinking coffee; for the Koran forbids the use of wine and other intoxicating liquors. It is rather disquieting to the Christian's sense of moral superiority to be told by Mr. Dwight, an American missionary, that "the syndicate of European officials [representatives of the Christian powers], who constitute the administrators of the Turkish national debt, have multiplied sevenfold the places in Constantinople where liquor is sold."[1] Smokers bring to the café their own mouthpieces and tobacco, and they rent for a penny the great smoking apparatus called the narghilé.

The Turks are inveterate coffee drinkers, and spend as much time and take as much enjoyment in sipping their coffee as Germans do their beer. The luxury was introduced

[1] "Constantinople and Its Problems." Chicago, 1901.

into Turkey during the reign of Suleiman the Magnificent and it immediately became indispensable to Moslem existence. Turkish coffee is an acquired taste. The berry is ground into a very fine powder and is boiled with sugar. Mark Twain was apparently not long enough in the country to acquire the taste, for he says of it: "Of all the unchristian beverages that ever passed my lips, Turkish coffee is the worst. The cup is small; it is smeared with grounds; the coffee is black, thick, unsavoury of smell, and execrable in taste. The bottom of the cup has a muddy sediment in it half an inch deep. This goes down your throat, and portions of it lodge by the way, and produce a tickling aggravation that keeps you barking and coughing for an hour."

CHAPTER XV

BAZAARS, KHANS, BATHS, AND FOUNTAINS

The bazaar an Oriental department store — The Grand Bazaar — Diversity of commodities — Egyptian Bazaar — Drugs and perfumes — Khans — Turkish baths — Their social function — What they are not — Fountains — Ahmed Fountain.

THE bazaar is the chief emporium of retail trade in a Turkish city; it is a sort of an Oriental department store. The word bazaar means " to bargain," and the institution has been appropriately named, for I found it infinitely easier to bargain than to buy at the great bazaars of Constantinople and Smyrna. The Grand Bazaar and the Egyptian Bazaar are the two best known in Constantinople. The former is really a city within a city, with arcaded streets, interminable lanes, alleys, and fountains; and all enclosed by high walls and covered by a vaulted roof that is studded with a hundred cupolas.

The business of the bazaar is classified, and a given commodity or guild has one or more streets for the display and traffic of its wares. The Grand Bazaar has something like three thousand separate shops, and it covers a space more than a mile in circuit. It was Théophile Gautier who remarked that " every one in the bazaars busies himself in doing nothing with a conscientiousness quite admirable." The shopkeepers sit cross-legged upon a bit of matting and carelessly smoke their pipes or play with their beads. There is no fixed price for anything, and every purchase involves a prolonged linguistic contest. Shopkeepers do not seem at all anxious to sell, and one may spend the whole day at the bazaar sipping coffee, eating sweetmeats, and conversing in a dozen languages. The bazaar, in fact, combines the features of a museum, theatre, and promenade, and its mercantile function seems quite secondary. As Turkish women are not allowed to be shopkeepers they revenge themselves by shopping.

The diversity of bazaar commodities is something astounding — pyramids of Persian shawls and brocades; mirrors inlaid with mother-of-pearl; perfume censers of gold, silver, and enamelled brass; sherbet salvers richly carved and inlaid; dainty hands of ivory for scratching one's back; choice muslins from Bengal

Bazaars, Khans, Baths 225

and brocades from India; limp dressing-gowns of Brusa silk; Indian and Persian cashmeres; embroidered slippers and handkerchiefs; dolmans stiff with gold; fans made of the plumage of argus pheasants; scent-boxes of gold; pearls of Ophir; opals from Bohemia; damasks, gauzes, carpets, rugs, and variegated and embroidered fabrics from every corner of the universe.

Mark Twain's description of a Turkish bazaar is directly to the point. He says: "The place is crowded with people all the time, and as the gay-coloured eastern fabrics are lavishly displayed before every shop, the Great Bazaar of Stambul is one of the sights worth seeing. It is full of life and stir and business, dirt, beggars, asses, yelling peddlers, porters, dervishes, high-born Turkish female shoppers, Greeks, and weird-looking and weirdly dressed Mohammedans from the mountains and the far provinces — and the only solitary thing one does not smell, when he is in the Great Bazaar, is something which smells good."

The Egyptian Bazaar, which adjoins the mosque of Yeni Valideh, is a miniature of "Araby the Blest." The building is covered by a vaulted roof and forms a street more than three hundred and fifty feet long, forty feet wide, and forty-five feet high. This is the drug and the perfume bazaar; and here are exposed for sale heaps and bags of every conceivable medicinal plant — dried, crushed, and powdered — coffee, gums, dates, opium, pepper, antimony, ginger, pistachio nuts, dye stuffs, cinnamon, cloves, sandalwood, attar of roses, essences of bergamot and jasmine, cosmetics of every imaginable variety — in fact a whole arsenal of Turkish coquetry.

Khans take the place of hotels in Turkey, and they are patronized by Christians and Jews, as well as by the Moslems. They are immense stone barracks and are built about courts. The courts contain fountains and are surrounded by stables and warerooms. The Valideh Khan, which is the centre of the Persian colony in Constantinople, will serve as a type. It was built by the mother of Sultan Mohammed IV. and is an immense fortress-like structure; it has a great court which is ornamented with trees and two fountains. Stables and warehouses are on the ground floor and above are three ranges of galleries, one above the other, which are partitioned into small rooms. They contain no furniture, for Oriental travellers carry their bedding with them; and

SPICE BAZAAR AT CONSTANTINOPLE.

Bazaars, Khans, Baths

food is always easily obtained at near-by soup-kitchens.

There are one hundred and eighty khans in Constantinople; some are connected with mosques and have endowments for their maintenance, for Moslems regard the foundation of khans as highly meritorious works of philanthropy. A small rent is generally paid for the use of the rooms and the occupant keeps his apartments in order so that the expense is reduced to a minimum. The Yeni Khan, the largest in Constantinople, has running water in all the rooms and a fire-proof magazine for the protection of merchandise; but all the khans are substantially fire-proof, and during fires and insurrections their iron gates are closed and they afford relative security to merchants and their goods.

With the Moslems cleanliness is not merely next to godliness, it *is* godliness. The Koran specifically enjoins regular and careful ablutions; and, in consequence, the Turks of Constantinople are said to be free from many of the physical ailments with which both the Christians and the Jews are habitually afflicted. Comparative immunity from disease, therefore, seems due to the large number and frequent use of Turkish baths. There are more than one hundred and thirty such baths at the capital. Every important mosque has its bath; and many of the mosque-baths have been endowed by philanthropic Moslems, so that the poor of the city may enjoy gratuitously the luxury of Turkish baths.

None of the great Turkish baths in Constantinople make any pretension to outward show. They are immense structures surmounted by great domes and lighted from above by numerous convex glasses. There are three main divisions to the bath: (1) the dressing-room, where the clothing is removed, the head wound with a broad band of cotton like a turban, the loins girt about by an abbreviated cotton petticoat, and the feet thrust in wooden sandals; (2) the steam-room, where the air is at a high temperature and where one is forced to undergo a series of plunges in basins filled with scalding water; and (3) the massage-room, where the patient is kneaded, pulled, pinched, pressed, and pounded, and then scraped and rubbed with gloves of coarse camel's hair. This done, the patient returns to the dressing-room where he is served with coffee or lemonade and a narghilé or cigarettes.

The Mahmud Pasha Hamman is the largest Turkish bath in Constantinople. There are numerous private baths where the charges vary from twenty-five to forty cents. In addition to being places for ablutions, Turkish baths serve the added purpose of clubs. Men and women — never together, of course — spend hours at the baths in social intercourse; and it is not uncommon for women to spend the entire day at the bath with friends. The men's baths are open in the evening, and here the Turks congregate much as men in America and England meet in clubs, and as Frenchmen gather at well-known cafés.

Most tourists who visit a Turkish bath for the first time in Constantinople suffer the disillusionment of Mark Twain. The great American humourist says: "For years and years I had dreamed of the wonders of the Turkish bath; for years and years I had promised myself that I would yet enjoy one. Many and many a time, in fancy, I have lain in the marble bath, and breathed the slumbrous fragrance of eastern spices that filled the air; then passed through a weird and complicated system of pulling and hauling, and drenching and scrubbing, by a gang of naked savages, who loomed vast and vaguely through the steaming mist, like demons; then rested for awhile on a divan fit for a king; then passed through another complex ordeal, and one more fearful than the first; and, finally, swathed in soft fabrics, been conveyed to a princely saloon and laid on a bed of eider-down, where eunuchs, gorgeous of costume, fanned me while I drowsed or dreamed, or contentedly gazed at the rich hangings of the apartment, the soft carpets, the sumptuous furniture, the pictures, and drank delicious coffee, smoked the soothing narghilé, and dropped at last, in tranquil repose, lulled by sensuous odours from unseen censers, by the gentle influence of the narghilé's Persian tobacco, and by the music of the fountains that counterfeited the pattering of summer rain. That was the picture, just as I got it from incendiary books of travel. The reality is no more like it than the Five Points are like the Garden of Eden. They received me in a great court, paved with marble slabs; around it were broad galleries, one above another, carpeted with seedy matting, railed with unpainted balustrades, and furnished with huge rickety chairs, cushioned with rusty old mattresses, indented with impressions left by the forms of nine successive generations of men who had reposed upon them. The place was vast, naked, dreary; its court a barn, its galleries stalls for human horses. The cadaverous, half-nude varlets that served in the establishment had nothing of poetry in their appearance, nothing of romance, nothing of Oriental splendour. They shed no entrancing odours — just the contrary. Their hungry eyes and their lank forms continually suggested one glaring, unsentimental fact — they wanted what they term in California ' a square meal.' "

Water is exalted by the Koran and it plays a significant rôle in the lives of the faithful. Ablutions must be performed five times daily before prayers, and the use of intoxicating beverages is forbidden by the Prophet. Hence, fountains are everywhere abundant in Moslem cities. Constantinople has hundreds; and many of them are spacious and handsome structures. Every mosque has its fountain; and sultans and pious persons have spent vast sums on the construction and endowment of fountains at the capital. Quite recently Emperor William of Germany, desirous of making some substantial evidence of his esteem for his friend Abdul-Hamid, erected a beautiful and costly fountain in Constantinople.

The handsomest fountain at the capital is that of Sultan Ahmed III., in a little square just back of St. Sophia. The building is constructed entirely of white marble; and the roof, turned up like a Chinese pagoda, is surmounted by five bell turrets which have domes bearing gilded pinnacles, each terminated by a crescent. The building is flanked at the corners by projecting rotundas having broad openings covered with wrought brass gratings. The plain spaces between the rotundas form the fountain proper. The base bears a trough of white marble into which the water falls from a faucet. The painted and gilded friezes form beautiful arabesques; and an inscription in gilt letters upon a green and red background gives the date of the dedication of the fountain, after the Oriental custom — that is, by counting the letters in the words of the inscription. Another beautiful fountain, erected by the same ruler, is that of Azab Kapu in Galata. It is smaller but more elaborately decorated with floral devices and gilt arabesques.

FOUNTAIN OF SULTAN AHMED III.

CHAPTER XVI

SULTAN ABDUL - HAMID AND HIS HAREM

Ancestry of the present Sultan — Early death of his parents — How his childhood was passed — Inaptitude for studies — Dorys's life of the Sultan — Varying estimates of Abdul-Hamid's character — Mental illness — Yildiz Kiosk — Why selected — The imperial harem — Its organization and administration — Education of the harem women — Occupations and amusements — The Sultan's sons — Fast of Ramazan — Feast of the Bairam — The Selamlik.

ABDUL - HAMID II. is the thirty-fourth sultan of the Ottoman Empire and the twenty-eighth since the conquest of Constantinople. He is a younger brother of Murad V., whom he deposed, and a nephew of Abdul-Aziz, whom the latter displaced. He has occupied the throne of Osman for thirty years. He was born September the 22d, 1842, and is the son of Abdul-Mejid and an Armenian slave. His paternity has been seriously questioned; some have maintained that his father was an Armenian cook who was employed in the palace of Abdul-Mejid, and others that he is the son of Garabet-Effendi-Balian, brother of the late Serkis Bey, the architect of the Cheragan Palace. The sultan's physical and mental characteristics are distinctly Armenian, facts which have given colour to the apocryphal version of his full Armenian ancestry. It seems altogether probable that his Armenian features and traits come entirely from his mother, and that he is the legitimate son of Abdul-Mejid.

His mother died when he was seven years old, of pulmonary trouble, and his father later of the same disease; and the young prince fought the progress of phthisis during his childhood and early manhood. As a lad he was sickly and taciturn, cunning and greedy, and he early developed a distrustful disposition which cost him the affection of his father and the good-will of the other princes. At the death of his mother he was placed successively under the care of two of the other wives of the Sultan Abdul-Mejid, who cared for him until the age of twelve, when, after the Turkish custom, he was transferred from the haremlik to the part of the seraglio occupied by the men. His life in the harem was, like that of other Turkish princes, spent chiefly in idleness with the women, the eunuchs, and the female slaves. He showed great aversion for languages and literary studies, after such studies were formally begun in the selamlik, and made little progress.

Sultan Abdul-Hamid

Later he became infatuated with a Belgian seamstress whom he admitted to his harem, and from whom he learned a little French, but he never mastered any language. He visited the capitals of Europe in company of his uncle, the Sultan Abdul-Aziz, but the trip did not noticeably broaden his mental horizon or overcome an instinctive aversion for intercourse with foreigners.

Georges Dorys in his " Private Life of the Sultan " has given the only available intimate pen-picture of the early life of the Padishah. Dorys is the son of Adossides Pasha, one of the former ministers of Abdul-Hamid and later governor of Crete. The young man spent his childhood about Yildiz Kiosk, and had exceptional opportunities for the accumulation of the materials of a biography of the sultan. He was for a time the Constantinople correspondent of the London *Times,* and in this position he familiarized himself with the political conditions of Turkey and the causes of governmental maladministration in the Ottoman Empire during recent years. His book is a scathing criticism of the life and character of Abdul-Hamid, and its publication in England, France, and the United States has been the subject of no little controversy. The author was sentenced to death but fled to Paris; the French government was asked to surrender him but declined to do so. The sultan asked the governments of Europe to make the sale of the book illegal; but Sweden was the only country to take steps in the matter, and the action of the Swedish government only served to advertise the book. Well-informed European residents at Constantinople are divided in their estimate of the worth of Dorys's biography. Many believe it a just and accurate statement of the character of the sultan, and others think that the author was actuated by prejudicial motives and that he failed to give Abdul-Hamid credit for the few virtues which he certainly possesses.

Concerning the sultan's childhood Dorys says: "The youthful misanthrope avoided his brothers' society and took no part in their games. Most of the time standing aloof in some dark corner, he would watch them laugh and play with a fixed stare and with an expression in his eyes of infinite sadness except when fear or malice lit them up with a furtive flame." With reference to Abdul-Hamid's inaptitude for school studies he says: "Studious and diligent as was his elder brother Murad, Abdul-Hamid displayed little aptitude for books. As is well known, he is to-day practically uneducated and ignorant even of his own tongue; and, although he has tried several times to improve it, he has never been able to restrain the excessive independence of his orthography." Commenting on the lack of paternal love of Abdul-Mejid for his son, Dorys adds: " His younger brothers, too, had no great love for Hamid; Murad alone, good-hearted and generous, worthy son of his father, showed him neither hatred nor contempt and urged the little princes to treat him in more brotherly fashion;" but " loving no one, feeling himself loved by no one, the pale and sickly child became each day more suspicious and morose, and all the evil there was in his soul developed rapidly in his gloomy solitude, as fermentation is favoured by darkness."

Of the sultan's use of his absolute power Dorys says: " Abdul-Hamid has never attempted to better his country. On the contrary, he has done everything for twenty-five years to ruin it. He stifled the budding liberalism which might be for his people a resurrection; he cut the throat of its independence in the cradle, seized power by intrigue, kept it by force and cunning, and concentrated it by violence. He has paralyzed patriotism, gagged truth, and put in chains independence of thought and conscience; he has massacred entire populations of his empire, parts of which also he has traded over to the foreigner. And busy only with strengthening the throne, on which he has promised himself to remain at all cost, he has drawn the elements of his oppressive power, favouritism, espionage, ignorance, tyranny, cruelties, corruption, from the rapes of his favourites gorged with gold, from their quarrels, and from every iniquity, violence, and injustice." Most of the Europeans with whom I discussed Abdul-Hamid in my travels in Turkey thought him a very bad man; and most of their characterizations of him were not less mild than those by Dorys.

This view-point, however, is not shared by all writers on Turkey. Prof. Edwin Augustus Grosvenor, of Amherst College, Massachusetts, who was seventeen years an instructor in Robert College, near Constantinople, regards Abdul-Hamid as a man of worthy character, good impulses, and a friend and patron of education and enlightenment. In his comprehensive work on " Constantinople," he says: " The new sultan manifested unusual talents in organization and administration. There was no problem too humble or detail too minute to receive his careful consideration. Sympathetic, generous, and large-hearted, he endeavoured to benefit as well as to rule his people. No other living sovereign has equalled him in gifts to the unfortunate and suffering. Not only the capital, but countless villages cherish tokens of his interest and regard."[1]

In the same strain G. des Godins de Souhesmes, a Greek writer residing in Constantinople, extols the virtues of the Padishah. He says: "The present sultan, His Imperial Highness Abdul-Hamid Khan II., is the most remarkable sovereign of his dynasty. Walking in the footsteps of Mohammed II., Suleiman the Great, and the glorious Mohammed, he has provided Turkey with excellent reforms, and has become the protector of sciences, letters, and arts. He undertook with courage to dispose of the past, a laborious undertaking, if ever such has been; and he has succeeded in clearing, in a great measure, a ground covered with ruins. Mild, good, generous, and enlightened, he joins to brilliant intellectual abilities, lofty views and a quick understanding, much wisdom, and the most sincere desire of accomplishing worthily his mission. History reserves undoubtedly one of its best pages for this seri-

[1] "Constantinople." Boston, 1895.

ous and laborious prince, whose resolutions ordinarily bear the impress of bright common sense, rare sagacity, and of a thoughtful character that is sure of itself."[1]

The anonymous author of "Sovereigns and Courts of Europe" holds "that the present sultan is a serious man, whose entire energy and ability are devoted to the affairs of government, the reforms he has instituted prove. That his private life resembles much more that of an English gentleman than the popular idea of an Oriental prince, is familiar to all who reside in Constantinople." And the Hon. Samuel S. Cox, who served the United States as minister to Turkey, says of Abdul-Hamid, "He is a king every inch, and without any dramatic ostentation. He deserves great credit for his great ability. He is his own adviser. Amid his troubles and cares, and with the populations of diverse religions and races, which he must reconcile to rule, he is not unworthy of the fame of Abdul-Mejid."[2] I have quoted at length from these well-known writers because their estimates of the character of Abdul-Hamid are so entirely at variance with facts presented in earlier chapters of this work.

[1] "A Guide to Constantinople." Constantinople, 1893.
[2] "Diversions of a Diplomat in Turkey." New York, 1893.

Sultan Abdul-Hamid

The sultan is a monomaniac on the subject of conspiracy; and the civil service of Turkey is a stupendous detective bureau. Vast sums are squandered to pay spies, and the major part of the sultan's energy is consumed in the receipt and disposition of the reports of his detectives. A physician in Constantinople, who has had abundant opportunities for the study of Abdul-Hamid, assured Mr. Curtis that the sultan is " a victim of neurasthenia, a nervous disease which is a form of insanity, and that his psychological condition presents a most interesting problem, for his symptoms are complex, and vary materially from time to time. He is naturally very intelligent, but, living in continual terror of assassination, being afflicted with chronic insomnia, and having a naturally suspicious nature abnormally developed, he has become a monomaniac on the subject of self-preservation. His disposition is gentle, and if he had lived like an ordinary man he might have escaped the disease from which he suffers almost continual agony; but his mistrust of every one around him has become chronic, and he has developed a cunning that is never at loss for expedients."[1]

Upon his accession to the throne Abdul-

[1] "The Turk and His Lost Provinces." Chicago, 1903.

Hamid took up his residence in the beautiful Dolme Bagtché Palace; but at the outbreak of the war with Russia, he transferred his residence to the Yildiz Kiosk on a hill overlooking the Bosporus. A small kiosk had been erected on the Bagtché hill by Sultan Mahmud as early as 1832; and Abdul-Mejid in 1884 pulled the kiosk down and erected a larger pavilion which he christened Yildiz in honour of one of his favourite Circassian women. The Yildiz estate is admirably situated from a strategetical viewpoint; and from the time of its occupation by the present sultan great numbers of kiosks, pavilions, and cottages sprang up about it.

The Yildiz Kiosk is not, as a critic has pointed out, a palace at all — it is simply a medley of incongruous buildings. The Ottoman rulers have long been afflicted with the building mania, and Abdul-Hamid has not escaped the disease. A Turkish proverb asserts that the more a man builds the longer he will live; and the present sultan, who has been building, tearing down, and rebuilding without interruption during the past thirty years, doubtless hopes to attain the reputed age of Methuselah.

The Yildiz estate is enclosed by an immense wall, which, in 1898, was largely rebuilt and

YILDIZ KIOSK AND MAMIDIEH JAM MOSQUE.

the walls raised thirty feet higher to render scaling impossible. The private residence of the sultan, his harem, and the residences of his sons are on the northern part of the estate and enclosed by a second wall twelve feet thick, and entered by strong iron doors which open without. The harem communicates with the sultan's pavilion by means of a gallery, but the quarters of the princes are separated by a high wall. His own pavilion is a graceful wooden building which contains only twenty-four rooms. In front is an artificial lake and at one side is his private theatre.

The estate also includes the Palace of Ceremonies, where Emperor William of Germany was lately entertained, parks and gardens, two mosques, the imperial stables, baths, a museum of natural history, the imperial library, a porcelain factory, dog kennels, aviaries, and the like. The Yildiz estate is a veritable city; and without counting the large imperial guard, it has something like five thousand permanent inhabitants within its walls, including the sultan's chamberlains, aides-de-camp, bodyguards, musicians, gardeners, cooks, grooms, domestics, stable-boys, the women of his harem with their suites of eunuchs and slaves, and the households of his sons. This does not include a large number of workmen who live outside the walls. The monthly salary list of the palace reaches the enormous sum of $160,000.

The harem is a state institution and all children born within its walls, whether the offspring of free women or of slaves, are legitimate and of equal lineage. The Prophet originally proclaimed monogamy to be superior to polygamy, but he subsequently modified his teaching so that "if one wife does not suffice, it is lawful to take four, but the four women must be treated with impartiality, each having her own special apartments and her jewels." Only three sultans have gone through the ceremony of a marriage: Orkhan wedded the Greek princess Theodora; Suleiman went through a marriage ceremony with Roxalana, and Abdul-Mejid legally married the bath woman Besma.

The harem of the sultan is administered by the Valideh-Sultan (sometimes called Sultana) and the Chief of the Eunuchs. The Valideh-Sultan is the mother or foster-mother of the reigning sovereign. Abdul-Hamid's mother died when he was a child; his first foster-mother was Hanum-Naavik-Missal, an old slave in his father's harem, and upon her death

Peresto-Hanum, his father's fourth wife, who was without child, succeeded to the office. She is the present Valideh-Sultan, and she is said to be a woman of excellent tact and highly respected in the seraglio. She has powerful authority and must be implicitly obeyed. The chief of the eunuchs and his colleagues serve the double rôle of police and guards; for seraglio rivalries and jealousies are numerous and violent; and harem rebellions must sometimes be quelled by force. The women of the harem are imprisoned within a double row of thick walls and they live in a world to which all men, except the Grand Turk and his eunuchs, are denied access.

The harem is organized into a hierarchy, at the head of which stand the kadine-consorts, or first four wives of the sultan; they are not women whom he has legally married, but they are the four women who have first borne him children. They have their own households, eunuchs, and slaves. The kadines come next; they are women who have given birth to children and are treated with the same consideration as the kadine-consorts, but they can only attain the latter dignity when vacancies occur by death among the first four wives. The ikbals or favourites come next. The moment an ikbal gives birth to a child she is elevated to the rank of a kadine. The gediklis, or "young women who are pleasant to the eye," are next. All the women in the imperial harem are of slave origin, and they come chiefly from Circassian and Georgian peasantry. Most of them enter the harem in childhood as gifts or purchases, and few of them have any notion of their ancestry. They receive their education in the harem and they are gradually promoted from the lower to the higher ranks.

During the annual Bairam festival it is the privilege of the Valideh-Sultan to present the Padishah with a beautiful adult girl (over twelve years of age); and relatives and powerful pashas are permitted to display a friendly rivalry by making him similar gifts. During the reign of previous sultans the harems sometimes reached the enormous size of 1,500 or 1,600 women. Abdul-Hamid, however, has never maintained a harem of more than 300 or 400 women; he is thrifty and he has not cared to give much of his time to his harem. In recent years, since he has grown insanely suspicious of every one, he has rarely visited his women. The Bairam gifts are generally sent to a Mohammedan institution in Scutari. Ikbals who have reached the age of thirty years

and have not given birth to children may be presented to court favourites and friends. Oddly enough such gifts are appreciated; because a woman who has once lived at the seraglio has free access for ever after to the imperial harem and she may thus materially advance the interests of her new husband. On the other hand, it is currently reported in Constantinople that harem women thus presented to ministers and officials act as spies for the sultan and that they often cause the downfall of their husbands.

The education of the harem women, for most of them enter as young girls, consists of the principles of the Mohammedan religion, the graces of deportment, the arts of pleasing the Padishah, conversation, dancing, singing; and, in modern times, a little French. The higher orders of the harem lead lives of enforced idleness. Kadines, for example, have their own private apartments, and maintain separate existences somewhat after the pattern of the sultan, — with a head treasurer, a keeper of the seals, a first secretary, a mistress of the robes, and a numerous staff, including eunuchs, housekeepers, and female slaves of the lower order. Kadines are not permitted to leave the imperial harem; and Abdul-Hamid has increased the rigour of seraglio discipline, and thus put an end to the scandals and intrigues which characterized the reigns of his father and uncle.

The women of the imperial harem spend most of their time lying on divans or silk covered sofas or squatting on Bokhara rugs. They smoke cigarettes, sip syrups or sherbets, nibble ice, munch sweetmeats, chew gum, and toy with chaplets of beads. Turkish women (and men) incessantly and nervously toy with chaplets of beads that resemble somewhat Roman Catholic rosaries, save that instead of terminating in a crucifix, or a knot of relics, they are merely a string of ninety-nine beads — one for each of the names of Allah — divided at intervals by some of larger size. They are made of sandal or other odorous woods; and, as they become heated by the rapid action of the fingers, they emit a delicious perfume. Dancing is one of the chief amusements at the harem, although in recent times such diversions as rowing, cycling, and photography have been provided. The women also are fond of pets — such as Angora cats, parrots, and doves — and they devote some time to their care; and many of the weary hours are passed in sipping coffee, playing cards, and relating suggestive stories. Although the kadines may not leave the imperial harem, they are frequently visited by the wives of the sultan's ministers and the leading women in Constantinople.

Harem life is not an antidote for race suicide. With a seraglio of three or four hundred women, Abdul-Hamid is the father of only thirteen children, five of whom are boys. Mohammed-Selim, the oldest, was born January the 11th, 1870. He does not maintain a harem, but has one wife whom he has married, and he is the father of one child, a daughter. Dorys says of him: "Although a thoroughly good man, a hard worker, and possessed of keen intelligence, Prince Selim, unfortunately, has not been able to turn his abilities to account, owing to the state of captivity in which he is kept. He is subjected to exasperating surveillance, deprived of all communication, not only with the outside world but with the people of the palace, and even his own brothers, and is furnished with a course of reading more apt to dull his intellect than to develop it."[1] Kadir, the fourth child and second son, was born February the 23d, 1878, and Ahmed, the third son, the 14th of March the same year. Both are studying military tactics. Burhan-Eddin, the

[1] "Private Life of the Sultan of Turkey." New York, 1901.

fourth son, was born December the 19th, 1885. He is his father's favourite and the only child to whom he introduces foreigners. Abdur, the fifth son, was born in 1892. Only two of his daughters are married.

The Koran and ecclesiastical traditions require the sultan to leave his palace at stated periods. On the fifteenth day of the fast of Ramazan he must go to the Old Seraglio in state to venerate the cloak, the beard, and a decayed tooth of the Prophet. This annual pilgrimage costs Abdul-Hamid untold agony, for he is in constant terror of losing his life by assassination. Every possible precaution is taken by the police — houses along the proposed route are searched, occupants are forbidden to appear at windows while the Padishah is passing, and druggists are required to remove from their shops any inflammable or explosive substances which they may have in stock. The route is protected by double rows of troops; the street covered with sand; and the sultan, generally accompanied by his favourite son Burhan-Eddin, rides at an enormous speed in an open carriage drawn by handsome white horses. Eunuchs and palace runners, attired in costly costumes, with their hands crossed on their breast in token of re-

ENTRANCE OF THE OLD SERAGLIO.

Sultan Abdul-Hamid

spect for the successor of the Prophet, precede the imperial carriage; and he is followed by high ecclesiastical dignitaries, functionaries of the government, the princes, the Valideh-Sultan, and the women of his harem. Another annual pilgrimage, although less painful because it is shorter, is the visit to the hall of the Dolme Bagtché Palace at the feast of the Bairam to receive the homage of the Moslem world. On this occasion a vast concourse of ecclesiastical and civil functionaries salute him as the Shadow of God.

He is also required to visit a mosque every Friday in celebration of the Selamlik; but he has reduced apprehension to a minimum by building a mosque at the entrance of the Yildiz Kiosk, and, since the assassination of the king of Italy, by limiting foreign visitors to those holding personal cards of introduction signed by the ambassadors. Former sultans went every Friday to the historic mosques in Stamboul, — some of them riding on horseback, — but Abdul-Hamid contents himself with a ride of a few rods to his private mosque of Mamidieh Jam. The ceremony, as it may be witnessed from the ambassadors' lodge, is not without interest. From six to ten thousand soldiers are present to guard the line from Yildiz Kiosk to the mosque, including the artillery on foot, the engineers, magnificent zouave regiments, the Albanians in white, and the green-turbaned Syrian battalions. To this military spectacle must be added a glittering company of staff officers — generals, marshals, colonels, and brigadiers; a vast concourse of elderly — and presumably respectable — gentleman ablaze in patent leather boots, brass buttons, and ugly red fezes, and an amused and curious lot of tourists.

The ninety yards of sandy street between the kiosk and the palace are swept, and a victoria, with the hood half-lowered, appears with the Padishah; as he approaches the mosque, a voice from the minaret calls, "There is no god but God and Mohammed is the Prophet of God;" the carriages of the kadine-consorts, guarded by black eunuchs, follow; and after a brief interval in the mosque for prayers, the imperial party reappears, the sultan enters his phaeton alone; and taking the reins of the richly harnessed white Arabian thoroughbreds, he drives back to the palace. The sultan dresses in a plain black suit and wears on his head the ugly red fez. After witnessing this ceremony, I am free to confess that I shared Théophile Gautier's lament. "I regret sin-

THE SELAMLIK: — THE SULTAN ENTERING HIS MOSQUE.

cerely the loss of Asiatic magnificence,'' he says. '' I admired the unapproachable sultans — installed, like idols, in shrines of precious stones — a kind of peacocks of power, displaying themselves amid a galaxy of stars. In a country governed by despotic power, the sovereign cannot too far separate himself from common humanity by solemn and imposing forms — by a luxury, dazzling, chimerical, and almost fabulous. He should be seen by his people only through an atmosphere blazing with gold and diamonds.''[1] The weekly Selamlik cannot be omitted, even though the sultan may be at the point of death. Mahmud I., son of Mustafa, actually died between the two gates of the Seraglio while returning from one of these Friday ceremonies.

[1] "Constantinople." New York, 1875.

CHAPTER XVII

PALACES OF THE SULTANS

The Seraglio a cluster of kiosks — Present uses of these — Chamber of Execution — Hall of the Divan — Library of Mustafa — Imperial palace treasury — The Bagdad Kiosk — Dolma Bagtché Palace — Palace of Beylerbey — Cheragan Palace — The Sublime Porte.

The Seraglio is the palace of greatest interest in Constantinople. It occupies the eastern end of the promontory of ancient Byzantium. Here once stood a temple of Jupiter, the Acropolis, the baths of Arcadius, the palace of the Empress Placidia, and the churches of St. Barbara, St. Demetrius, and the Virgin. When the Turks conquered Constantinople, the Conqueror took up his residence in an old palace which was on the site now occupied by the Seraskerat. In 1468 the present Seraglio was begun and it was much enlarged by Suleiman I. For more than three centuries this was the chief residence of the Ottoman sultans. Abdul-Mejid moved his residence to Dolme Bagtché Palace

SERAGLIO POINT.

Palaces of the Sultans 255

in 1853 and henceforth the Seraglio became the residence of the widows of the sultans.

The Seraglio, like most of the other imperial palaces, is a community of buildings. It is separated from Stambul by a battlemented wall provided with square towers. The great inclosure is planted with venerable cypresses and plane-trees; and kiosks rise on every side. The grounds of the Seraglio rise in three terraces: the upper terrace contains the palace proper and the court of the Janissaries, and the middle and lower terraces contain numerous buildings and gardens. On the lower terrace are some huge vaults (which are doubtless of Byzantine construction), the Imperial School of Fine Arts, and the Chinili Kiosk which now houses the Museum of Antiquities. On the middle terrace is the Kiosk of Roses, where Abdul-Mejid signed his famous decree extending religious equality to his non-Moslem subjects. This is now used as a powder magazine. Just beyond is the ancient Church of St. Irene, now converted into an armory for rifles and bayonets and a museum for historical weapons. Among its objects of interest are the swords of the Conqueror, an armlet of Tamerlane, the drums and soup-kettles of the Janissaries, the standards of Ali, the keys of conquered cities, suits of chain mail, swords, etc.

The palace proper — a maze of small buildings on the upper terrace — may only be entered by special permission from the sultan. This, however, is easily obtained, but it involves an expense of about twenty-five dollars in gratuities to the imperial aides-de-camp. The Chamber of Execution is at the entrance of the main kiosk; here grand viziers, ministers, and court officials, who incurred royal displeasure, were formerly executed. Next come the palace kitchens, a series of nine buildings covered with domes, with holes in the centre for the escape of smoke. The first building of interest shown the visitor is the Hall of the Divan, or throne-room; it is adorned with porcelain tiles and the ceiling is covered with magnificent arabesques. The room is almost entirely occupied by a mammoth couch or divan on which the sultans reposed while receiving their ministers and foreign ambassadors. The divan is surmounted by a canopy, supported by gilt pillars that are adorned with precious stones. At the corners of the great divan are balls surmounted by the crescent and trimmed with long horse tails. The room has a latticed window, behind which sultans could sit when

Palaces of the Sultans

they desired to assume the rôle of unapproachable Oriental potentates.

The library of Mustafa III. is the next kiosk of interest. It has a handsome bronze door that is artistically decorated, and it contains more than three thousand Arabic, Persian, Greek, and Turkish manuscripts of unknown value. Some of them belonged to the kings of Hungary and were brought to Constantinople when Budapest was sacked. The imperial treasury is shown next; and its doors may be opened only by the second in authority of the imperial eunuchs "while a crowd of black-coated and fezzed officials stand on each side." Among the treasures are the great golden throne, incrusted with mosaics of rubies, emeralds, and pearls, that was taken from the shah of Persia in the war of 1514; another throne made of ebony and sandalwood and incrusted with mother-of-pearl, gold, rubies, emeralds, and sapphires; the coat of mail of damask plates and the scimitar adorned with diamonds worn by Murad IV. at the siege of Bagdad; a collection of robes of state, of thick brocades and covered with rich embroideries, worn by Ottoman sultans from 1433 to 1830; turbans ornamented with plumes and held in place by costly jewels; jars, cups, and bottles of gold, onyx, and crystal, and numerous objects of art dating from the Byzantine period.

The Bagdad Kiosk is the last of the Seraglio buildings shown to visitors. It is a beautiful structure and is said to be a copy of a kiosk that Murad IV. saw at Bagdad. Both the outside and the inside walls are covered with beautiful blue tiles; the dome is of gilded copper; the doors are inlaid with ivory and mother-of-pearl, and the furnishings include costly carpets, draperies, and divan coverings. There are two buildings on the Seraglio grounds which visitors are not permitted to approach; one of these is the former imperial harem; another contains the relics of the Prophet — his standard and beard, a tooth, and an impression of his foot in a block of limestone. But the Seraglio is now merely a matter of history. Some of the buildings were destroyed by the earthquake of 1865. The railway from Vienna passes through the outer walls. Military schools, hospitals, and barracks have invaded its once exclusive precincts; its kiosks have been transformed into a variety of governmental uses; and only its great walls have a semblance of the Seraglio in the time of Ottoman greatness.

The Dolma Bagtché Palace, on the European

DOLMA BAGTCHE PALACE.

side of the Bosporus north of the Golden Horn, was erected by Sultan Abdul-Mejid in 1853. It is a strange confusion and mingling of many orders of architecture — Arabic, Greek, Roman, Gothic, and Renaissance. When seen from the water-side at a distance, the effect is not unpleasing; but a nearer view reveals its conglomerate nature. There are two richly decorated gates on the land side, but these are hidden by the huge walls. The interior is more sumptuous and costly than the outside. Its carved and gilded doors are of mahogany and cedar; bathrooms, the tubs cut from single blocks of Parian marble, are gorgeously frescoed; chimneypieces are made from costly malachite; there are mirrors with a hundred square feet of surface; a crystal candelabrum with two hundred and fifty candles; there are costly bronzes, Sèvres porcelains, and rare paintings. Sultans Abdul-Mejid and Abdul-Aziz made Dolma Bagtché their residence; but at the outbreak of the war with Russia Abdul-Hamid retreated to the security of the Yildiz Kiosk, and the costly palace has been unoccupied for thirty years.

Beyond Dolma Bagtché, on the Asiatic side of the Bosporus, is the Palace of Beylerbey. It was erected by Abdul-Aziz in 1865. It is a white marble structure and has a marble quay, broken by steps leading to the Bosporus, on the water side. The interior is profusely decorated, and the ground floor is one great hall of columns, flagged with marble, from which leads a beautiful staircase. About the palace are beautiful gardéns and graceful kiosks. Foreign sovereigns are sometimes entertained at Beylerbey.

The Palace of Cheragan is also the creation of that spendthrift Sultan Abdul-Aziz. It cost more than $30,000,000. Stone and stucco were disdained and only the costliest marbles were used. When Abdul-Hamid deposed Murad in 1876 he imprisoned him in this palace and no one but the confidential eunuchs of the sultan have been permitted to see the interior of Cheragan for thirty years. The enthusiastic Edmondo de Amicis visited it while Abdul-Aziz lived and gives this account of it: " Nothing of all the splendour remains in my memory except the sultan's bath, made of whitest marble, sculptured with pendent flowers and stalactites, and decorated with fringes and embroideries that one feared to touch, so fragile did they seem. The disposition of the rooms reminded me vaguely of the Alhambra. Our steps made no sound on the rich carpets spread

PALACE OF BEYLERBEY.

everywhere. Now and then a eunuch pulled a cord, and a green curtain rose and displayed the Bosporus, Asia, a thousand ships, a great light; and then all vanished again as in a flash of lightning. The rooms seemed endless, and as each door appeared we hastened our steps."[1]
Abdul-Aziz met his tragic end at Cheragan in 1876; and after he was deposed Murad remained a prisoner here until his recent death.

Yildiz Kiosk is described in another chapter; and the only public building in Constantinople worthy to rank with the palaces of the sultans is the Sublime Porte. It is a large modern building, in the Italian style, adorned with a colonnade and surmounted by a pediment. The east entrance has a monumental gateway which is flanked by fountains and marble pillars. It contains the quarters of the grand vizier, the foreign minister, the minister of the interior, and the hall for the meetings of the council of state.

[1] "Constantinople." New York [1896].

CHAPTER XVIII

SANCTA SOPHIA AND OTHER MOSQUES

Origin of the mosques of Constantinople — Their dependencies — St. Sophia — Some of its materials — Its dedication by Justinian — Capture by the Turks — The disappointing exterior — Beauty of the interior — Mosque of Sultan Ahmed — — Its minarets — Richness of its decorations — Its tombs — Mosque of Mohammed the Conqueror — Its impressive size — Mosque of Suleiman the Magnificent — Interior decorations — Mosque of Eyub, and other mosques.

THE mosques of Constantinople are of three kinds: **(1) those built by the Christians and after the conquest transformed to suit the needs of Moslem worship, as St. Sophia;** (2) those founded by reigning sultans, as the mosques of Ahmed, Suleiman, and Bayezid; (3) those built by humbler persons, as the mosque of Yeni Valideh Djami. Most of the mosques have a court and a fountain in the centre for ablutions. The larger mosques have endowed dependencies, such as colleges, schools, libraries, hospitals, baths, khans, and soup-kitchens. The royal mosques have mortuary chapels (turbehs) in the courtyard, as

St. Sophia and Other Mosques

tombs are never placed in the mosques. All mosques must have at least one minaret, and royal mosques have more than one. The mosque of Sultan Ahmed has six minarets and St. Sophia and the mosque of Suleiman have four each. Five times a day the voice of the muezzin is heard in the minaret calling the faithful to prayer. Since the Crimean war Christians have been permitted to visit St. Sophia, so that at the present time the mosque of Eyub is the only one at the capital that is closed to non-Moslems. The shoes must be removed, or some covering worn over them, on entering a mosque. Constantinople has three hundred and seventy-nine mosques; and I have selected for brief description the half-dozen most likely to interest the general reader and tourist. In point of historic interest St. Sophia naturally comes first, although judged by æsthetic standards the mosque of Sultan Ahmed takes highest rank. The mosques of the Conqueror, of Suleiman, and of Eyub are peculiarly related to the theocratic government; and the special points of interest of the others described in this chapter will be noted later.

The original St. Sophia [1] was erected by Constantine in the year 325. In the riots which

---
[1] St. Sophia means divine wisdom, and not the name of a saint.

followed the exile of Chrysostom in 404, the building was partly destroyed by fire. It was rebuilt eleven years later by Pulcheria; but in the conflagrations which accompanied the religious riots of Neka from January the 13th to 20th in the year 532, the church was entirely destroyed. The cathedral (mosque of to-day) was at once rebuilt by Justinian; and he aimed to make it the most magnificent and enduring edifice of all ages. To accomplish this his vast empire was laid under contribution. Eight columns of green marble were brought from the temple of Diana at Ephesus; Rome supplied as many more of green porphyry which had been taken by Aurelian from the temple of the Sun at Heliopolis; and Athens, Baalbek, Delos, and twenty other temples were robbed of their richest ornaments and most precious marbles that Justinian might make his Christian basilica the most admired in the world. Ten thousand workmen were employed on the building, and it was completed in the surprisingly brief period of sixteen years.

On the 27th day of February in the year 537 a splendid ecclesiastical pageant marched from the church of Anastasia to the new basilica of St. Sophia to dedicate it to the service of the God of the Christians. Leading the procession

MOSQUE OF ST. SOPHIA.

St. Sophia and Other Mosques 265

and in the imperial chariot rode the Patriarch of the Orthodox church; after him came the high ecclesiastical dignitaries of the empire and the imperial city; and following on foot, at the head of a vast concourse of people, came the Emperor Justinian. As the procession marched up to the richly carved and gold-gilded high altar, it beheld the handsomest and costliest sanctuary known to man. The massive brick walls, covered with precious slabs and incrusted with forty thousand pounds of silver, rested upon huge blocks of calcarious stone; the great dome constructed of bricks from Rhodes, so light that twelve were no heavier than an ordinary brick, was embellished with gold and coloured mosaics; the capitals and the cornices were likewise covered with gold; the doors were of amber and ivory and cedar; the holy table was one mass of jewels held together by gold; the great branched candlesticks and the crosses were also of solid gold; the altar was of gold and silver with incrustations of pearls and diamonds; a thousand silver lamps were suspended from the arches and domes and a hundred candles burned in silver standards on the floor; the tabernacle containing the host was of solid silver, and it was supported by a golden cupola weighing one hundred and eighteen pounds and surmounted by a gold cross weighing eighty pounds.

In this magnificent edifice, surrounded by bishops and courtiers, soldiers and common people, the great Emperor Justinian uttered the words of dedication: " Glory to God, who has judged me worthy to accomplish this great work, I have vanquished thee, O Solomon;" and the vast concourse of bishops and priests, senators, soldiers, and common people echoed and reëchoed the jubilante, " Glory to God, who has judged him worthy to accomplish this great work, he has vanquished thee, O Solomon."

Another ceremony, not less significant but more dolorous, took place in St. Sophia on the 29th day of May in the year 1453. The last of the Greek emperors, with bishops and priests, senators and courtiers, soldiers and common people, celebrated for the last time at the high altar the communion of the Lord's body and blood; and with agonizing supplications they chanted " Kyrie eleison, kyrie eleison " ("Have mercy on us, O Lord, have mercy"), after which they abandoned the beautiful sanctuary that Justinian a thousand years before had dedicated to the followers

St. Sophia and Other Mosques 267

of the Man of Nazareth. And an advancing army of three hundred thousand Osmanli Turks, followers of the militant Prophet of Mecca, took possession of St. Sophia.

The exterior of St. Sophia is disappointing, for it is surrounded by a confused mass of mean buildings, — tombs, hospitals, baths, schools, soup-kitchens, and the like. The enormous dome is dwarfed by the ponderous buttresses which Sultan Ahmed II. added to protect it from earthquakes; the four heavy and inelegant minarets, added by various sultans since the time of the conquest, increase the confusion; the porticos are dingy and suggest entrances to tumble-down bazaars; and the strawberry coloured plaster, as Davey wittily remarks, suggests " a huge pink blancmange, flanked by four colossal white china candlesticks, a centrepiece for some giant's banqueting table."

Once inside the mosque, however, disappointment vanishes. While the outer vestibule no longer has its beautiful marbles and rare mosaics, those of the inner vestibule, together with the splendid bronze doors, are still intact. Formerly there was a cross on each door, the arms of which the Turks have removed; but curiously enough the Christian inscriptions which surround the crosses have been left untouched. The centre of St. Sophia, like the heavenly Jerusalem, "lieth four square and the length is as large as the breadth." The great dome rises over the centre of the mosque to a height of one hundred and seventy-nine feet. It is supported by four arches which rest upon four massive piers. Between the piers stand the eight great columns from Ephesus; and the numerous columns, brought from other renowned temples, support the galleries and the vaulted roof. The walls are veneered with jasper, and the ceilings adorned with mosaics. The latter are hidden behind a layer of plaster which may easily be removed when Constantinople comes into the hands of the Christians again.

The Mohammedan Turks, it must be confessed, have done less harm to St. Sophia than those godly thieves who masquerade in history under the name of crusaders. Davey truly says: "The blood-stained soldiers of the cross swarmed like ants in the sanctuaries, not of Sancta Sophia alone, but of the thousand four hundred and fifty churches of the holy city," and wherever they swarmed they pilfered. None of the movable adornments of St. Sophia remain. To except two huge ala-

St. Sophia and Other Mosques

baster jars from Pergamus, the steep pulpit with its canopy-cover and its delicately chiselled balustrade, a cupboard-like stall in which former sultans performed their devotions, and a few platforms for readers of the Koran, St. Sophia is practically empty. Among the alleged relics are a prayer carpet used by the Prophet, a basin in which the infant Jesus was washed, and the cradle in which he was rocked in Bethlehem.

Although erected so late as the early years of the seventeenth century, the mosque of Sultan Ahmed is one of the noblest specimens of Arabic architecture in the Ottoman Empire. It occupies the site of the palace of the Greek emperors and a part of the ancient Hippodrome. It cost an immense sum of money and is unquestionably the handsomest mosque in Constantinople. There is a beautiful court in front of the mosque, surrounded by columns of black and white, having bases of bronze. The lofty dome rises majestically in the midst of several lesser ones and is surrounded by six superb minarets. The two minarets which face the At Meidan square have two balconies and the other four minarets two each. The ten balconies are gracefully carved and rest upon beautiful corbels. When Sultan Ahmed I. erected this mosque in 1610, the only ecclesiastical edifice in the Moslem world with six minarets was the sacred mosque at Mecca; and the audacity of the sultan was subjected to such adverse criticism that he was compelled to order a seventh minaret for the Kaaba.

The mosque is rectangular in form, two hundred and thirty-seven feet long and two hundred and seventeen feet wide. A beautiful bronze door, reached by three steps, leads to the interior of the mosque. The principal dome is supported by four fluted columns, each measuring nearly one hundred feet in circumference, and at the corners rise small octagonal towers with surbased domes. Besides the four great pillars there are numerous other columns of granite and marble, supporting beautifully pointed arches. The walls of the mosque are covered with tiles that are gilded and adorned with gems. The mihrab, which indicates the direction of Mecca, is incrusted with lapis lazuli, agate, and jasper. There is a sameness, a lack of variety and contrast, which lessens somewhat the beauty of the interior. The mosque of Sultan Ahmed occupies an exalted place in the religious life of the capital, because here is generally cele-

MOSQUE OF SULTAN AHMED.

St. Sophia and Other Mosques 271

brated the feast of Bairam and the birthday of the Prophet; and it is the customary starting-point of the annual caravan for Mecca.

In the garden of the mosque is the turbeh of its founder, a rectangular building with an anteroom and a tomb-chamber covered by a dome and artistically decorated with tiles. Besides the great and glorious Sultan Ahmed, here repose Osman II., Murad IV., and thirty lesser personages, including their favourite wives and children. Ahmed's coffin is covered with the most costly shawls and embroideries from Persia and India. At his head is his turban with its jewelled aigrette, and at his feet two gigantic tapers. At one end of the turbeh is a cabinet which contains his sabres, kandjars, and other weapons which blaze with jewels.

The mosque of the Conqueror crowns the fourth hill of the ancient city, and occupies the site of the historic church of the Holy Angels. Here were buried the rulers of the Byzantine empire in sarcophagi of porphyry, granite, serpentine, and marble; but their tombs were desecrated by the Latin vandals, the cruusaders, who pillaged Constantinople in 1204. They converted the holy vessels into troughs for their horses; the mitres and vestments of the bishops, they made into helmets and halters; and the body of Justinian, which had reposed in the vault of the church for seven hundred years, they desecrated and robbed of its jewels.

The Conqueror's mosque covers the elevated terrace and it is surrounded by eight colleges, schools, residences for the imams, baths, a soup-kitchen, turbeh, hospital, khan, and fountain. The court is surrounded by cloisters, roofed by domes and supported by eighteen columns which doubtless came from the original church of the Holy Angels. Six are of red granite and twelve of verde antique, and the carvings on the capitals belong to the best period of Byzantine art. In the court is an octagonal fountain with twenty-four washing-places, into which water rushes by many spouts through a bronze grating, and all overshadowed by numerous cypress-trees.

The size of the mosque makes it impressive, but it has suffered severely from earthquakes and subsequent restorations. Above the entrance on a blue lapis lazuli slab, is inscribed the traditional prophecy of the Prophet: "They shall conquer Constantinople; happy the prince, happy the army, which shall achieve the conquest." The turbeh of the Conqueror

St. Sophia and Other Mosques

is in the garden of the mosque. It is a plain octagonal building, with a porch and two rows of windows, and it contains only one tomb — that of Mohammed II., the Conqueror. His tomb is enclosed by a railing inlaid with mother-of-pearl; at the head hangs his enormous turban and at the foot two big brass candlesticks. The reliquary of the turbeh contains a tooth of the Conqueror and a copy of the Koran said to have been made by himself.

The mosque of Suleiman the Magnificent occupies the third hill of the ancient city. It was constructed from plans drawn up by the great architect Sinan; and both its design and details may be traced to Christian sources. Most of the blocks of marble used in its construction and many of the great pillars came from the church of St. Euphemia at Chalcedon. It was built after the pattern of St. Sophia and is nearly square — two hundred and twenty-six feet long and two hundred and six feet wide. The mosque is entered by a monumental gate of white marble and adorned with mitre-shaped and delicately carved alcoves. The interior forms a rectangle and is divided into three naves. The great dome, supported by four square piers, rises in the centre; and on each side, between the piers, are enormous columns of porphyry one hundred and twenty-five feet high. The dome has a diameter of eighty-eight feet; and it rises two hundred and thirty-two feet above the ground, or nearly twenty feet higher than that of St. Sophia. It is surrounded at its base by a narrow gallery that is reached by a staircase from the roof outside. One may hear distinctly in this gallery everything that is said in the nave and aisles, so perfectly are the sounds concentrated in the dome.

The interior decorations are in blue, white, and gold. The four large windows of the apse at the end of the mosque have beautifully stained glass, and two windows are set with ground glass said to have been taken from the Persians. Other windows are ornamented with floral decorations and pious inscriptions. The walls and pillars are veneered with coloured marbles; the mihrab is of white marble, bordered with choice Persian tiles, and flanked by enormous gilt candelabra; and the pulpit and the praying-place of the sultan are delicately carved in white marble. In the right wing of the mosque, and behind a copper grating, may be seen piles of boxes and bundles. These are the treasures of the faithful. In a country where banks are few and private safe

TURKISH BEGGARS IN FRONT OF THE MOSQUE OF SULEIMAN THE MAGNIFICENT.

St. Sophia and Other Mosques 275

trust boxes unknown, the mosque assumes the guardianship of the valuables of its parishioners. The crypt of this mosque is traversed by an aqueduct which supplies the neighbourhood with water and which keeps the atmosphere cool even in the hottest days of summer.

The mosque of Suleiman is surrounded by cypresses and plane-trees and a great number of dependencies, — four mosque colleges, three mosque schools, soup-kitchens for the students and the poor of the neighbourhood, hospitals, baths, libraries, fountains, turbehs, and the residence of the Sheik-ul-Islam. The court in front of the mosque is paved with white marble and in the middle is a fountain for ablutions. The court is surrounded by a cloister formed by twenty-four columns, — two of porphyry, ten of white marble, and twelve of rose-coloured granite, — the columns placed alternately and supporting pointed arches of red and white marble. The turbeh of Suleiman I. is on the east side of the mosque. It is an octagonal building, with one large dome, and supported by twenty-nine columns. The turbeh is entered by a vestibule embellished by four columns of verd-antique. The great dome is decorated with arabesques of red and blue and large blocks of rock crystal which simulate diamonds and other precious stones. The walls are covered with blue and white tiles; and lamps, covered with gems, hang from the vault. The tomb of Suleiman the Magnificent is surrounded by a wooden balustrade inlaid with mother-of-pearl. Near him are the tombs of his sons and of Sultans Suleiman II. and Ahmed II. A less pretentious turbeh near by contains the tomb of Roxalana, the favourite wife of Suleiman I.

The mosque of Eyub is the only one in Constantinople which may not be visited by Christians. Eyub Ansari, whom the mosque commemorates, was the standard-bearer and companion of the Prophet; and it is supposed that he was killed at the first siege of Constantinople in 668 by the Arabs. The mosque is a handsome white marble building with a large dome, several small domes, and two minarets. The tomb of Eyub, which is held in high veneration, is in the court on the west side of the mosque. At the time of their accession to the throne, the sultans come here to be girded with the sword of Osman. The honour of girding the successor of the Prophet with the sabre of the founder of the present dynasty falls to the chief of the whirling der-

St. Sophia and Other Mosques 277

vishes, who comes from Konia expressly for the purpose.

Yeni Valideh Djami, or the New Mosque of the Valideh Sultan (sometimes called the little St. Sophia), stands opposite the large bridge and at the rear of the Balouk Bazaar square. It was begun by the mother of Sultan Ahmed I. in 1615, and completed by the mother of Sultan Mohammed IV. in 1665. The mosque is a square building, surrounded by two concentric rows of wings of decreasing height. The centre is surmounted by a huge hemispherical dome, flanked by four half-domes resting on the first range of wings. Four octagonal turrets rise at the corners. The west façade has a beautiful marble portico and above it rises two minarets, each bearing three galleries with elegant balustrades. The interior is entirely veneered with white, blue, and gold tiles, and there are some fine stained glass windows. The court at the south of the mosque contains hospitals, schools, fountains, turbehs, and a bazaar where fezes, beads, and tobacco-pipes are sold. There are two turbehs — both heavy buildings and without character. The first contains the tombs of Sultans Mohammed IV., Ahmed III., Mahmud I., and Osman III., and the latter the tomb of the mother of Ahmed I., the original founder of the mosque.

The mosque of Sultan Bayezid, sometimes called the Mosque of the Pigeons, wears a decidedly commercial aspect, and the court is generally filled with buyers and sellers of diverse commodities. The court contains some fine cypresses and plane-trees, an octagonal marble fountain, and a fine portico with pointed arches of red and white marble, supported by twenty monolith columns, ten of verd antique, four of jasper, and six of granite. The interior is not distinctive. Behind the mosque is the turbeh of Sultan Bayezid II. Pigeons live in the court of the mosque, and they are cared for by a foundation left by Bayezid. The legend relates that when the sultan was building the mosque, an impoverished old woman brought him a pair of pigeons as her free-will offering. He was touched by the incident and decreed that the pigeons and their offspring should be regarded as sacred, and he set aside a fund for their maintenance.

PIGEON COURT OF THE MOSQUE OF SULTAN BAYEZID.

CHAPTER XIX

WHIRLING AND HOWLING DERVISHES

Monastic orders not recognized by the Koran — Opposition of Turkey — The Turlakis, or nude dervishes — Bektashee, or free-thinkers — Whirling dervishes — Their movements — Religious significance — Howling dervishes — Nature and purpose of the religious excitement — Its counterpart in Protestant and Roman Catholic churches.

ALTHOUGH the Koran expressly forbids monasticism, the prohibition of the founder of Islam has not been sufficient to stem the ascetic tendency in the Moslem world. Orders of dervishes appeared first in Persia; and although the Ottoman sultans have always opposed their progress, their membership is reckoned by thousands in Turkey, and at least twelve strong orders are entrenched in the empire. The dervishes correspond to the regular clergy of the Roman Catholic and Greek Orthodox churches. Each order has its general or sheik whose office is hereditary, and only elective when a given dynasty becomes extinct.

The dervishes are bound by no laws of poverty or celibacy. The Turlakis alone of the numerous Moslem orders of dervishes do not marry. The members of this rapidly disappearing order take vows as rigorous as those of the Trappists in the Roman Catholic church. The Turlakis wear no clothing — not even the loin-cloth. Richard Davey, in his discriminating chapter on the " Sultan and His Priests," says of them: " They never partook of meat, or even fish, but lived entirely on herbs, and held women in holy horror, a fact which did not, however, prevent their having such an abominable reputation that early in the last century they were nearly exterminated. A few, however, of these extraordinary creatures still exist, and only three years ago one of them was still to be seen, wandering stark naked about the streets of Constantinople. He was held in such veneration that, in the low quarters of the city, men and women would run out to touch and embrace him in the most repulsive manner. I saw him once, but he was arrested shortly afterward at the request of the ambassadors, and placed in some charitable institution. Old residents in Constantinople assured me that in their youth there were a great many of these half-crazed creatures, popularly known as Abdals, to be seen. They are even now frequently to be met on the country highroads and in the provincial towns, and are always treated by the natives with scrupulous respect, and even with awe."[1]

The Bektashee dervishes, with headquarters at Rumili Hissar, are of special interest because of the alliance of the order with the Young Turk party and the well-known liberal political views which they hold. While professing Moslems, they hold to a refined form of philosophical deism. They are rationalistic in their habits of thought and they engage in philosophical, political, and scientific studies. Members of the order are even affiliated with French masonic lodges. For many years the order was recruited almost entirely from military ranks, and at one time it formed a part of the Janissaries. In recent times the order has grown more distinctly literary and political, in consequence of which its members are constantly watched by the police and the palace spies sent out by Abdul-Hamid.

An interesting ceremony that may be witnessed in Constantinople every Tuesday and Friday is that of the whirling or dancing dervishes. A revolving movement on the toes,

[1] "The Sultan and His Subjects." New York, 1892.

and at the same time going round the room, circle within circle, to music, is the form of religious worship peculiar to this order. Although the Koran prohibits the use of musical instruments in divine worship, the whirling dervishes persistently evade the Prophet's injunction. They have an orchestra of six or eight pieces, including the tabour, the tambourine, the dulcimer, the mandolin, a one-stringed violin, and a small Egyptian harp. Mevlevi, the mystical founder of the order, says concerning the symbolical religious significance of movements: "You speak of the sea and its waves; but in so speaking you do not mean two different things, for the sea in its rising and falling makes waves; and the waves when they have fallen return to the sea. So it is with men, who are the waves of God; they are resolved after death into Him."

The chapel of the whirling dervishes in Constantinople is an unpretentious octagonal building with a highly polished circular platform in the middle for the pious gyrations of the dervishes. The low balustrade is surrounded by a balcony for the musicians and the general public, and a latticed gallery in one corner is reserved for the use of Moslem

WHIRLING DERVISHES.

women. After saluting their sheik, the dervishes, with arms spread, the palms of the right hand upward and of the left hand downward, begin their revolving motions. The music of the orchestra marks the time to which they move. They whirl round on the bare feet with marvellous rapidity, each dervish preserving his own place as if revolving on an axis, and yet all waltzing in the prescribed circle. After about five minutes of rapid whirling, the name of the Prophet appears in the chant, and they pause, fold their hands on their breasts, and bow in reverence at the sound. The interval for prayer is followed by a repetition of the previous movements; and at the third performance all fall prostrate.

The whirling dervishes wear jackets and immense white petticoats much resembling the accordion-plaited tunics of the Albanians, but longer. Under the petticoats they wear tight-fitting white trousers. As the rotary movements become more rapid, their immense petticoats present the aspect of a whirlwind of snow or inverted mammoth white tops. As they drop one by one, mantles are thrown over them, and they kneel and a long monotonous prayer is recited. I believe that they maintain that the movement produces an ecstatic state necessary for the highest spiritual communion with God. As an exercise in motor dexterity and the unerring rhythm of movement, the ceremonies of the whirling dervishes are truly wonderful.

A curious religious ceremony is that of the howling dervishes at Scutari on Thursday afternoons from one to two. The sheik of the order seats himself on a carpet near the mihrab and the members range themselves in front of him, and together they repeat portions of the Koran. This is followed by a litany or profession of faith. They bend forward as they pronounce the first syllable, raise themselves up at the second, and bend backward at the third. These motions are repeated with the following syllables. The musicians with cymbals and tambourines begin and the dervishes cry out, "Allah Akbar, ya Allah, ya hu." As the chant grows louder, the movements of the head quicken, the chests pant, and the faces grow more livid. The signal for the quickest movement is when the sheik begins to stamp. They recite the ninety-nine names of God ninety-nine times, the sheik meanwhile counting his long chaplet of beads. At the last bead, in a frenzy of excitement,

Whirling and Howling Dervishes 285

they form a chain by putting their hands on each other's shoulders and swing to and fro; and from the depths of their vocal organs they utter prolonged cries of "Allah hu," until they fall to the floor swooning, as in an epileptic fit. The movements and frantic cries and sobs exhaust them, and exhaustion brings religious ecstasy, spiritual bliss, and "oneness with God."

Devout Moslems — men, women, and children — then prostrate themselves on sheepskins, and the dervishes walk lightly over their bodies. The foot of the holy man when in this ecstatic state is a cure for disease and bodily infirmity. I recall an Ethiopian eunuch who turned slightly after each tread, and he remained prostrate for a long time and required the dervishes to step on his body again and again. I was told that he was a severe sufferer from rheumatism and he wished the holy feet to come in contact with all the aching parts of his body. Small children were thus trampled on by able-bodied dervishes, and they naturally wept bitterly, although I had been told that children never wept. The adults, I must confess, bore the torture stoically. When I related the ceremony to a New England audience, a man, who stands well in his community as a pillar of church and state, remarked that such religious practices alone justified the annihilation of the Turks. But I called his attention to the fact that emotional excess formed a feature of the religious life of his own community; that frenzied ejaculations to the Deity constituted a part of the paraphernalia at camp-meetings, revivals, and the like, and that the ecstatic state which followed physical exhaustion and emotional fatigue was still esteemed in Massachusetts as well as in Turkey.

Théophile Gautier administered a deserved rebuke to two Capuchin monks who ridiculed the ceremony as foolish and absurd, " forgetting," as he remarks, " that they are a kind of Catholic dervishes, mortifying themselves in another manner to approach a Deity of different attributes. The dervishes seek Allah and address him in their howlings, as the Capuchins seek Jehovah in their prayers, their fasts, and their ascetic exercises. I confess that this want of tolerance, nay, even of intelligence, annoyed me excessively; for sincerity deserves respect everywhere, and however mistaken in its manifestations. For I can appreciate alike the Hindu fakir, the Trappist, and the dervish writhing beneath the immense pressure of the vague Infinite and seeking to appease 'the unknown God whom they ignorantly worship,' by the immolation of their bodies and libations of their blood."[1]

[1] "Constantinople." New York, 1875.

CHAPTER XX

MITYLENE, SMYRNA, AND EPHESUS

The ancient Lesbos — Nature of the island — Its prominence in Greek history — Mitylene to-day — Smyrna — Foundation of the city — Early history — Ancient ruins — Character of the population — Commercial importance of the city — Ephesus — The ancient city — Temple of Diana — Other ruins at Ephesus — Connection of Ephesus with Christianity.

MITYLENE, the ancient Lesbos, is one of the most historic of the islands of the Greek archipelago. It is separated from the mainland of Asia Minor by a channel seven miles broad and is traversed by mountain ridges, three of whose peaks attain elevations, respectively, of 1,780, 2,750, and 3,080 feet. The higher slopes of the ridges are covered with pine-trees, the lower slopes with olive orchards, and the bases with vineyards. Mitylene has the most equable temperature and the healthiest climate of all the islands of the archipelago, and it once produced the best wine in Greece. Under the Turkish government the taxes have grown oppressive and the wine has degenerated.

Mitylene, Smyrna, and Ephesus

Grapes, figs, gall nuts, cotton, wine, olive-oil, pitch, and pine timber are the chief products of the island. The area is two hundred and seventy-six square miles and the population one hundred and seven thousand, three-fourths of whom are Greeks. The southern coast is indented by two bays, which form excellent harbours. The city of Mitylene, sometimes called Kastro, with a population of twenty thousand, is on one of these bays.

The frequent mention of Lesbos in the Iliad and Odyssey would suggest that it was a populous and flourishing island at an early historic period. It was likewise one of the most ancient Hellenic culture spots. No island of Greece did so much for lyric poetry, the lyric art song, and the music drama as Mitylene. During the mythical period the head and lyre of Orpheus are said to have been carried to its shores. Lesches, the cyclic minstrel, was the first of its authentic poets; Terpander and Arion, the two foremost names in the history of Greek music, were natives of Lesbos; and Sappho and Alcæus, the founders of schools of letters and music, have given the island imperishable fame. Pittacus, the famous legislator, Theophanes, the friend of Pompey, and Cratippus, who was distinguished in Greek philosophy and science, were also natives of Mitylene. But its intellectual greatness is only a memory; for, while still a beautiful island, it is inhabited by a mere handful of illiterate Greeks and stupid Turkish officials who are entirely oblivious of the large part it has played in the mental history of the world.

Smyrna, the great emporium of western Asia Minor, lies at the head of the gulf of the same name and east of the mouth of the Hermus River. The city is built about the slopes of Mt. Pagus, a conical hill six hundred feet high, which, in ancient times, was renowned for a chapel of Nemesis and a spring of excellent water. Smyrna is said to have been founded by an Amazon of that name who had previously conquered Ephesus. It early came into the possession of the Æolians and continued in the confederacy down to 688 B.C., when, by an act of treachery, it fell into the hands of the Ionians and became the thirteenth city of the League. The original Smyrna was subsequently destroyed, but Lysimachus, the Thracian king, rebuilt it, and he made the new city the most magnificent in Asia Minor.

Smyrna is one of the numerous Greek cities

RIVER MELES, NEAR SMYRNA, THE REPUTED BIRTHPLACE OF HOMER.

Mitylene, Smyrna, and Ephesus

which claims to be the birthplace of Homer; and a little rivulet, which flows to the northeast of the town under the caravan bridge, is pointed out as the true Meles. Anaxagoras, the philosopher, was born on a little island in the outer gulf, — now used as a quarantine station, — and near Smyrna is the imposing ruin of the Ionian city of Teos, the birthplace of Anacreon, the lyric poet. Smyrna was not only distinguished as a commercial centre during the early Greek period, but it was also renowned for its schools of rhetoric and philosophy and other higher institutions of learning. The Christian church flourished here at an early period, largely through the zeal of its first bishop Polycarp, who was put to death A. D. 166.

In spite of the frequent sieges which the city has undergone, and its later vicissitudes under Roman, Byzantine, and Turkish rulers, a few relics of antiquity are still to be seen. The walls of the acropolis, in the ancient Cyclopean style, are in a tolerable state of preservation; the stadium, between the western gate and the sea, has been stripped of its marble seats and decorations, but is still an object of interest to the antiquarian; and the theatre, on the side of a hill fronting the bay, retains some of its ancient features. The present citadel dates from the thirteenth century. The view from Mt. Pagus, the site of the ancient acropolis, is superb, and is thus described by the poetic Gautier: "Smyrna lies extended below, with its houses of red and white, its tiled roofs, its screens of cypresses, its tufts of verdure, its white domes rising like pillars of ivory, its environs with their variety of culture, and its harbour forming a sort of liquid sky, yet more blue than the one above, — and all this bathed in a fresh and silvery light and pervaded by an air of unequalled transparency."[1]

Smyrna has a population of two hundred and five thousand, one-half of whom are Greeks, one-fifth Turks, one-tenth Jews, one-twentieth Armenians, and the balance Levantines and other foreigners. The city has suffered greatly from destructive earthquakes and visitations of the plague; but it has an excellent harbour, well-built docks, and in late years the railways have supplemented the caravan trade with Asia Minor. The Smyrna and Kassaba Railway extends east from the city to Manissa, up the valley of the Hermus to Kassaba and Alashehr, and connects at

[1] "Constantinople." New York, 1875.

GENERAL VIEW OF SMYRNA AND THE ACROPOLIS.

Mitylene, Smyrna, and Ephesus

Afion Kara-hissar with the Anatolian Railway for Constantinople. It has branches near Smyrna to Soma and Burnabat. There is also a railway line from Smyrna to Ayasoluk (and Ephesus), Aidin, and Dinair. It has direct and regular steamship connection from Liverpool by the Cunard, Leyland, and other lines; from Marseilles by the Messagerie Maritime line; and numerous cross communications with Brindisi, Trieste, Messina, Corfu, the Piræus, Saloniki, Constantinople, and Alexandria. Smyrna continues to have a relatively large caravan trade with the plateau of eastern Asia Minor, and the arrival and departure of the long trains of camels are still matters of interest for the tourist.

Although one of the first shipping cities in the Ottoman Empire, Smyrna has few industries. The manufactures include coarse cotton cloth, wicker-work, light silken fabrics interwoven with gold thread, and hava, a paste made of sesame, flour, and honey. The so-called Smyrna rugs and carpets come almost entirely from the interior. The export trade of the city consists of agricultural and industrial products from Asia Minor, such as grapes, figs, cereals, oils, cotton, tobacco, hides, skins, carpets, and rugs. The import trade includes cotton and linen cloth from England, woollens from Germany, silks and brocades from France, and hardware and other manufactured articles from the different countries of Europe.

The city is built almost entirely of wood, but the large Vizier Khan is constructed from the marble ruins of the ancient theatre; there are large bazaars and market-places; twenty mosques; Greek and Roman Catholic churches, several important cafés, and the Greeks have many notable elementary and secondary schools. The quays along the beautiful water front are paved with lava blocks from Vesuvius. Several summer retreats and health resorts — Burnabat, Kakluja, and Bunar-Bashi — are picturesquely situated among the hills and valleys that stretch eastward from the Gulf of Smyrna.

The ancient city of Ephesus, the traditional birthplace of the goddess Diana and the seat of her famous temple, may now be reached from Smyrna by railway to Ayasoluk. Ephesus was one of the twelve cities of the Ionian Federation and was founded about 1044 B. C. According to Pausanius, Androclus was the first great Ephesian ruler to give the city renown and to extend the worship of the god-

THE QUAYS OF SMYRNA.

Mitylene, Smyrna, and Ephesus

dess to Samos and the neighbouring Greek islands. The city was besieged by Crœsus in 562 B.C.; but he had respect for the temple of Diana and granted the citizens their liberty. For two centuries — from 548 to the time of Alexander the Great — Ephesus was subject to Persia; but Alexander succeeded in freeing the city from the Persian yoke. It was successively ruled by the kings of Syria and Pergamus, and in the year 41 B.C. it was subdued by the Romans under Antony. Cleopatra later joined him, and in Ephesus they lived the life of luxury which is familiar to students of history.

Ephesus is located on the Cayster River where it falls into the canal that connected the city with the Scala Nova Bay. The main part of the ancient city was built on the slopes of Mt. Prion and Mt. Coressus. The walls, which may still be traced, follow the jagged edge of Mt. Prion, which bounds the city on the south side, and thence westward to the mouth of the Cayster. Then turning eastward they enclose the ancient fort, the so-called prison of St. Paul. Aside from its religious significance Ephesus occupied a commanding position in the history of ancient commerce. It was the natural port and landing-place for Sardes, the capital of the

Lydian kings, and it was the mart for a large caravan and maritime trade.

Diana, the priestess of the Asiatic Artemis, and her temple — referred to by ancient writers as one of the seven wonders of the world — gave the city its renown. "The city was proud to be termed neocorus, or servant of the goddess," says Percy Gardner, "Roman emperors vied with wealthy natives in lavish gifts to her, one Vibius Salutaris among the latter presenting a quantity of gold and silver images to be carried annually in procession. Ephesus contested stoutly with Smyrna and Pergamus the honour of being called the first city of Asia; each city appealed to Rome, and we still possess rescripts in which the emperors endeavour to mitigate the bitterness of the rivalry."

The priestesses of Diana were virgins who were supposed to possess occult powers over woods, plains, and water, and their aid was particularly sought by women in childbirth. Runaway female slaves were also prominently identified with the worship of Diana. The temple was rich in lands and possessed the revenues from the fisheries of the Selinusian lakes. Another important privilege which the goddess and her priestesses possessed was that of affording an asylum for fugitives from justice or

EPHESUS AND THE SO-CALLED PRISON OF ST. PAUL.

vengeance. All such who reached her precincts were absolutely safe from pursuit or capture. The temple also served the function of a bank, and nowhere was money regarded so safe as here, in consequence of which kings and wealthy persons entrusted their treasures and riches to the safe-keeping of the temple priestesses.

The temple was presumably one of the handsomest structures produced by the ancient Greeks. According to Pliny, the platform on which it stood was four hundred and eighteen feet long and two hundred and thirty-nine feet wide, and it was approached by ten steps. The temple proper was three hundred and forty-three feet long and one hundred and sixty-four feet wide. There were eight columns in front, and double ranks of fluted columns formed the outer structure. In all there were one hundred columns, fifty-six feet high, including the base, and six feet in diameter, and thirty-six of the columns were sculptured. The roof was covered with large white marble tiles; and the statue of the goddess, which was the temple's treasure, was said to have "fallen from heaven." After its destruction the temple lay buried for centuries, and even its exact location was unknown. Forty years ago John Turtle Wood, an English archæologist, obtained permission to excavate for its site. Aided by the trustees of the British Museum and other archæological interests in England, he not only succeeded in locating the ancient temple but in uncovering other historic buildings in the old city, including the Great Theatre, the Lyric Theatre, the Great Gymnasium, the Stadium, the Tyrant's Palace, and numerous Christian antiquities.

Ephesus has numerous Christian associations. Here the church which St. Paul planted was nurtured by St. John; and the enormous success of the Apostle's preaching provoked the disturbances led by Demetrius and his fellow shrine-makers. The making of shrines and images of the goddess gave employment to many people. About the time the Goths sacked the city (A. D. 262), the Christians determined to extirpate the last vestiges of the pagan worship, and they completed the destruction of the temple. Some of the marbles in the walls were used to repair the proscenium in the theatre, others were utilized for building purposes, and the beautiful sculptures were burned into lime!

Churches at Ephesus were dedicated to St. Luke, St. John, and St. Mark; and on the slope of Mt. Coressus, where a cleft in the rock may still be seen, was the church of the Seven Sleep-

EPHESUS AND THE RUINS OF THE TEMPLE OF DIANA.

Mitylene, Smyrna, and Ephesus

ers. Timothy, the first bishop of the church at Ephesus, is supposed to be the angel of the church referred to in the Revelation of St. John. The famous council of four hundred and thirty-one, which met to settle the question of the Nestorian heresy, held its sessions in the church of St. John.

The destruction of the temple of Diana marks the decline of the city; commerce waned; and it ceased to be a city of renown. It fell successively into the hands of divers adventurers and pirates; and in the thirteenth century it was captured by the Turks, who built the present town of Ayasoluk, near the ancient city. Both Ayasoluk and Ephesus fell into the hands of the Knights of St. John of Rhodes in the fourteenth century. They were later taken by Timour, the Tatar; and early in the fifteenth century both places were captured by the Turks, their present masters. Ephesus was by degrees deserted, and Ayasoluk later was depopulated by deaths caused by the malarious marshes of the Cayster. The uncovering of the ruins at Ephesus, and the subsequent tourist trade, has given Ayasoluk the semblance of life again. It has a badly kept and high-priced inn, coffee-houses, provision dealers, and livery stables. The growing of tobacco among the ruins of

Ephesus gives employment to a few people. But the chief objects of interest at Ayasoluk are the numerous storks who nest on the piers of the ancient aqueducts.

CHAPTER XXI

THE NEAR-EASTERN QUESTION [1]

Triangular nature of the question — Three sides of the triangle — Nations interested — Russia's foothold on the Black Sea — The policy of Catherine — Appearance of England — Pitt's failure — The Greek war of liberation — The Crimean war — Duke of Argyll's defence of England's attitude — — Bulgarian barbarities — Congress of the Powers — Porte rejects suggested reforms — War with Russia — Treaty of San Stefano — Shameful policy of England — Congress and treaty of Berlin — The defenseless Armenians — The subsequent massacres — Austria, Germany, France, and Italy.

VICTOR HUGO once remarked that when a man was killed in France it was called a murder, but when fifty thousand throats were cut in the Ottoman Empire it was called a question.

The Near-Eastern Question is triangular. The long side of the triangle is a straight line from St. Petersburg to Constantinople; and, while an altogether imaginary line to the general public, it has been very real to the Russian

[1] Now that there is an Eastern Question in China, the present title seems more appropriate. For a fuller discussion see the authoritative book by the Duke of Argyll: "Our Responsibilities for Turkey," from which I have quoted liberally in this chapter.

sovereigns since the days of the wily Empress Catherine. Before her day — as early as the time of Ivan the Terrible — the Muscovite boundaries began to encroach upon the Ottoman dominions. Ten times — an average of once in every twenty years — during the past two centuries, Russia has been at war with Turkey. She has generally been the aggressor, and seven of these wars she has fought single-handed. The shortest side of the triangle is the Macedonian question; and its solution at this writing (1907), as pointed out in the chapter "The Ottoman Empire To-day," seems temporarily adjusted. The third, or intermediate side, and touching the triangular question on all its sides, is the oppression of the Christian Armenians in Asia Minor. Russia and England — after Turkey — are the chief factors in the question, although Austria, Germany, France, and Italy have played secondary rôles.

Russia gained a foothold on the shores of the Black Sea as early as 1696 when Peter the Great captured Azov; he continued his attacks on the Danube provinces, and suffered a humiliating defeat beside the river Pruth. But " the quick wit and the heavy bribes of Catherine extricated her consort and saved Russia." Peter found it to his advantage to make an alliance with

The Near-Eastern Question 303

Turkey, and the two countries joined in a scheme for the partition of Persia. But the humiliation of Peter was not forgotten; and the Empress Anne in 1736 sent her troops into the dominions of Sultan Mahmud I., with results not entirely satisfactory to Russian revenge.

The determination to make the Black Sea a Russian lake probably originated in the fertile brain of the crafty Empress Catherine II. Turkey opposed her occupation of Poland and the fraudulent election which she had secured for a favourite as Polish king. Mustafa III. entered upon war before he was prepared, and in the peace of Kaynarji, which temporarily closed the struggle, Russia was permitted not only to retain the fortress on the Sea of Azov and several strong fortresses which she had erected on the Black Sea, but the Crimean kahnate and the Danubian principalities were made practically independent. Catherine saw in this defeat the downfall of the Ottoman Empire in Europe; she resolved* that the possessions of the sultans should become the heritage of the czars; and, as an expression of her faith in Russian destiny, she christened a grandchild Constantine, and had a gate at Moscow that opened toward Turkey named "The Way to Constantinople." She renewed hostilities in

1787, in alliance with the Emperor Joseph of Austria, and she pushed the boundaries of Russia into Moldavia and Wallachia. By the conditions of the treaty of Jassy in 1792, " In the name of the Almighty " she entered into a solemn compact with Selim III. to make enduring " peace, friendship, and good understanding; " but she immediately began preparations for a most formidable war against Turkey. Death fortunately interrupted her schemes.

England, whose diplomatic reaction time has always been that of the proverbial snail, at last in 1791 grew conscious of the fact that Turkey was in the clutches of Russia. Accordingly she formed a tripartite alliance with Holland and Prussia and tried to make Catherine disgorge some of her Turkish conquests, which the proud and self-sufficing empress quite naturally refused to do. The House of Commons was asked to furnish the sinews of war to bring Catherine to terms. The measure was violently opposed by Charles James Fox and Edmund Burke. The former declared that it was absurd for Pitt to assume that Russia was a great power or for England to regard her as an object of dread; and Burke denounced the squandering of British blood and treasure in bringing or keeping Christian nations under the yoke of a savage and inhuman Moslem government.

Pitt carried his motion in the House of Commons, but was defeated in the country. The action of Pitt marks the appearance of England as an active factor in the Near-Eastern Question. The overweening power which Russia acquired by her great share in the overthrow of Napoleon caused a popular feeling of dislike for her in England, as the Duke of Argyll has pointed out. "For then came the new spirit breathed into our foreign policy by George Canning," he says, "and especially our national and popular antipathy to the Holy Alliance. Russia was the head and front of that offending. That she should be allowed to seat herself on the throne of Constantinople — to make the whole Black Sea a Russian lake, to command the Bosporus and the Dardanelles, and to issue from them into the Mediterranean with fleets powerful in action and inaccessible in retreat — this would indeed be a menace and a danger to the western world. To avert this danger, or at least to postpone it, the easiest plan was to keep up the Turkish empire as long as possible."

And this has been the policy of the English government from the time of the Great Commoner to our own day. This policy, admits the Duke of Argyll, is only to be defended on the supposition that the government of Turkey could be made at least a decent and tolerable government toward its own subjects. On any other supposition, he affirms, the new British policy would have been unprincipled and atrocious. "We may have been all fools in entertaining the more hopeful supposition," he adds, "but, as a matter of fact, the people of this country have entertained it, and have acted on it, at least in so far as they thought at all. They did actually, and with passion, abandon the policy of protecting Turkey when they were roused to sympathy with the insurgent Greeks, and when all Europe was horrified by the atrocious massacres perpetrated by the Turks between 1821 and 1827. Yet the moment Canning died British politicians betrayed the undercurrent of their feeling by the famous sentence in a king's speech which deplored the destruction of the Turkish fleet at Navarino as an 'untoward event.'"

England, it will be remembered, suspended her antipathy for Russia and her friendship for Turkey long enough to act with the former and France to free the Greeks from the intolerable Ottoman yoke. It should be noted in this connection that while the policy of British statesmen on the Near-Eastern Question has not been above suspicion at all times, that at this period, and during the Crimean war, England maintained that the fate of Turkey should be regarded as a European and not a mere Russian question. The incessant attacks of Russia on Turkey and her constant movements in the directions of Persia and India have, it must be confessed in recent times, powerfully influenced the British mind; and the question of Turkey's qualifications for domestic government has had secondary importance, if considered at all. Bluntly stated, the most recent British policy has simply regarded Turkey as a buffer state against the designs of Russia and as such to be upheld in the face of manifest maladministration.

But for the timely aid of England, and the allies she was able to secure, the Crimean war would have annihilated Ottoman power in Europe. The subsequent Turkish policy of massacre and pillage has subjected the friendly aid of Lord Palmerston's government to harsh criticism. Lord Salisbury in 1858 gave expression to international judgment when he asserted that "on the continent of Europe. our claims to be regarded as the champions of liberty were looked upon as hypocritical boastings — for, while we were loud in our professions, we were lax in our practises."

It is manifestly unfair, however, to interpret the alliance of England with Turkey during the Crimean war in the light of the later wavering and selfish policy of British politicians. William E. Gladstone, the honest and sturdy champion of civil liberty, was one of the statesmen directly responsible for the British policy of the Crimean war. The Duke of Argyll, who, with Gladstone, was a member of the Palmerston cabinet, says in defence of the policy, " On my own behalf, and on behalf of colleagues who cannot now vindicate their own reputation — on behalf, too, of a whole generation of the British people in whose name we acted — I emphatically deny that such was our conduct or our position in the war of 1854-55, or in the treaty of 1856. For myself, indeed, I never did believe in the regeneration of Turkey; I doubt if any one of my colleagues did — even Lord Palmerston. But we did hope that her government might at least be rendered tolerable, for a time, if it could be made to feel its dependence on a united Europe instead of on Russia alone, and if some time were given to it to initiate and carry into effect certain reforms which might be of a very simple character, but which, nevertheless, might be far-reaching. I see now that it was a gross delusion to believe even this. But, at all events, this is the idea on which we did actually proceed, and which did underlie the whole policy both of the war and the treaty. We never did, even for a moment, entertain the iniquitous policy of strengthening a government irredeemably vicious, corrupt, and cruel, without caring at all for the sufferings it would inflict on millions of subject populations.''

Whatever the motives which may have prompted the policy of England at the time of the Crimean war — and before — it must be confessed that her conduct during the last forty years has been characterized by criminal selfishness and statesmanship — measured by ethical standards — that is singularly mean. English statesmen during the first half of the last century held honestly to the conviction that the united action of the Great Powers of Europe would enable Turkey to reform her glaring abuses. The aim of the Crimean war alliance was to cripple Russia so that Turkey might have time to reform. But it was a time of grace the sultans did not improve. They did not put their disorderly governmental houses in order. They did not carry out any of the reforms which they had promised in the treaty of Paris. The treaty had specifically prohibited Russian naval armaments on the Black Sea. It was widely recognized that the wily Muscovite would improve the earliest opportunity of escaping from the restrictive obligation; and the friendly powers repeatedly warned both Abdul-Mejid and Abdul-Aziz that if Turkish officials continued to oppress and slaughter Orthodox Christians in the Balkan provinces, that Russia was sooner or later certain to renounce the Paris treaty and plunge the Ottoman Empire in another hazardous war.

So late as October the 6th, 1870, Lord Granville informed the Sublime Porte that unless the unjust oppression of Christian subjects ceased, changes were imminent; and he warned Abdul-Aziz that his government would not again be defended as it had been fifteen years earlier. But the stupid successor of the Prophet turned a deaf ear to these timely warnings. The continuous infamy of the governors sent out by the Sublime Porte, the misery of the people, and the increasing desolation of the Christian provinces finally brought matters to a climax. As early as 1860 Russia represented to England, the sultan's friend, that Turkey had not lifted a finger to improve the infamous misgovernment in Bosnia, Herzegovina, and Bulgaria; and an English consul on the ground confirmed the charges and added that "the rapacity and corruption of the governing classes keep the country in a state of penury and misery." He further informed his home government that the lower grades of Turkish functionaries had not the means of living without extortion, "whilst the Porte seemed knowingly to encourage the oppressions by which they really live."

The story of the notorious misdeeds that led to the last great war with Russia, which so signally dismembered the Ottoman Empire, is too long to tell in this connection. It is sufficient to remark in passing that the twenty years which followed the Crimean war, in the Baltic provinces, as elsewhere in Turkey, were years of untold oppression and suffering for the Christian subjects of the sultans. Life, property, and family honour were all at the mercy of an organized system of villainy. While England continued to rebuke the Porte, she took no steps to enforce her rebukes; worse, she regarded the rebelling Christians as a lot of naughty and disobedient children. After the bombardment of Belgrade in 1862, the Servians made a desperate effort to arm themselves; they contracted with an English firm for a quantity of firearms, but when the incident reached the ears of the queen's government, the firm was forced to cancel the contract. Some old arms were then purchased in Russia, but English consuls did all in their power to stop their conveyance across Wallachia. When the Bosnians revolted in 1876 England did her utmost to injure the cause of the insurgents and to assist the Sublime Porte. The English consul-general at Sarajevo wrote that he was in bed very ill, but he added, " I intend to take an early opporunity of urging the vali to take steps at once, if possible, to sweep these bands of brigands out of Bosnia." A distinguished English statesman very bluntly says: " Although we knew that the insurgents had frightful grievances, and that they demanded nothing more than the most elementary benefits of a civilized government; although we knew that the Turks were, as usual, committing against them acts of perfidy and deeds of butchery, we actually implored the Porte to hasten to put down the insurrection with their own forces, so as to prevent it from being made the subject of foreign intervention."

The horrible massacres in Bulgaria began in May, 1876. The manly and humane Gladstone came out in September with his celebrated pamphlet denouncing the atrocities and character-

The Near-Eastern Question 313

izing Abdul-Hamid as "The Great Assassin." Public sentiment in England was with Mr. Gladstone, but the British government did not join the rest of Europe in intervention, but simply told the Turks "that if they were attacked by Russia, it had now become practically impossible — owing to the state of public feeling — for us to intervene to save them!" Russia, it must be said to her lasting credit, played the part of the humanitarian, whatever may have been her ulterior motives. She begged England and the other powers to aid her in putting an end to these massacres. She suggested that Austria should occupy Bosnia, that she would occupy Bulgaria, and that the combined fleets of the Great Powers of Europe should occupy the Bosporus and the Dardanelles. But England refused. She then asked if England would join a combined action of the fleets without any territorial occupation. And England refused this.

It was finally arranged that there should be a congress of the Great Powers at Constantinople in the hope that moral suasion would settle the difficulty. England made this proposition! The congress met December the 23d, 1876. The English envoy, Lord Salisbury, pursued the flabby moral suasion tactics of his home government.

He told Abdul-Hamid that it was his country that had saved Turkey from destruction twenty years earlier; that the Ottoman Empire was now at the mercy of other nations for protection, and that all foreign designs against the Turks derived their power from "the profound misgovernment which the inhabitants of the empire had suffered." The congress formulated certain reforms which the Porte promptly and unreservedly rejected January the 18th, 1877. The astute Abdul-Hamid knew, says an English writer, "the long-established dislike and fear of Russia which dominated the English people. He had good reason to know that among almost all the politicians in England that feeling was as strong as ever. He therefore heard with absolute incredulity our threats to abandon him to the armies and fleets of Russia. He calculated that when it came to the point we would not allow it, but would be forced to intervene on his behalf. He therefore resolutely refused to yield." The Duke of Argyll says of the event, "The Turk was astute enough to see the advantage of his position. It is a law of nature that creatures which cannot live by strength are obliged to live by cunning. The Turk is an animal in whom this faculty has acquired an almost preternatural development. For many years he has lived on the jealousy existing between the Christian powers. He has watched it constantly in the rivalries for influence of the embassies of Constantinople.''

England took the policy of peace at any price; and, but for the strong feeling occasioned by Mr. Gladstone's pamphlet, which tied the government's hands, it seems altogether likely that she would have fulfilled Abdul-Hamid's cunning anticipations. Russia stood firm; she resigned from the concert; she concluded a convention with Rumania the 6th of April, and eighteen days later she declared war against Turkey. The story of the war has been briefly told in an earlier chapter. The Turks were vanquished in both Europe and Asia. Adrianople was occupied January the 20th, 1878, and a week later the Russian troops were within gunshot of the capital. An armistice was declared January the 21st, and the treaty of San Stefano was signed March the 3d. After having crushed the Turkish armies in both Europe and Asia, and with a great army before the walls of the undefended city of Constantinople, Russia once more acted a manly and honest part. She required the liberation of her Christian kinsmen in Bosnia, Herzegovina, Montenegro, Servia, Rumania, and Bulgaria; the maintenance of a

Russian army in Armenia as a guarantee against the slaughter of Armenians by the Moslem Kurds and Circassians; retention of a portion of the Asiatic provinces which she had wrested from Turkey by hard fighting, and the free access of the Black Sea to all nations, both in time of war and in time of peace.

To the eternal disgrace of English statesmanship, it must be said that the queen's government acted shamefully. It was angry and jealous, and forthwith voted $30,000,000 for armaments and ordered troops from India. Russia was informed that the treaty of San Stefano could not stand, but that the whole matter must be submitted to a congress of the Great Powers of Europe. Russia did not object to a congress, in spite of the fact that she had fought this war for Christian liberation single-handed and that it had cost her many millions in dollars and many thousands in lives. The congress of the Powers met at Berlin June the 8th, 1878; they tore up the treaty of San Stefano, and a month later they announced the treaty of Berlin. It was not so good a treaty as that of San Stefano because it left the province of eastern Rumelia nominally in the hands of the Turks and it declined to give the Armenians the protection of Russia. This stupid blunder, the work of

England, is directly responsible for those barbaric massacres which have horrified the civilized world during the past dozen years. Russia is the only country that is capable of guaranteeing the security of life and property to the helpless Armenians against the cruel Kurds and Circassians. With Batoum as a naval base and Kars as a land key, she is the only one of the six Great Powers that has the ghost of a chance of making the protection of the Armenians a reality.

Nine days before the meeting of the congress at Berlin, England had concluded a secret treaty with Turkey in which she promised to maintain the integrity of the Ottoman Empire in Asia and in consideration for this service she was permitted to occupy the island of Cyprus and hold the same in fee for the sultan! It delighted the low cunning of Abdul-Hamid to make this deal rather than permit Russia to protect his Christian subjects in Armenia. The Duke of Argyll remarks: "The Turk could see at a glance that, whilst it relieved him of the dangerous pressure of Russia, it substituted no other pressure which his own infinite dexterity in delays could not make abortive. As for the unfortunate Armenians, the change was simply one which must tend to expose them to the increased enmity of their tyrants, whilst it damaged and discouraged the only protection which was possible under the inexorable conditions of the physical geography of the country."

The awful butchery of thousands — probably more than a hundred thousand — of innocent men, women, and children in Armenia, and the burning of more than forty Armenian towns and villages are the logical consequences of the abrogation of the treaty of San Stefano and the substitution of the treaty of Berlin; and however much English politicians may wince under the charge, it is so plainly recorded in the history of the last quarter-century that whoever runs may read.

So much space has been given to the part played by England and Russia in the Near-Eastern Question that the other members of the concert — Austria, France, Germany, and Italy — must be passed over briefly. In spite of the fact that Austria is a sluggish power and interests herself little in the sufferings of the Armenians and other distant Christians, it must be admitted that she has acted in the interest of humanity in the recent Macedonian oppressions and that she has made an excellent foster parent for both Bosnia and Herzegovina. The inhabitants of these provinces were certainly unfit for self-

The Near-Eastern Question 319

government at the time of the treaty of Berlin. Mr. Thomson, an English traveller who has been much among these people, says: "They could never have united to form one nation, and to them the gift of liberty would have been but the prolonging of misery. What they were in immediate need of was a strong, firm government such as Austria has given them. The proclamation, announcing the occupation, undertook that all the people of the land should enjoy equal rights before the law, and that they should be protected in life, in belief, in property, and in estate. This undertaking Austria has kept. She has established peace where there was never-ending strife. She has evolved government and order out of anarchy and chaos; and, under her rule, all races and all religions are not only tolerated but protected. A Catholic country herself — an ardently Catholic country — she is making no attempt to favour the Catholics at the expense of either the Turks or the Orthodox Christians."[1] It will be remembered that England took charge of Cyprus the same time that Austria assumed the care of Bosnia and Herzegovina, and yet the same traveller laments that "it is humiliating to contrast what she has done with what we have done in Cy-

[1] "The Outgoing Turk." New York, 1897.

prus." Germany has nothing to her credit in the account of the Near-Eastern Question. She has at no time shown an interest in humanity, and her emperor has played a very selfish and reprehensible rôle in his defence of the crimes of *his friend* Sultan Abdul-Hamid. The part played by France, in recent years at least, is altogether negative. Italy, while her rôle has been small, has conducted herself throughout with dignity; and, during the recent horrible Armenian massacres, she was the only one of the six Great Powers that had the temerity to tell Abdul-Hamid that she could place absolutely no reliance upon his account of the causes and extent of the troubles.

THE END.

APPENDIXES

(a) BRIEF SUGGESTIONS FOR TRAVELLERS

1. *General Remarks.* — These brief suggestions are not intended to supersede guide-books, but rather as preliminary aids to the prospective traveller in Turkey. A course of travel-reading is helpful in visits to any country; and, as in Turkey, where the languages are so numerous (and generally unknown) and the guides and dragomen so ignorant, a preliminary course of careful reading is a necessity. A following appendix gives the most important American and English books on the subject.

2. *Guide-books.* — Murray's "Constantinople" is the only standard convenient hand-book in English. It does not, however, include Saloniki, Smyrna, and other parts of the empire. There is a little "Guide to Constantinople and Its Environs," by G. des Godins de Souhesmes, a native Greek, which travellers have told me they have found helpful. Those who read German will find the Baedeker and the Meyer excel-

lent supplements to the Murray. But travellers are warned against taking many books with them to Turkey, as all printed matter is liable to confiscation. Even guide-books are subject to the examination of the customs officials; they are often kept for days and weeks; and when they are returned to the owners the maps are generally missing and the books otherwise mutilated.

3. *Seasons for Travel.* — Constantinople is dryest and healthiest — and the temperature most equable — from May to September, although it is never absolutely free from the cold, moist winds from the Black Sea. March and April are not disagreeable months in Turkey. Because of its splendid natural drainage, Constantinople is not an unhealthy city, in spite of the absence of a sewerage system.

4. *Mediums of Exchange.* — The monetary system of Turkey is most complex, and travellers will find it to their comfort to master its elementary principles before visiting the country. The Osmanli lira (sometimes called the Turkish pound) is the monetary standard. It is equivalent in value to $4.36. The Osmanli lira is divided into forty paras. The silver coins include the Mejideh (worth about eighty cents in American money), the half and quarter

Appendixes 323

Mejideh, and the piastre, the latter worth about four cents. The gold coins of France and England circulate freely in Turkey. Whenever a purchase is made or a bill paid, the traveller is required to give the exact change. The short-sighted government does not put sufficient small change in circulation, with the result that one must continually pay Hebrew, Greek, and Armenian money-changers a premium for small change. But money-changers in Constantinople are as numerous as saloons in an American city.

5. *Passports and Teskere.* — It is not possible to enter Turkey without a duly countersigned passport; and Turkish police agents being incompetent to pass upon the validity of passports, these documents must be countersigned by a Turkish ambassador or consul in some foreign country before reaching the frontier. The teskere is a travelling passport and a countersign is required for every fresh start while in the Ottoman Empire. A teskere to a given point once issued, the journey cannot be broken. Applications for teskeres must be made through the consulates of one's country.

6. *Hotels.* — The leading hotels in Constantinople are in Pera, and the charges are from $3 to $4 a day for rather ordinary accommodations. There are a few satisfactory boarding-

houses in the city where the rates are from $2 to $2.50 a day. But Turkey is an expensive country in which to travel; and in dealing with Greek and Armenian innkeepers travellers, who do not wish to be fleeced, must be on the constant lookout for extortioners.

7. *Cabs and Boats.* — There are now a few cabs in Constantinople. For a short drive (not exceeding twenty minutes) the charge is twenty cents. By the hour the charge is sixty cents for the first hour; but it is always important to settle the price when the cab is engaged. Travellers are in addition required to pay the bridge tolls. Sedan-chairs are still used in Constantinople, but they are expensive.

Boats — caïques and barcas — are the cheapest and quickest public conveyances. They have no fixed rates; but long trips may be made in a caïque for twenty to thirty cents and in a barca for thirty to forty cents.

(*b*) SELECT ANNOTATED BIBLIOGRAPHY

(1) DE AMICIS, EDMONDO. *Constantinople.* New York: G. P. Putnam's Sons [1896]. pp. 327. A rather brilliant popular book on Constantinople by an enthusiastic traveller. Very readable.

(2) BAKER, JAMES. *Turkey.* New York: Henry Holt & Co., 1877. pp. 495. The writer is familiar with his subject, but his judgment on many topics — political and otherwise — is open to question.

(3) CLEMENT, CLARA ERSKINE. *Constantinople: the city of the sultans.* Boston: Estes & Lauriat [1885]. pp. 309. An incoherent book that contains a lot of useful information.

(4) COX, SAMUEL S. *Diversions of a diplomat in Turkey.* New York: Charles L. Webster & Co., 1893. Diffuse, scattering, and inconsequential.

(5) CRAWFORD, F. MARION. *Constantinople.* New York: Charles Scribner's Sons, 1895. pp. 79. Brief but bright.

(6) CURTIS, WILLIAM ELEROY. *The Turk and his lost provinces.* Chicago: Fleming H. Revell Co., 1903. pp. 396. Result of a journey undertaken for the *Chicago Record-Herald* at the time of the Macedonian disturbances. Excellent account of the social and political conditions in the Balkan states.

(7) DAVEY, RICHARD. *The sultan and his subjects.* New York: E. P. Dutton & Co., 1892. 2 volumes, pp. 364 and 371. Complete and scholarly. One of the most useful books on the subject.

(8) DODD, ANNA BOWMAN. *In the palaces of the sultan.* New York: Dodd, Mead & Co., 1903. pp. 492. Contains some popular information of a rather superficial nature.

(9) DORYS, GEORGES [ADOSSIDES]. *Private life of the sultan of Turkey.* New York: D. Appleton & Co., 1901. pp. 277. An intimate and scathing account of Abdul-Hamid II. The author's father was for many years one of the sultan's ministers and later governor of Crete. Bad as the present sultan doubtless is, Dorys has failed to credit him with the few good qualities which the sultan probably possesses.

(10) DUKE OF ARGYLL [GEORGE DOUGLAS CAMPBELL]. *Our responsibilities for Turkey: facts and memories of forty years.* London: John Murray, 1896. pp. 196. A frank and comprehensive statement of the Near-Eastern Question by an able English statesman.

(11) DWIGHT, HENRY OTIS. *Constantinople and its problems: its people, customs, religion, and progress.* Chicago: Fleming H. Revell Co., 1901. pp. 291. Discussion of Turkish problems by an American missionary.

(12) FIELD, HENRY M. *The Greek islands and Turkey after the war.* Charles Scribner's Sons, 1885. pp. 228. Readable bits of travel.

(13) GARNETT, LUCY M. J. *Turkish life in town and country.*

London: George Newnes, n.d., pp. 228. A small but very useful book on the inhabitants and institutions of the Ottoman Empire. Brief but valuable chapters on harem, monastic, nomadic, and brigand life in Turkey.

(14) GAUTIER, THÉOPHILE. *Constantinople.* New York: Henry Holt & Co., 1875. pp. 363. An altogether brilliant book by one of the first literary men of France.

(15) DES GODINS DE SOUHESMES, G. *A guide to Constantinople and its environs.* Constantinople: A. Zellich Sons & Co., 1893. pp. 288. A guide-book by a native.

(16) GROSVENOR, EDWIN A. *Constantinople.* Boston: Roberts Brothers, 1895. 2 volumes. pp. 811. A comprehensive work. The author was a professor in Robert College near Constantinople for seventeen years, and his book is the result of personal investigation.

(17) HALID HALID. *Diary of a Turk.* London: A. & C. Black, 1903. pp. 269. An intimate account of Turkish life by a Turk. Valuable chapter on boy life and training.

(18) HAMLIN, CYRUS. *Among the Turks.* New York: Robert Carter & Brothers, 1878. pp. 378. The author was an American missionary and teacher in Turkey — the first president of Robert College.

(19) HOGARTH, DAVID G. *A wandering scholar in the Levant.* New York: Charles Scribner's Sons, 1896. pp. 206. Good account of Anatolia and its inhabitants.

(20) HUTTON, WILLIAM HOLDEN. *Constantinople: the story of the old capital of the empire.* London: J. M. Dent & Co., 1900. pp. 341. Best brief historical guide of Constantinople.

(21) KESNIN BEY. *The evil of the east, or facts about Turkey.* London: Vizetelly & Co., 1888. pp. 327. A pessimistic book, but it shows familiarity with political conditions in Turkey.

(22) LANE-POOLE, STANLEY. *The story of Turkey.* New York: G. P. Putnam's Sons, 1888. pp. 373. Best short history of the Ottoman empire.

(23) LATIMER, ELIZABETH WORMELEY. *Russia and Turkey in the nineteenth century.* Chicago: A. C. McClurg & Co., 1893. pp. 413. Contains some interesting facts bearing on the Near-Eastern Question.

(24) MILLINGEN, FREDERICK. *Wild life among the Koords.* London: Hurst & Blackett, 1870. pp. 380. An excellent dis-

cussion of the Kurds and Armenians, among whom the author lived in a military capacity for some time.

(25) *Murray's Handbook of Constantinople, Brusa, and the Troad.* London: John Murray, 1893. pp. 166. Indispensable for the English-speaking traveller as there is no Baedeker for Constantinople and Turkey in English.

(26) ODYSSEUS [CHARLES NORTON EDGECUMBE ELIOT]. *Turkey in Europe.* London. Edwin Arnold, 1900. pp. 47. An authoritative work on the diverse races of European Turkey.

(27) PARDŒ, JULIA. *The city of the sultan : domestic manners of the Turks.* Philadelphia: Adam Waldie, 1837. An intimate but discursive account of domestic life at Constantinople.

(28) RAMSAY, WILLIAM MITCHELL. *Impressions of Turkey during twelve years' wanderings.* New York: G. P. Putnam's Sons, 1897. pp. 296. Discriminating impression, by a Scotch archæologist.

(29) SYKES, MARK. *Dur-ul-Islam : record of a journey through ten of the Asiatic provinces of Turkey.* London: Bickers & Son, 1904. pp. 294. Readable travel notes.

(30) THOMSON, H. C. *The outgoing Turk : impressions of a journey through the western Balkans.* New York: D. Appleton & Co., 1897. pp. 281. Discriminating discussion of the Macedonian question and related Balkan problems.

(31) THORNBURY, WALTER. *Turkish life and character.* London: Smith, Elder & Co., 1860. 2 volumes. pp. 283 and 293. Travel notes of passing interest.

INDEX

A

Abdul-Aziz, 38, 39-40, 162, 259, 310.
Abdul-Hamid I., 31.
Abdul-Hamid II., succeeds Murad V., 40; promulgates and revokes constitution, 41; war with Russia, 43, 313; responsibility for Armenian massacres, 47; opposition to Macedonian reforms, 53; friendship with William II. of Germany, 57; wealth, 147; press censorship, 178; parentage, 233; education, 234; mental alienation, 241; palaces, 242; harem, 244; children, 249; religious life, 250; detective service, 281.
Abdul-Mejid, 37-38, 215, 234, 244, 259, 310.
Aboukir, battle of, 33.
Aboul-Turk, 59.
Abu-Bekr, 120.
Adabazar, 158.
Adana, 159.
Admiralty. See Navy.
A d o s s i d e s. See Dorys, Georges.
Adrianople, 4, 8, 16, 141, 158, 315.
Afion Kara-hissar, 156, 293.
Agia Sophia. See Sancta Sophia.
Agriculture, 105, 150-152.
Ahmed I., 26-28, 271.

Ahmed II., 29-30, 276.
Ahmed III., 29, 231, 277.
Ahmed fountain, 231.
Ahmed mosque, 269-271.
Ahmed, son of Abdul-Hamid II., 249.
Aidin, 80, 159, 293.
Aintab, 154, 176, 177.
Albania, 13, 16.
Albanians in Turkey, habitat, 3, 103; religion, 104; occupations, 105; physical and mental characteristics, 106.
Alashehr, 292.
Alcæus, 289.
Aleppo, 86, 156.
Alexander the Great, 192, 295.
Alexandretta, 156.
Algiers, 13, 22, 26.
Ali-Ibn-Abu-Talib, 132.
Almsgiving. See Charities.
American College for Women at Scutari, 176-177.
American missions in Turkey, 92.
de Amicis, Edmondo, quoted, 72, 93, 116, 211; bibliography, 324.
Anacreon, 291.
Anastasia, church of, 264.
Anatolia, 13, 155, 157.
Anatolia college, 176.
Anatolian railway, 156, 158, 293.
Anaxagoras, 291.
Androclus, 294.
Angora, 16, 17, 86, 152, 58.

Index

Animals, treatment of, 74, 75, 214.
Anne, empress of Russia, 302.
Antioch, 183.
Antony, Mark, 295.
Appendixes, 321-327.
Arabas, 73, 201.
Arabia, 13, 64, 120.
Arabic architecture, 269.
Arabic language, 73, 164, 168, 169.
Arabs, 61, 129, 141, 170, 171, 276.
Arcadius, column of, 191.
Archæological institute, 170.
Area of Turkey, 8.
Argos, 182.
Argyll, Duke of, quoted, 302, 305, 306, 325; bibliography, 325.
Armenia, 13, 16, 85-86, 120.
Armenians, geographic distribution, 85; ethnic stock, 86; character, 87; lack of personal courage, 89; religion, 90; education, 92; intellectual progress, 172; moral lapses, 202; porters, 215; in Smyrna, 292.
Armenian massacres, 47-51, 193, 318.
Army, 141.
Astrakhan, 23.
Athanasian creed, 129.
Athens, 25, 183, 264.
Athos mountain, 5.
At Meidan, 188.
Augustine Fathers, 177.
Augustine, St., 183.
Aurelian, 264.
Austria, 23, 24, 29, 30, 45, 154, 318-320.
Avars, 108.
Avicenna, 131.
Ayasoluk, 159, 293, 294, 299.
Azov, 28, 30, 302, 303.
Azhar mosque college, 131.

B

Baalbek, 264.
Backsheesh, 135.
Bagdad, 13, 28, 141, 154, 157, 166.
Bagdad Kiosk, 258.
Bairam feast,130, 246, 251, 271.
Baker, James, bibliography, 324.
Balat, Jewish quarter of Constantinople, 197.
Balkan mountains, 2-3.
Balkan peninsula, geography of, 1-11.
Barcas, 217, 324.
Baths, 71, 227-231.
Batoum, 317.
Bayezid I., 17.
Bayezid II., 19-21, 278.
Bazaars, 223-226.
Beaconsfield, Earl of, 45, 46.
Bedouins, 9, 212.
Beirut, 154, 157, 175, 177.
Bektashee dervishes, 281.
Belgrade, 4, 30, 175, 311.
Berlin, treaty of, 44, 316.
Bessarabia, 37.
Beylerbey palace, 259.
Bibliography, 324-327.
Bitlis, 86, 154.
Black Sea, 1, 6, 38, 303, 305, 316.
Boats. See Barcas and Caïques.
Borgia, Alexander, 20.
Books, censorship of, 180.
Books on Turkey, 324-327.
Bosnia, 7, 13, 16, 30, 40, 46, 311, 312, 315.
Bossora, 157.
Bridges in Constantinople, 20.
Brinton, Daniel G., 60.
Bronze horses of Lysippus, 188, 190.
Brusa, 15, 17, 86, 154, 159.
Budget. See Finances.
Bulgaria, 2, 13, 16, 40, 46, 311, 315.

Index

Bulgarian massacres, 40, 312.
Bulgarians in Turkey, where found, 111; peasant characteristics, 112; religion, 112.
Bunar-Bashi, 294.
Burgas, 3, 158.
Burke, Edmund, 304.
Burnabat, 156, 295.
Burhan-Eddin, son of Sultan Abdul-Hamid II., 249.
Burnt column, 190.
Byron, George Gordon, Lord, 181.
Byzantine art, 272.
Byzantium. See Constantinople.
Byzas, 182.

C

Cabinet officers, 134.
Cabs in Constantinople, 216, 324.
Cafés, 221, 294.
Caïques, 216, 324.
Cairo, 9, 22, 25.
Caliph, 22, 118, 120, 132.
Campbell, George Douglas. See Duke of Argyll.
Canning, George, 305.
Canon law, 138.
Capuchin monks, 286.
Caravan routes, 157, 293.
Carlowitz, treaty of, 29.
Carlyle, Thomas, 76, 123.
Catherine II., empress of Russia, 31, 32, 33, 302, 304.
Cayster river, 295, 299.
Celibacy, 127, 280. See also Marriage.
Cemeteries. See Fields of the Dead.
Censorship of the press, 178, 180.
Central Turkey College, 176.
Chalcedon, 182, 273.
Chaplets of beads, 248.
Charities, 130, 167.
Charles VIII., of France, 20.
Charles XII., of Sweden, 30.

Cheragan palace, 260.
Chief of eunuchs. See Kislar Agassi.
Children of Abdul-Hamid II., 249.
Christ. See Jesus Christ.
Chryses, 203.
Chrysopolis, 203.
Chrysostom, St., 264.
Circassians in Turkey, migration from Russia, 107; ethnic stock, 108; mental traits, 109; cruelties toward the Armenians, 317.
Cisterns in Constantinople, 192-193.
Civil service, 135.
Clarendon, Earl of, 149.
Clarke, James Freeman, 117, 122.
Cleanliness, 74, 227.
Clemens, Samuel L. See Mark Twain.
Clement, Clara Erskine, bibliography, 325.
Cleopatra at Ephesus, 295.
Climate of Turkey, 6-7.
Clothing. See Dress.
Clubs, baths as substitutes for, 229.
Coffee, Turkish, 221.
Colleges. See Education.
Columns in Constantinople, Serpent, 188; Egyptian, 189; Burnt, 190; Marcian, 191; Arcadius, 191.
Congo Free State, 77.
Constantine the Great, 183, 190.
Constantinople, climate, 6, 322; conquest of, 18; prison of Seven Towers, 73, 187; Greeks, 80; Armenians, 86; Persians, 107; admiralty, 143; commerce, 155; railways, 158; post-offices, 159; mosque schools, 167; technical schools, 169; Greek schools, 173; newspapers,

179; Hippodrome, 183, 188; Golden Horn, 186; historic monuments, 189-191; museum, 192; cisterns, 192; characteristic quarters, 194-207; street scenes, 208-222; bridges, 210; dogs, 213; Fields of the Dead, 217-220; fires, 220; cafés, 221; bazaars, 223-226; khans, 226; baths, 227-231; fountains, 231; palaces, 254-261; mosques, 262-278; hotels, 323.
Constitutions promulgated, 41, 134.
Costumes. See Dress.
Cox, Samuel S., quoted, 240; bibliography, 325.
Cradle of Jesus, 269.
Crawford, F., Marion, quoted, 202; bibliography, 325.
Creed of Mohammedans, 129.
Cretan rebellion, 47, 51.
Crete, 8, 23, 29, 80.
Crimea, 13, 19, 26, 31.
Crimean war, 37, 38, 204, 308, 310-311.
Croatia, 3, 104.
Crœsus, 295.
Crusaders, 91, 186, 187, 268, 271.
Curtis, William Eleroy, quoted, 49, 53, 57, 210; bibliography, 325.
Curzon on moral traits of people of Turkey, 80.
Cypress-trees, 217, 272, 278.
Cyprus, 8, 23, 80, 120, 317.

D

Dacians, 109.
Dalmatia, 3, 29.
Damascus, 141, 153, 157, 159, 166.
Dancing dervishes. See Whirling dervishes.
Dandolo, 187, 190.

Dante, Alighieri, 181.
Danube river, 1.
Darius, 183.
Davey, Richard, quoted, 96, 199, 268, 280; bibliography, 325.
Debt. See National debt.
Dedeagatch, 11, 156, 158.
Delos, 264.
Delphi, 183.
Demetrius, 298.
Dervishes, Turlakis, 279-281; Bektashee, 281; whirling dervishes, 281-284; howling dervishes, 284-287.
Dinaric Alps, 3, 103.
Diana of Ephesus, 264, 296-298.
Diarbekr, 86, 99, 154.
Dinair, 293.
Divorce, 67.
Dodd, Anna Bowman, bibliography, 325.
Dogs of Constantinople, 213-216.
Dolma Bagtché palace, 251, 258-260
Dorys, Georges, quoted, 48, 235; bibliography, 325.
Dress, 71-73, 106, 111, 283.
Drin river, 3.
Dwight, Henry Otis, quoted, 68, 121, 128; bibliography, 325.

E

Earthquakes, 258, 267, 292.
East Indies, 77.
Education in Turkey, 161-181.
Egypt, 13, 22, 33, 34, 120, 127.
Egyptian obelisk, 189.
Elementary schools, 162.
Eliot, Sir Charles Norton Edgecumbe, quoted; 64, 142, bibliography, 327.
England, 29, 33, 37, 44, 93, 140, 154, 304.
English cemetery at Scutari. 204.

Index

Ephesus, early history, 294; walls, 295; temple of Diana, 264, 296-298; Christian churches, 298; downfall of the city, 299-300.
Epirotes, 103.
Ertoghrul, 14.
Erzerum, 47, 86, 91, 99, 154.
Eski-Shehr, 14, 158.
Etchmiadzin, 91.
Ethiopians in Turkey, African origin, 115; the eunuch type, 116.
Eunuchs, 115-116, 136, 201.
Euphrates college, 175.
Exarch of the Bulgarian church, 113.
Expenditures of Turkey, 144.
Exports of Turkey, 154.
Eyub, 184, 196, 199, 276.
Eyub Ansari, 276.

F

Faith of Islam, 117-132.
Fatalism of the Turks, 62.
Fez, the emblem of Turkish nationality, 153, 209, 218, 252.
Field, Henry M., quoted, 63; bibliography, 325.
Fields of the Dead, 204, 217-220.
Finances of Turkey, 144.
Fires in Constantinople, 220.
Fisheries of Turkey, 152.
Fiume, gulf of, 1.
Foreigners, legal rights of, 139.
Forests of Turkey, 151.
Fountains in Constantinople, 231.
Fox, Charles James, 304.
France, 33, 37, 51-52, 154, 306, 320.
Francis, Joseph, emperor of Austria, 53.
Fruits of Turkey, 7.
Furniture in the Turkish home, 70, 75.

G

Galata, 185, 201, 202, 210, 220.
Gardner, Percy, quoted, 296.
Garnett, Lucy M. J., quoted, 104, 161, 210; bibliography, 325.
Gates, C. Frank, 174.
Gautier, Théophile, quoted, 286, 292; bibliography, 326.
Gedıklis, 246.
Geography of the Balkan peninsula, 1-11.
Georgia, 23, 108.
Germany, 55, 56, 57, 320.
Gershom, Rabbi, 96.
Gladstone, William E., 41, 134, 308, 312.
des Godins de Soushesmes, G., quoted, 239; bibliography, 326.
Goethe, Johann Wolfgang, 124.
Golden Horn, 6, 185, 200.
Government of Turkey, 133-149.
Grand Bazaar, 225.
Grand Eunuch. See Kislar Agassi.
Grand Vizier, 134.
Granville, Earl of, 310.
Great Britain. See England.
Great Powers of Europe, 42, 44, 54, 134, 316.
Greece, 7, 13, 32, 34, 45, 84, 157.
Greeks in Turkey, geographic distribution, 80; diverse occupations, 81; physical and mental traits, 82; religion, 84; schools, 196; quarters in Constantinople, 196-197; Smyrna, 292.
Gregorian church, 90.
Grosvenor, Edwin A., quoted, 238; bibliography, 326.
Guide books, 178, 321.
Gymnasium at Ephesus, 298.
Gypsies in Turkey, physical traits, 113; mental condition, 114.

H

Hafiz, 132.
Haidar-Pasha, 158.
Halid Halid, bibliography, 326.
Halki, 169, 170, 206.
Hall, G. Stanley, quoted, 89.
Hama, 159.
Hamals, 87, 215.
Hamdy Bey, 192.
Hamlin, Cyrus, 174, 326.
Hanefites, 131.
Hannbelites, 131.
Harbours of Turkey, 155.
Harem, 6, 7, 244.
Harput, 86, 175.
Harrison, Frederic, quoted, 185.
Hassan Pasha, 144.
Hebrews in Turkey, numerical strength, 93; social condition, 94; ignorance, 95, 172; religion, 96; quarters in Constantinople, 197-199; Smyrna, 292.
Hegira, flight of the Prophet, 127.
Heliopolis, 189.
Hereditary rank in Turkey, 71.
Hermus river, 290.
Herzegovina, 3, 8, 13, 40, 46, 47, 311, 315.
Hippodrome, 183, 188.
Hodeida, 157.
Hogarth, David G., bibliography, 326.
Holland, 29, 33, 154, 304.
Holy Alliance, 305.
Holy Inquisition, 95.
Homer, birthplace of, 291.
Hotels in Constantinople, 323.
Howling dervishes, 284-287.
Hugo, Victor, 301.
Hungary, 13, 18, 22, 24, 29, 32, 154.
Hunyadi, Jonas, 18.
Hutton, William Holden, quoted, 195; bibliography, 326.

I

Ibrahim, 28.
Ikbals, 244.
Illyrians, 103, 109.
Imams, 128, 272.
Imperial city, 182-190.
Imperial museum, 192.
Imports of Turkey, 154.
Index Expurgatorius, 181.
Indo-Eranic peoples, 98, 113.
Industries of Turkey, 153.
Innocent III., 186.
Innocent VIII., 20.
Interregnum, 17.
Ireland, William W., quoted, 125, 127.
Irene, church of, 255.
Islands in the sea of Marmora, 205.
Istillar, gulf of, 5.
Italy, 37, 155, 320.
Ivan the Terrible, 23, 302.

J

Jaffa, 159.
James, William, quoted, 76.
Janissaries, 16, 23, 27, 28, 35-37, 187, 255, 281.
Jassy, treaty of, 304.
Jemshid, brother of Bayezid II., 19.
Jerusalem, 95, 159.
Jesuit schools in Turkey, 177.
Jesus Christ, 75, 118, 121, 127 267.
Jews. See Hebrews.
Johnson, Samuel, 118.
Joseph II., emperor of Austria, 304.
Journals. See Newspapers.
Julian Alps, 3.
Justinian, 264, 265, 272

K

Kadija, wife of Mohammed the Prophet, 125.

Kadines, 245, 247, 249.
Kadir, son of Sultan Abdul-Hamid II., 249.
Kairwan, 120, 166.
Kakluja, 294.
Kamerun, 77.
Kara Hissar, 15.
Karaites, 96.
Karaman, 13, 80.
Kars, 149.
Kartalinia, 33.
Kassaba, 158, 292.
Kastro (Mitylene), 289.
Kaynarji, 302.
Kesnin Bey, quoted, 74, 113; bibliography, 326.
Khans in Constantinople, 226; in Smyrna, 294.
Kiamil Pasha, 199.
Kislar Agassi, chief of the eunuchs, 115, 136, 244, 245.
Knights of St. John, 19-20, 299.
Konia, 15, 158, 277.
Koran, 67, 132, 161, 167, 214, 219, 227, 269, 273, 282.
Kosova, 16.
Kreka river, 3.
Kulpa river, 1.
Kurdistan, 9, 13, 22, 86, 98, 170.
Kurds in Turkey, origin, 98; population, 99; rural life, 100; conflicts with the Armenians, 101.
Kurins, 108.

L

Lamartine, Alphonse, 87.
Landsturm, 141.
Land tenure in Turkey, 150.
Landwehr, 141.
Lane-Poole, Stanley, quoted, 12, 20, 57; bibliography, 326.
Latimer, Elizabeth Wormley, bibliography, 326.
Latin kings of Constantinople, 184.

Law, Moslem, 138.
Law of succession, 24.
Lepanto, battle of, 23, 143.
Leprosy, 95, 198.
Lesbos. See Mitylene.
Lesches, 289.
Lewes, George Henry, 124.
Libraries in Constantinople, 170, 257.
Lycurgus, 84.
Lyric theatre at Ephesus, 298.
Lysimachus, 290.
Lysippus, bronze horses of, 188.

M

Macedonia, 4, 5, 53-56, 302.
Mahmud I., 30-31, 253, 277, 302.
Mahmud II., 34-37, 215.
Malta, 22, 23, 26.
Mamidieh Jam mosque, 251.
Mamins, 96.
Manissa, 292.
Manuscripts in Turkish libraries, 257.
Manufactures in Turkey, 153.
Marash, 177.
Marcian, column of, 191.
Marmora, sea of, 6.
Marriage, 66, 75, 96, 244, 249.
Marsovan, 176.
Masonic lodges in Turkey, 281.
Mecca, 118, 120, 170.
Medina, 119, 123.
Mediums of exchange, 322.
Megara, 182.
Mehemet Ali, 34.
Mektebs, 163.
Meles (Smyrna), birthplace of Homer, 291.
Mental alienation of Murad V., 40; of the Prophet, 125; of Abdul-Hamid II., 241.
Mercantile navy of Turkey, 157.
Mesopotamia, 9, 170.
Messina, 159.

Mevlevi, quoted, 282.
Meyerbeer, Giacomo, 181.
Midhat Pasha, 41.
Mihrab, the Mecca indicator, 270, 274, 284.
Military service. See Army.
Military reforms, 142.
Miller, Joaquin, quoted, 78.
Milligen, Frederick, bibliography, 326.
Minerals of Turkey, 152.
Ministry of the government, 135.
Mission schools, 173.
Mitrovitza, 158.
Mitylene, physiography of the island, 288; products and trade, 289; place in the history of ancient Greek culture, 289-290.
Man of Nazareth. See Jesus Christ.
Mohammed the Prophet, 118-127, 244, 250, 267.
Mohammed II., the Conqueror, 18-19, 191, 271.
Mohammed III., 24 25.
Mohammed IV., 29, 277.
Mohammed-Selim, son of Abdul-Hamid II., 249.
Mohammedan religion, 117-132.
Moldavia, 13, 24.
Molière's "L'Avare" in Turkish, 180.
Monasteries, Christian, 5, 127, 206; Mohammedan, see Dervishes.
Monastir, 8, 141, 158.
Money, Turkish, 322.
Monier's report on Turkish education, 171.
Monopolies granted by the government, 155.
Montenegro, 45, 46, 315.
Monte Santo, gulf of, 5.
Morava river, 4.
Morocco, 132, 140.

Mortuary chapels. See Turbehs.
Mosque colleges, 163, 167.
Mosques of Constantinople, Mamidieh Jam, 251; St. Sophia, 263-269; Ahmed, 269-271; Conqueror, 271-273; Suleiman, 273-276; Eyub, 276-277; Yeni Valideh Djami, 277; Bayezid, 278.
Mosul, 154, 157.
Mudania, 159.
Muderris, 128.
Muezzin, 263.
Mufti, 129, 135.
Murad I., 16-17.
Murad II., 17-18, 104.
Murad III., 23.
Murad IV., 28, 257, 258, 271.
Murad V., 38, 236, 237, 260.
Murray's Handbook of Constantinople, 327.
Musical instruments, 282, 284.
Muss-Alla mountain, 5.
Mustafa I., 28.
Mustafa II., 29.
Mustafa III., 31, 257, 303.
Mustafa IV., 34.

N

Napoleon I., 33, 34, 304.
Narenta river, 3.
Narghilé, 221, 228, 230.
National debt, 146, 148.
Navarino, 143, 306.
Navy, 143.
Near-Eastern question, 301-320.
Neka, riots of, 264.
Nestorian heresy, 299.
Netherlands. See Holland.
Newspapers, 177-180.
Newton, Sir C., 189.
Nicæa, 15.
Nicholas I., czar of Russia, 37.
Nicholas II., czar of Russia, 53.
Nicomedia, 15.

Index

Nightingale, Florence, 204.
Nude dervishes. See Turlakis.

O

Odalisques. See Gediklis.
Old Seraglio. See Seraglio.
Olympus, mount, 4.
Orkhan, 15-16, 244.
Oriental railway, 158.
Orpheus, lyre of, 289.
Orsova, 30.
Orthodox Greek church, 85.
Osman I., 15-16.
Osman II., 28, 271.
Osman III., 31, 277.
Osmanli Turks, origin of, 13-14.
Otchakov, 33.
Ottoman debt administration, 146.
Ottoman Empire, rise, 12-25; decline, 26-38; present conditions, 39-58.
Ox-carts in Turkey, 205.
Oxia, island of, 207.

P

Palaces of the sultans, 254-261.
Palmerston, Earl of, 307.
Pamir plateau, 60.
Pardoe, Julia, quoted, 218; bibliography, 327.
Paris, treaty of, 310.
Parthians, 98.
Passports, 140, 323.
Patent medicines, 155.
Patriarch of the Orthodox church, 265.
Patrick, Mary Mills, 176.
Paul I., czar of Russia, 33.
Pausanias, Greek general, 183.
Pausanius, Greek historian, 294.
Pentateuch, 96.
People of Turkey, the Turks, 59-78; Greeks, 79-85; Armenians, 85-93; Hebrews, 93-97; Kurds, 98-103; Albanians, 103-106; Persians, 106-107; Circassians, 107-109; Wallachians, 109-111; Bulgarians, 111-113; Gypsies, 113-114; Ethiopians, 115-116.
Pera, 185, 201, 202.
Perfume bazaar, 225.
Pergamus, 269, 295, 296.
Persia, 14, 22, 28, 120.
Persians in Turkey, ethnic stock, 106; Constantinople colony, 107.
Peter the Great, 30, 302.
Phanar, 82, 172, 173, 196.
Phidias, 188.
Philip of Macedon, 183.
Philippopolis, 16.
Pigeons, mosque of, 278.
Pitt, William, 305.
Pittacus, 289.
Pius V., 143.
Platæa, 189.
Platy, island of, 206.
Plevna, capture of, 43, 44.
Pliny, quoted, 6, 297.
Poland, 28, 29, 33, 302.
Political divisions of Turkey, 136.
Polycarp, 291.
Polygamy, 65, 96, 109, 244.
Population of Turkey, 10-11, 46.
Porters. See Hamals.
Portugal, 95.
Postal service, 159.
Prayers, 130.
Praxiteles, 188.
Press censorship, 178.
Priests. See Imams.
Prime Minister. See Grand Vizier.
Princes' Islands, 205.
Prinkipo, 205.
Prisons, 187, 206.
Professional schools in Turkey, 169-171.

Prophet. See Mohammed the Prophet.
Protestant Armenian church, 92.
Protestant mission schools, 173.
Provincial governors, 136.
Prussia, 33, 304.
Public debt. See National debt.
Pulcheria, 264.

Q

Quarters in Constantinople, 194-207.

R

Races. See People.
Ragusa, 13.
Railways, 156, 158, 292-293.
Rainfall in Turkey, 6-7.
Ramazan fast, 96, 129, 130, 250.
Ramsay, William Mitchell, quoted, 89; bibliography, 327.
Rawlinson, H. C., quoted, 99.
Reclus, Elisée, quoted, 74, 137.
Relics of the Prophet, 258.
Religion. See Faith of Islam.
Renan, Ernest, 123.
Revenues of Turkey, 144.
Rilodagh mountain, 5.
Rhodes, 22, 80, 265, 299.
Robert, Christopher R., 173.
Robert college, 173-175.
Robes of state, 257.
Roman Catholic Armenian church, 91.
Roman Catholic schools, 177.
Rome, 183, 264.
Roumania. See Rumania.
Roumanians. See Wallachians.
Roxalana, 244, 276.
Rumania, 7, 43, 45, 46, 110, 315.

Rumanians. See Wallachians.
Rumelia, 7, 13, 316.
Rumili Hissar, 92, 173, 281.
Russia, 23, 29, 31, 32, 37, 38, 42, 45, 302, 315.

S

Sadi, 132.
Salaries of officials, 147.
Salisbury, Earl of, 308, 313.
Saloniki, 8, 10, 51, 81, 96, 155.
Samos, 8.
Sancta Sophia, 263-269.
San Stefano, treaty of, 44, 315.
Sapienza, 21.
Sappho, 289.
Saracens, 120.
Sarajevo, 312.
Sardes, 295.
Save river, 1, 3.
Scala Nova bay, 295.
Scanderbeg, 104.
Schafiyites, 131.
Schiller, Johann Christoph Friedrich, 181.
Schools. See Education.
Scio, 143.
Scutari, 176, 203-205, 220, 246, 284.
Sedan chairs, 216.
Selamlik, ceremony of, 251.
Self-government in Turkey, 138.
Selim I., 21.
Selim II., 23.
Selim III., 32, 304.
Semen river, 3.
Sennacherib, 192.
Seraglio palace, 253-258.
Serasker tower, 184.
Serpent column, 189.
Servia, 2, 7, 13, 16, 30, 34, 41, 45, 104, 315.
Seven Sleepers, church of, 298.
Seven Towers, prison of, 73, 187.
Severus, Septimius, 183.
Shakespeare, William, 181.

Index

Shardagh mountain, 5.
Sheik-ul-Islam, 129, 134, 135, 138, 275.
Shi'ites, 99, 106, 131.
Silk industries in Turkey, 154.
Sinan, 273.
Sivas, 86, 154.
Slavic people, 109, 110, 112.
Smyrna, trade, 156, 293; geographic position, 290; birthplace of Homer, 291; historic monuments, 291; people, 292; railways, 293; former rivalry with Ephesus, 296.
Solon, 84.
Soma, 293.
Sophia (Bulgaria), 4, 175.
Spain, 2, 95.
Spanish Jews in Turkey, 95.
Stadium at Smyrna, 291; at Ephesus, 298.
Stambul, 185, 188, 196, 199, 202, 210, 219, 220.
Statesman's Year-book, 144.
Stores. See Bazaars.
Street scenes in Constantinople, 208-222.
Sublime Porte, 261.
Succession, law of, 24.
Sudan, 9.
Suggestions for travellers, 321-324.
Sugut, 14.
Suleiman I., the Magnificent, 22-23, 244, 254, 273, 275.
Suleiman II., 29, 276.
Sultan, official titles of, 133.
Sultana. See Valideh Sultan.
Sunnites, 99, 130, 167.
Sweet Waters of Europe, 200.
Sykes, Mark, bibliography, 327.
Syracuse, 183.
Syria, 8, 13, 22, 120, 127, 295.
Syrian Protestant college, 175.

T

Tabnith, 192.
Talmud, 96.
Tamerlane, 255.
Tariff, 146, 152.
Tartars. See Tatars.
Tatars, 14, 59, 132, 213.
Taxes, 47, 54, 135, 145.
Teachers, 164.
Technical schools, 169-170.
Telegraph service, 159.
Temple of Diana at Ephesus, 296-298.
Teos, birthplace of Anacreon, 291.
Teskere, 323.
Terpander, 289.
Theodosius, 189.
Theophanes, 289.
Thessaly, 45, 46.
Thornbury, Walter, bibliography, 327.
Thrace, highland of, 4.
Thomson, H. C., quoted, 319; bibliography, 327.
Tiflis, 33.
Timothy, the first bishop of Ephesus, 299.
Tirnova, 158.
Tithes. See Taxes.
Trade. See Commerce.
Trajan, 109.
Transylvania, 13, 29, 113.
Trappist monks, 280.
Trebizond, 13, 80, 93, 157.
Tribute duties, 146.
Tripoli, 9, 13, 120, 132.
Tunis, 13, 23, 27, 120, 132.
Turbans, 257, 271, 273.
Turbehs, or mortuary chapels, 262, 275, 277.
Turkestan, 59.
Turkey, geography, 1-11; history, 12-58; people, 59-116; religion, 117-132; government, 133-149; agriculture, 150-152; industries, 153-155; commerce, 155-160; education, 161-181; capital, 182-278; bibliography, 324-327.

Turks, origin, 59; physical type, 61; mental characteristics, 63; home life, 65; dress, 71; moral qualities, 74.
Turkish baths, 227-231.
Turkish coffee, 221.
Turlakis, or nude dervishes, 280-281.
Twain, Mark (Samuel L. Clemens), quoted, 83, 209, 222, 225, 229.
Tyrant's Palace at Ephesus, 298.

U

Ulema, or Moslem priests, 128, 129, 167, 169.
Underground Palace. See Cisterns.
United States, 140, 155.
Universal Israelitish Alliance, 95.
University of Constantinople, 171.
Uskup, 158.
Usurers among the Armenians, 102.

V

Vali, or governor-general, 136.
Valideh Khan, 107.
Valideh Sultan, 66, 226, 244, 251.
Valonia oak, 152.
Van (Armenia), 86, 93, 216.
Vardar river, 4.
Vekil, head of Armenian Protestant church, 92.
Veneration of the relics, 250.
Venice, 19, 23, 29, 190.
Verdi, Giuseppe, 181.
Vienna, 4, 158, 172.
Vilayet, political division of empire, 136.
Vincent, Sir Edgar, 144.
Vlachs. See Wallachians.

W

Wallachia (now Rumania), 13, 16, 31.
Wallachians in Turkey, origin, 109; physical and mental traits, 110; occupations, 111.
War-ships in Turkish navy, 143.
Washburn, George, 174.
Whirling dervishes, 281-284.
Williams, Sir Fenwick, 51, 148.
William II., emperor of Germany, 49, 51, 55, 231, 243.
Women, Turkish, 64-71, 200, 248; recreations of, 200; Hebrew, 96; Kurd, 101; Albanian, 104; Circassian, 107; Wallachian, 110; Gypsy, 114; Protestant schools for, 176; imperial harem, 244.
Wood, John Turtle, 297.

X

Xenophon concerning the Armenians, 90.
Xerxes, 5, 189.

Y

Yashmak, or face-covering of the women, 65, 201.
Yemen, 47, 141.
Yeni Khan, 227.
Yeni Valideh Djami mosque, 277-278.
Yildiz Kiosk, 242, 251, 259.
Young Turk party, 40, 281.

Z

Zappion College in Constantinople, 82, 173.
Zapties, or Turkish police, 51.